The Invitation

DERICK BINGHAM

AMBASSADOR

BELFAST ◆ GREENVILLE
NORTHERN IRELAND   SOUTH CAROLINA

The Invitation
© 1996 Derick Bingham

Cover photo: Rowland Davidson

First published 1996

ISBN   1 898787 81 6

AMBASSADOR PRODUCTIONS LTD,
Providence House
16 Hillview Avenue,
Belfast, BT5 6JR
Northern Ireland

Emerald House,
1 Chick Springs Road, Suite 206
Greenville,
South Carolina 29609
United States of America

To the memory of my uncle
John McNeil
1903- 1995

The following poem was written by his granddaughter and
perfectly sums up his life and witness.

To Us

To us he was our grandfather
Held our hands when we were small
A loving smile, a warm embrace
An example to us all.

To us he was a gentle spirit
Saying little and meaning well
Always clothed with love and mercy
A tower of strength, a faithful friend.

To us he was a peacemaker
Loved even those who let him down
One who never bore false witness
Wearing forgiveness as his crown.

To us he was a visionary
Believed in the coming of the Lord
Dreamed of heaven's glory
The best being on before.

And now he is our teacher
Preparing all our ways ahead
Telling Him whom we love about us
Our loving grandfather to the end.

~ Judith McLoughlin

Preface

We face in our generation a colossal ethical crises that afflicts our society from the top to the bottom. Violence haunts our streets. Drunkenness is rampant. Language is foul. One commentator spoke of a recent flare-up at a football match where seats were being hurled about and blamed the stadium authorities for not having their seats screwed down tightly enough! Self discipline, respect for the law, concern for others and individual responsibility are values long abandoned by many. At the back of it all is the sinister rise of moral relativism summed up by one judge who stated that the moral basis for his judicial decision in a certain case was that "One man's vulgarity is another's lyric". Indeed the only absolute law that a lot of people follow nowadays is that there is no law that must be followed absolutely!

In the midst of all the moral chaos comes the lovely Gospel of Jesus Christ. He was not the first Christian but He was and is the Christ. He is in every respect unique and nothing can be compared to Him. They do not love Christ who love anything more than Christ. He is the end because He is the beginning and He is the beginning because He is the end. To be "In Christ" is to be a Christian. Nobody can be a Christian without it. Baptism, church membership, Christian conduct are empty without a living union in your life with Jesus Christ. 164 times the expressions "In Christ", "In the Lord", "In Him" occur in the New Testament. It does not mean to be inside Him, as say, you would be said to be "In the house". No. It is, according to the Bible to be as a branch is united to a tree, as a limb is united to a body, as a husband is united to his wife, as the Father and Son are united in the Trinity, so is a Christian said to be "In Christ".

To be "In Christ" is to know Him. Mohammadens do not claim to know Mohammed. Buddhists do not claim to know the Buddah. Communists do not claim to know Lenin or Karl Marx but every Christian claims to know Jesus Christ. For a Christian to be "In Christ" is their status. Their status is not found in their car, or house, or school, or university or in the friends they know. It is not found in their social position. Their place in life and in eternity is to be "In Christ". He redeems them, justifies them, adopts them, and forgives them. To those who are "In Christ Jesus" there is, Paul writes, "No condemnation".

So then, how can this Christ be known? How can a person "out of Christ" come to be "in Christ"? What basis do we have for believing that Christ is who He says He is? Do we have proof? The answer is that we do. John wrote his Gospel highlighting the great proofs of Christ's claims that we "Might believe that Jesus is the Christ, the Son of God and that believing we might have life through His Name". This book is a year's readings in what is for many one of the most precious books of the New Testament. I have, quite frankly, found studying it has made me view the loveliness of Christ in a clearer way, and, somehow, I have found not only my mind fed but my spirit soar.

It is my prayer that if you are "in Christ" this book of readings will show you that despite all of the uncertainties of life around you, knowing Christ gives you a place and a purpose in God's great plan for the Universe. For, be sure of this, He has refurbishment plans and you have a place in them. If you are not yet "In Christ", may you soon be found in Him, "Not having your own righteousness which is from the law but that which is through faith in Christ, the righteousness which is from God by faith". Millions have found Christ through reading St. John's Gospel. May you be another one of them.

I invite you, then, to join me for a year of looking at Christ through the eyes of the disciple whom Jesus loved. May your life and mine be more Christlike as a result.

Derick Bingham
Winter of 1995-1996.

*Y*ou are facing some frightening task, today? Some deep sorrow, perhaps? Some overwhelming situation which you are powerless to change? You may even feel intimiated by having to face someone today whom you would rather not face; true? The Lord has promised to give you His grace for your situation and emphasises that His strength is made perfect in weakness.

January first

"In the Beginning was the Word" (John 1:1).

N o book in history has ever begun with a more incredible statement. Talk about going in at the deep end? John is like an eagle, for it is the only living creature which can look straight into the sun and not be dazzled. In his opening statement John penetrates his gaze into eternity past and says, without a flinch, that there never was a time when Christ did not exist. A literal translation reads, "In the beginning was continuing the Word".

This year may bring all kinds of changes and challenges in your life but if you are trusting in Christ, you are trusting in One who never ends with an end. He always ends with a beginning. Whether you have to face life or death, He brings fresh, new, invigorating beginnings, every morning. He always has done, He always will.

January second

"And the Word was with God" (John 1: 1).

I f you are with someone, you must be distinct from him. John is telling us that Christ is distinct, with infinite personality. He is no mere emination from the Father. Before time ever existed, Christ had face-to-face fellowship with His Father.

As you go through all that today holds for you, remember that you have access to the One who has always been near to the heart of God. What a Mediator! You might not be able to get in touch with your country's President or King or Prime Minister today, but, you can, by prayer, touch God the Father through the Man Christ Jesus. Talk to Him!

January third

"And the Word was God" (John 1: 1).

T hink of it: the One who was born of a woman, made her. The One who wept made the lachrymal duct. The One who was spiked to a cross made the very hill on which the cross stood and the very iron that made the nails which held Him there.

Back to basics, indeed! If Christ be God, then one thing is certain; all fear is folly! If God be for us, show me who can be against us? If Christ be God, then, lovely thought, God was always like the Lord Jesus. In a single sentence John has given us the most compact theological statement in all of the Scriptures. Yet, it is more than that; it is the unbreakable rock on which our future rests. So, Christian, cheer up! Today is the tomorrow you worried about yesterday - and all is well, for Christ is very God, today and yesterday, and for ever.

January fourth

"All things were made through Him" (John 1: 3).

I could live with the 'big bang' theory", a man commented to me one day in the town of Newtownards in County Down. "Yet, what I want to ask is; 'who lit the fuse?' I smiled at his direct speaking! Yet, the Scriptures do not teach that the world was shaped out of some pre-existing primeval material.It distinctly teaches that God spoke to nothing and it became something. We do not, like Buddhism or Hinduism, which now influences New Age thinking, say that nature is God.

God is distinct from His creation and above it, yet, "not a flower but shows some touch, in freckle, streak or stain, of his unrivalled pencil". No force in heaven or earth is a match for Christ.

January fifth

"Without Him nothing was made that was made" (John 1: 3).

*T*he average galaxy contains about 100 billion stars and there are at least 100 million galaxies known in space. Einstein believed that we have scanned with our largest telescopes only one billion'th of theoretical space.

That means there are probably something like ten octillion stars in space. How many is that? One thousand thousand is one million; one thousand million is one billion; one thousand billion is one trillion; one thousand trillion is one quadrillion; one thousand quadrillion is one quintillion; one thousand quintillion is one sextillion: one thousand sextillion is one septillion and one thousand septillion is one octillion, and there are at least ten of those in space!

In Genesis we read that He "made the stars, also". That sentence is a half of a verse long. There are two whole chapters on the creation of man and woman in the Bible and only half of a verse on the stars and every one of them is bigger than the earth! So, you must be a priority. Think about that when you are called for everything by someone today.

January sixth

"In Him was life" (John 1: 4).

If you were to take a cup of water from the Nile or the Amazon or the Mississippi, that river would be diminished by what you took from it, no matter how small. Not so if you take from Christ. All life, natural, physical, animal or intellectual is in Him. He not only created life, He sustains it. But more. If you have accepted Christ as Saviour, He gives you spiritual life. Life more abundant. Are you reluctant to give up living for yourself? You are foolish. As the chippings fell thick on Michael Angelo's studio floor, he would say, "While the marble wastes, the image grows". Yield to the Master and it will be, as Paul put it, no longer you, but Christ that lives in you. Altogether a better life.

January seventh

"And the life was the light of men" (John 1: 4).

What does this little expression mean? It means that only in human kind does life become light. Scripture teaches that only human kind has understanding; it also berates us when we fail to do by understanding what lesser creation does by instinct. Ants are industrious, storks know the times and seasons, oxen know their Master's crib, and, birds are without anxious care. When human beings fail to do by consent and mind what animals do by instinct they are contradicting themselves. They are contradicting their creation and their distinctive humanity and missing God's best in their lives. In fact humans often stoop so low, these days, that animals wouldn't do by instinct what humans do with all their understanding. Selah.

January eighth

"And the Light shines in the darkness, and the darkness did not overcome it" (John 1: 5; F. F. Bruce's translation from the Greek).

One of John's chief aims is to show the inability of spiritual darkness to triumph over spiritual light. Just as it is true that a little candle can dispel a room full of darkness and not be dimmed by it, so the light of Christ will not be captured, overwhelmed, or overpowered by the darkness presided over by the Prince of Darkness. It is very important to understand that while light and darkness are opposites, they are not opposites of equal power. Light is stronger than darkness and darkness cannot prevail against it. Let your light of Christian witness shine today no matter how great the opposition, whether you are at school, in a hospital ward, in the university or on the farm, at home or in the boardroom, working on the factory floor or maybe in your office. It is better to light a candle than to curse the darkness.

January ninth

"There was a man sent from God, whose name was John" (John 1: 6).

Tell me, are prophets the only ones sent from God? Could a little baby from a couple's love not be sent from God to be a blessing, even if only lent by God for a little while? Could a letter arrive in through your letter-box speaking a word of encouragement and kindness not be sent from God to encourage you to go on with a task, yet unfinished? Just as surely as John the Baptist was sent by God from his desert school to serve Israel, so you, too, could be sent by God to cheer someone who needs cheered, to soothe a bereaved heart with a word of hope, to urge a word of caution to someone heading for disaster, or, to lay your cool hand on some hot head. If God sent you; would you go? John did.

January tenth

"This man came for a witness" (John 1: 7).

In my experience all the seminars in the world don't make a true Christian witness. All the books you could ever read about Christian witnessing don't give you the vital spark that makes you an effective Christian witness, either. It is love for Christ that makes all the difference. If you are truly in love with someone you cannot hide it.

Your love will surface sooner or later. I say, love Christ and you will witness. A friend of mine once brought me a little present from Austria. It was a statement written in work on wood which I put on my fireplace. It reads, "If your heart is cold, this fire will not warm it". Provoking words, yes?

January eleventh

"That all through Him might believe" (John 1: 7).

What a truly beautiful ministry John the Baptist had. The purpose of his life was that others might believe in Christ through him. Is there any work greater in all the world than to be used by God to cause others to believe in Christ? You might say that you know of no-one who has come to believe in Christ through you. That may be true, but, surely, the important word is that you do not "know" of anyone . But then you don't know everything, do you? That money you gave to send Bibles to Russia or Africa may have resulted in the conversion of someone that you know nothing about. That word you spoke to those young people years ago might lead to their conversion years later.

John Flavell spoke a word for Christ in the South of England, and the person who heard him remembered the word he gave seventy years later while sitting in the middle of a field in the United States and was converted through it.

Don't get discouraged just because you don't see the seed you sowed in the autumn sprouting in the chill of winter. Spring is coming!

January twelfth

"He was not that Light, but was sent to bear witness of that Light"
(John 1: 8).

John the Baptist was God's Morning Star. Have you ever seen the Morning Star? There it shines brightly in the sky, though solitary, though singular. Even as you look at it you are aware that it is but the forerunner of a greater light that will soon come up. When the sun does rise, the Morning Star and the sun do shine for a little while together but then the sun's light overwhelms the starlight. That is as it should be.

So be a "Morning Star" light today. When people see you coming may they know that your witness shines to be eclipsed by the greater Light of which you are a forerunner. Now, that's living!

January thirteenth

"That was the true Light which gives light to every person who comes into the world" (John 1: 9).

The light John the Baptist was witnessing to was the same light that shines across every human being's path at some time or other since the beginning of time. Soon people began to realise it. People like old Simeon and Anna, who had followed divine light given to them for years, recognised Christ as being the same as the light they had followed up until then. When you speak of Christ to others you will be amazed that from time to time people will respond by receiving him as Simeon and Anna did through your witness. I know of a tribe in the Chad who used to worship one God long before they heard of Christ. When the Gospel was preached to them, practically the whole tribe was converted on the spot. They said, in effect, "This is the same true light as has already crossed our path".

There never was a time when divine light did not shine in the world. No place with the slightest crack is safe from its presence. It shines continually in the darkness, through nature, through conscience, through the Scriptures, through God's chosen people, Israel, and now, through the Gospel, also. It is a revelation which leaves people without excuse.

January fourteenth

"... and the world knew Him not" (John 1:10).

J ust as the world around Christ did not recognise Him for who He was, don't you think we are just as blind, at times? You visited someone who was sick. According to Christ you were visiting Him. You went to see someone in prison. "You did it to Me", says Christ. You clothed and fed some people in the Third World through the money you gave to some aid agency, recently; right? You gave your money so that they could dig wells for water; right? You might as well have fed a hungry Christ, personally, and given Him water to drink. That lonely young student you showed kindness to?; you were taking Christ in. So, watch how you go, today, you may meet Christ in disguise.

January fifteenth

"As many as received Him to them He gave the right to become children of God, even to those who believe on His Name" (John 1: 12).

I leave today's reading in the capable hands of Her Majesty, Queen Elizabeth II. Of this verse she said, in her Christmas broadcast of 1993, "For all the inhumanity around us, let us be grateful for those who have received Him and who go about quietly doing their work and His Will without thought of reward or recognition. They know that there is an eternal truth of much greater significance than our own triumphs and tragedies, and it is embodied by the Child in the manger. That is their message of hope. We can all try to reflect that message of hope in our own lives, in our actions and in our prayers. If we do, that reflection may light the way for others and help them to read the message too".

January sixteenth

"Who were born, not of blood, nor of the will of the flesh, nor of the will of man, but of God" (John 1: 13).

T he new birth is to be radically distinguished from human birth. Human birth has to do with "natural descent" being a member of the human family is a matter of a blood-relationship. It has to do with "human decision", that is, sexual desire. It has to do with "A husband's will" in agreement with his wife, on the assumption that the male partner takes the initiative in sexual matters. All of these things are irrelevant when it comes to spiritual rebirth.

We must always remember it was the Lord who found us. It was the Lord who was reaching down to us long before we ever thought of reaching up to Him. The Lord's true children owe their origin to the Lord alone. That is why we must always give the Lord the glory when conversions occur. He started this new creation and to everyone who receives Him to them He gives the right to become the children of God. Jean Rees wrote a book a few years back called "Danger saints at work". In it she had a spoof of an Evangelist whose card read, "Results assured. Terms reasonable"! True evangelists and Christian workers all have their place but it is the Lord and the Lord alone who brings about the miracle of the new birth.

January seventeenth

"And the Word became flesh and dwelt among us" (John 1: 14).

*T*he Lord Jesus is no aloof, unsympathetic Diety, interested only in Heavenly affairs. Here is God, not just present in finer symbol but in person. We cannot say that God is cut off from suffering; here is Christ, made flesh and, suffering with us. We cannot say our Lord Jesus knows nothing of every-day temptations; here is the Lord Jesus, made flesh, and, tempted as we are. We cannot complain that God knows nothing of the frightening power of death and all that comes with it; in the person of His Son, He died for us. We live in a world that has known brutal World Wars sweeping across it and the horrors of such unspeakable events as the Holocaust. We live in a world that is steeped in tragedy and sorrow, disease and catastrophes. God's only self-justification in a world that has known such horrors is the Cross of Calvary. God forbid that Christians should glory in anything else.

January eighteenth

"And we beheld His glory, the glory as of the only begotten of the Father, full of grace and truth" (John 1: 14).

*T*he glory of God we imagine to be blinding light surrounded by choirs of angels. We imagine the glory of God to be unapproachable, unearthly, away beyond us. John knew different. He will tell us, soon, that Christ manifested His glory in a humble home at a wedding, moving freely amongst people as one of themselves. His glory was full of grace and truth. He did not wait for the great occasion, he made every occasion, great. So it should be with His followers; if you want God's glory to be displayed in your life, show it by displaying grace and truth. Do you doubt me? It is reckoned that every single conversion to Christ can be traced to a Christian, somewhere, who did a kind act to the person who was eventually converted.Christ does the saving but again and again He uses the conduit of Christlike lives to draw people to Himself.

January nineteenth

"John bore witness of Him and cried out saying ....." (John 1: 15).

You could almost sum up today's text with the phrase, "As John used to say". Phrases have a way of remaining in people's minds long after the person who said them has passed out of your circle or acquaintance. I was talking with a lady just yesterday and she was describing the horse and long cart that used to pick up children at the farms in her primary school district, long years ago. Her school was a place where children were flailed for the least mistake in a test which came every Friday. She told me of one lad who, when they stopped at one farm to pick up some children, rocked back and forward on his seat in fear of the coming school day."I wish I was here coming back", he kept saying. "I wish I was here coming back". Sad words? I wonder what phrase they will remember you and me for?

January twentieth

"This was He of whom I said, 'He who comes after me is preferred before me for He was before me'" (John 1: 15).

Tens of thousands flocked to hear John the Baptist preach. The banks of the Jordan were black with people from all walks of life, of every kind of background and with people from all over the known world. Even Apollos, the great Christian future orator and preacher was there and, he hailed from Alexandra in Egypt.

John was centre-stage for sure, and his audiences hung on his every word. It would have been so easy in such a situation, to draw attention to himself. You know, the odd word that would have grabbed a little bit of glory for himself in the hour of power. But no, John drew everyone's attention to Christ and to Christ alone. That's why centuries later we remember him and praise him for it.

Rome and its glory was all around John in that hour. Its great amphitheatres and coliseums streched across continents. Where is all that glory now? Mere Mediterranean rubble. No great Emperor's word comforts you and me as we face today's problems, but, the humble John's exhaltation of Christ burns in our souls today. Right? So, be like John wherever you are found in today's busy round. Put the preference on Christ and live.

January twenty-first

> *"And of His fullness we have all received, and grace for grace"*
> *(John 1: 16).*

You are facing some frightening task, today? Some deep sorrow, perhaps? Some overwhelming situation which you are powerless to change? You may even feel intimiated by having to face someone today whom you would rather not face; true? The Lord has promised to give you His grace for your situation and emphasises that His strength is made perfect in weakness.

Our text literally means "Grace instead of grace". How do we get grace instead of his grace? As the grace we receive is appropriated, more will come and then more and even more. Grace following grace! Grace heaped upon grace! Wave upon wave of grace. Where sin abounds, grace abounds much more. Got it? Good. Now prove and enjoy it, today.

January twenty-second

> *"For the law was given through Moses but grace and truth came through Jesus Christ" (John 1: 17).*

The law of God is perfect. The problem is, I am not. Even before I get out of my bed in the morning the law of God has me cornered before I do anything. I simply cannot keep it for, as in a chain, if I break it at one point, I break it all. I come short of God's glory every time. But the law is a schoolteacher who points me to Christ. I find that He, God's Son, kept God's law perfectly, died for my sins and rose again for my justification. I trust him as my Saviour.

Now I take, grace and truth, not from the law which was given through Moses, but from Jesus Christ, my Saviour. You could light a million candles from one candle and it wouldn't lose any of its brilliance. So, take from Christ, In fact, reverently speaking, Christian, you have a whole Christ to yourself!

January twenty-third

"No-one has seen God at any time. The only begotten Son, who is in the bosom of the Father, He has declared Him" (John 1: 18).

I study the stars and they make me stand in wonder. But, it is a scary kind of wonder. I study the history of the Children of Israel from the Red Sea to Auschwitz to the Six Day War to Entebbe and in and out of Camp David. I say, "Look at them, despised and rejected by men and there they are, distinct, indestructible". It makes me worship their God, whom no-one has ever seen.

I study the Bible and it fills me with a staggering awe at its power. I feel a bit like J. B. Phillips who, when he did his translation of the Scripture, said it was like trying to rewire a house with the mains still switched on. But still, for all I see in nature, in the Children of Israel, in the Scriptures, my heart is still lonely. I am only in an inn by the side of the road on the way, somewhere. How can I know the God behind all this? Through the Lord Jesus Christ! He has declared Him. He has revealed His secret. I get to know Christ and I get to call God, the Father, Abba. What a way to finish a prologue! What a text to begin your day with or to go to sleep on!

January twenty-fourth

"....the Jews sent priests and Levites from Jerusalem to ask Him, Who are you?" (John 1: 19).

I t is not easy to answer the question "What do you say about yourself?" We live in an age of C.V.'s and an age where image is all important. Asked to preach at a certain venture I was requested to send in a "potted history" of myself "listing your accomplishments, so far". I cringed. As for denominational pigeon-holing, the Christian seems to be no longer able to simply say, "I am a Christian", (though, I like the story of the little girl who asked, "I am Church of England, what abomination are you?"). John was human but he was not ordinary. He was a lamp but he was not the light. He was a witness but he was not the object of worship. He answered the questions from the Sanhedrin delegation, quietly and firmly. He knew who he was. What about you? I like my friend, Neville Taylor's answer. He said, "I am a person unfairly discriminated for!" (Got it?).

January twenty-fifth

"He said; I am the voice of One crying in the wilderness" (John 1: 23).

When you are talking about John the Baptist you are talking about someone of whom Christ said, "Of those born of women there is none greater". Here is the greatest of all the prophets. Here is the man, of all men, chosen by Almighty God to be the forerunner of His Son on earth, and, when asked who he was simply replied that he was a voice! Here is sublime humility if ever there was humility. He is saying that the prophet Isaiah wrote his job description. He was a voice telling people to get ready for the coming of the King.

In a generation when via satellites and cables, ten thousand voices vie for our attention, how about being a voice for the Lord today? Go on, raise it in the office or classroom or university high table. Raise it down on the factory floor where you work or on the aircraft to Brussels. When one of the first great international communication cables was laid under the ocean, someone asked a very simple question; "And what are they going to say to each other?" Indeed.

January twenty-sixth

"'Make straight the way of the Lord', as the prophet Isaiah said" (John 1: 23).

In olden times when a king wanted to visit a foreign country, he always sent his representative to the country and waited to see how he was received. If he was received with a warm welcome, then the King knew all was well and followed on. Out of the desert came Christ's herald crying, "Make straight the way of the Lord". How was he received? At the end of the day he was beheaded, and the One he heralded was crucified.

Now, Christian, you have a representative who has gone ahead into the presence of God to represent you; He is your great High Priest, the Lord Jesus. What we want to know is, how is He being received there? It all depends on that. The answer is that He is being received as your representative and mediator with a welcome beyond description Is it any wonder the Bible teaches that you have been "accepted in the Beloved"?

January twenty-seventh

"Now those who were sent were from the Pharisees and they asked Him, saying, "Why then do you baptise if you are not the Christ, nor Elijah nor the Prophet?"(John 1: 24-25).

Obviously when those who were sent from the Pharisees heard John simply say that he was a voice crying for the way to be prepared for the Lord, they were surprised. What do people do when they are surprised? They raise a ritualistic technicality. "I am a preacher", I tell them. "What kind of a preacher are you?", they ask. "Are you a Calvanist preacher, an Arminian preacher, a Presbyterian preacher, or a Baptist preacher, a.....". "I preach Christ", I tell them. "Yes", they say, "but do you preach the necessity of ...." Don't be diverted by ritualistic technicalities.

Be like John and give them spiritual, Biblical answers. There is nothing more powerful. Like Billy Graham at Sandringham when the B.B.C. asked him what it was like to preach in front of Her Majesty the Queen, he replied, "I preach in front of the King of all the Kings and the Lord of all the Lords, every day". I didn't hear one reporter follow on with a ritualistic technicality that day!

January twenty-eighth

"John answered them, saying, 'I baptize with water...." (John 1: 26).

John was a superb spiritual leader. Even this simple answer to his questioners proves that. They knew what he meant; his baptism was a sign of repentance. That's all. He was saying, "I am useful but I am not indispensible". No-one is. Notice the superb leadership qualities John shows. As a herald of Christ he did not highlight his own importance. As a leader he did not exploit other people's ignorance; many would have believed anything he said but he resisted the temptation to use their ignorance to his advantage. In public and in private John was Christ's man through and through. If you were to be put in court on the charge of being a Christian, would there be enough evidence to convict you? Even more, if your life were put under the scrutiny of a private investigator, what would he find?

January twenty-ninth

"But there stands One among you whom you do not know"
(John 1: 26).

on't you think this statement should be taken literally? John knew that the Messiah was standing in the crowd that day. But, he didn't identify him! No, John wasn't Elijah. No, he wasn't the second Moses, the prophet. He was a voice crying, "Make straight the way of the Lord" and he was affirming that He had already come, that He was there, undiscovered at Bethabara where John was preaching. Why did John not identify Christ that day? Because it wasn't God's time. As we shall see, later, John identified the Messiah the very next day. Let's learn the lesson; there is a time for everything under the sun. What will suit God's will tomorrow, will not suit today. Be careful, then, do not rush into things. Timing, it's all in the timing.

January thirtieth

"It is He who, coming after me, is preferred before me, whose sandal strap I am not worthy to loose" (John 1: 27).

here was a saying that stated, "Every service which a slave performs for his master shall a disciple do for his teacher except the loosing of his sandal thong". In the service of Christ, though, there was no duty too low for John. There is something incredibly moving about today's text. Though Disraeli, the famous British Prime Minister once said, "Everyone likes flattery; and when you come to Royalty, you should lay it on with a trowel", I am quite sure Royalty are sickened by flattery as anyone else. This statement of John's is no flattery;

he was speaking of the most perfect and lovely One who ever walked on our earth. He meant every word of this statement; no duty is too servile in Christ's service. Agreed?

January thirty-first

"The next day John saw Jesus coming towards him, and said, 'Behold, the Lamb of God'" (John 1: 29).

ere we have the remarkable public identification by John of the Lamb of God. Notice the change, the new note. Up until now John said Christ was like a fan, purging wheat from chaff. He saw Him as a fire burning up chaff, talked of Him as being like an axe levelling trees. He said Christ would lower mountains and exhalt valleys. It was all here, but, now John calls Him the Lamb of God; the sinless One who would take the place of the sinful. With all the changes, recently, in the world, new countries are emerging with new national symbols. Even Russia has a new symbol: the two-headed eagle, one head looking east and the other west. Have you, though, ever seen any nation choose a lamb as its symbol? It would look too weak, too innocent, too shy, too timid to symbolize a nation. Not so in the church of Jesus Christ. Not so in Heaven, for the Lamb is the light thereof. Glory to the Lamb!

*T*he Bible tells us we should care for one another, be devoted to one another, encourage one another, have fellowship with one another, forbear one another, forgive one another, greet one another, honour one another, be hospitable to one another, pray for one another and be of the same mind with one another. That's enough to be going on with!

FEBRUARY

February first

".....who takes away the sin of the world!" (John 1: 29).

What a text with which to begin a new month! Notice the emphasis on the word "sin". If a little baby dies it has not yet committed sins, in the plural, a baby has not reached the years of moral responsibility. Yes, the Scripture teaches we are "born in sin and shapen in iniquity", but, the word is "sin", not "sins". Are you a sinner because you sin or do you sin because you are a sinner? The latter, surely.

All born have a natural bias towards sin and commit sins quite naturally. But a baby has not committed sins because, I repeat, it has not reached the years of moral responsibility when it can choose to sin. Wonderful word, then, that the Lamb of God, takes away the sin of the world. The little one who has died is safe with Him because He is the sin-bearer. Comfort, indeed!

February second

"I did not know Him, but He who sent me to baptise with water said to me, 'Upon whom you see the Spirit descending, and remaining on Him, this is He who baptizes with the Holy Spirit'. And I have seen and testified that this is the Son of God" (John 1: 32-33).

I "I did not know Him", says John. What can he mean? His own cousin and he did not know Him until the day he baptized Him? It means that John did not know that his cousin was the Son of God until the day he baptized him. He knew He was the child who had done no wrong; he knew He was the teenager who had done no wrong: he knew He was the adult who had done no wrong. When Christ came to be baptized John said, "I have need to be baptized by you and are you coming to me?" Why would he say that if he had not believed Christ to be very special? Note Christ's answer; "Permit it to be so now, for thus it is fitting for us to fulfil all righteousness", i.e. by the very thing from which you are shrinking, the sinless taking the place of the sinful, is all righteousness fulfilled. Then the sign fell from Heaven on his cousin and he knew He was the Son of God.

February third

"Again the next day, John stood with two of His disciples. And looking at Jesus as He walked, he said, 'Behold the Lamb of God'" (John 1: 35-36).

See here the truth of the progress of doctrine. Not from error to truth, but progress from the dimness of the dawn to the brightness of the noon. Away at the dawn of time is Abel and his lamb; a lamb offered for one man. Come later to the night of the avenging angel. The Passover lamb is slain; a lamb for a family. Come to Leviticus and see the lamb on the altar; a lamb for a nation. Come now to the Lamb of God identified for a second time by John the Baptist; as John had said earlier, a lamb for the whole world. Come to Revelation 21 - 22. See who reigns in endless glory; and the city had no need of the sun, neither of the moon, to shine in it; for the glory of God did lighten it and the Lamb is the light thereof; a Lamb for all eternity.

February fourth

"The two disciples heard him speak. And they followed Jesus. Then Jesus turning, and seeing them following, said to them 'What do you seek?' They said to Him, 'Rabbi, (which is to say, when translated, Teacher) where are you staying?' He said to them, 'Come and see'"
(John 1: 37-39).

There is a very famous television programme here in the West called, "Through the Keyhole". A panel of people are shown a film of the house of a famous celebrity and they have to guess by the contents of the house who the celebrity is. Millions of people are intrigued by where a person lives. Is that all these disciples of John were interested in when they asked the Saviour, "Where are you staying?".

Certainly not. John in his prologue had said, "The Word was made flesh and dwelt among us". Realising who He was, they wished to find out where He stayed because where He stayed they wanted to stay too. Every Christian knows that He who, in the beginning dwelt with God, now dwells in their heart. Walking through the city of Nazareth the late Dr. Harry Ironside and his wife were greatly moved by the poverty of the inner city. I have been there myself and I have seen the open sewer running down the middle of the street of the old city. Dr. Ironside's wife turned to him and said, "Harry, to think that my Lord lived here". Pointing to his heart, Dr. Ironside said, "He lives in a far worse place now".

February fifth

"One of the two who heard John speak, and followed Him, was Andrew, Simon Peter's brother. He first found his own brother Simon, and said to him, 'We have found the Messiah' (which is translated, the Christ). And he brought him to Jesus." (John 1: 40-42).

*B*oswell called him "The shrimp who became a whale." The shrimp? Little William Wilberforce, small of stature, witty, gregarious, the life and soul of the aristocratic social round of the London of his day, and, at 21 a Member of Parliament. Rich by inheritance, alert by nature, he was introduced to the Gospel in depth by his friend Isaac Milner while on a holiday in Europe. Milner, a tutor of Queen's College, Cambridge, had a clear grasp of the intellectual heart of Christianity and as he and Wilberforce crossed Europe in a chaise, he helped him to understand its message. By the time Milner deposited Wilberforce at No. 10 Downing Street on 22nd February, 1758, Wilberforce was a changed man. With Christian dedication he was to assiduously pursue the abolition of the slave trade in the British Empire. His success has become a legend in history. Could Milner ever have calculated what would be accomplished through bringing one soul to Christ?

Could you?

February sixth

"The following day Jesus wanted to go to Galilee, and He found Philip and said to him, 'Follow Me' (John 1:43).

*C*hrist was the one people followed. Notice with these followers there was no theological examination, first. Christ didn't publish a manifesto. People were attracted to Him. Not the man through the doctrine but the doctrine through the man. "Follow Me", was the call. When the Apollo mission took astronauts from earth to the moon, the astronauts never identified with the moon. If they had they would have been dead in seconds.

Instead they took with them all the paraphernalia of earth. They took their own equipment, oxygen, clothes, and food and established a kind of earth colony on the moon. When Christ came to earth, He brought nothing with Him but Himself. Sometimes I feel like saying to many gimmick-laden, celebrity-orientated, business-managed churches of our day: "Tell me, is Christ not enough for you, anymore?" He is enough.

February seventh

"Philip found Nathanael and said to him, 'We have found Him of whom Moses in the law, and also the prophets, wrote - Jesus of Nazareth, the son of Joseph'. And Nathanael said to him, 'Can any good thing come out of Nazareth'? Philip said to him, 'Come and see'"
(John 1:45-46).

*D*on't be too quick to judge a small community. I happened to be teaching the Scriptures in one, once, in New Zealand. I was taken for a drive one afternoon by a gentleman and, looking for an "angle" for a newspaper column I had to write I asked the man who was driving me if anyone "different" had ever come out of the little place.

I expected a shrug of the shoulders. But no, he immediately drove the car around the corner and pointed to a sign which indicated the birthplace of Lord Rutherford whose research into the structure of atoms led to the splitting of the atom and the "nuclear age".

Be kind to that small child who interrupts your schedule today. That child may one day rise to become the greatest influence in their day and generation for God. Nazareth was to find that one of its carpenters was God Incarnate.

February eighth

"Jesus saw Nathanael coming toward Him, and said of him, 'Behold, an Israelite indeed, in whom is no guile!' Nathanael said to him, 'How do you know me?' Jesus answered and said to him, 'Before Philip called you, when you were under the fig tree, I saw you'. Nathaneal answered and said to Him, "Rabbi, you are the Son of God! You are the King of Israel!"' (John 1: 47-49).

*N*athanael became a Christian because he was shown Christ's omnipresence. It absolutely thrilled him and he was converted on the spot. Christ immediately informed him that what he had just experienced was only the start of a great adventure.

He would see far greater things. Are you discouraged, today? Is there lead in your heart, an inch missing from your step? Are your critics hounding you? And even speaking the truth, about you, in part. Is despair wanting to be your friend? Oh! Christian, listen to the word of Christ today. You are His child, you have peace with God, you have the forgiveness of sins, the Holy Spirit indwells you, you have God's Word to guide you but that is only the start. There is a vast adventure ahead of you away beyond this life in a world unseen to you now. God is not hard up for ideas as to what to keep you occupied with throughout Eternity.

Cheer up! The best is yet to be.

February ninth

"And He said to him, 'Most assuredly, I say to you, hereafter you shall see heaven open, and the angels of God ascending and descending upon the Son of Man'" (John 1: 51).

In his conversation with Nathanael, Christ alludes to the story of Jacob's ladder. Note that Jacob in his dream did not find God at the top of the ladder in heaven, he found Him, the original Hebrew tells us, "by the side of it", on earth. It so surprised Jacob that he said, "Surely the Lord is in this place and I did not know it". In the dream the angels were going out from God and back to God, as God stood on earth. Jacob had never imagined God ever visited the earth and, truth is, the way Jacob had been behaving he probably would have loved God to have been in His heaven and not so close. He soon learned that God's visit to earth would change his life.

The message to Nathanael was, of course, extremely pertinent. He would see Heaven opened and the Lord Jesus come down to earth with angels ascending and descending upon Him. Nathanael was amazed that Christ had known him without having ever been physically present with him; "Before Philip called you, when you were under the fig tree, I saw you," Christ had said. Nathanael was now told that he would see far greater things than these. And so will you. You have seen in your life many amazing things that the Lord has done for you, but these, in a sense, are but the edges of His ways. Soon you will be at the very heart of God's ways with a multitude that no man can number. Believe me, Christian, out there beyond the eyes horizon there's more for you, incalculably more.

February tenth

"This beginning of signs Jesus did in Cana of Galilee, and manifested His glory" (John 2: 11).

John calls Christ's miracles, signs. In other words he believes the supernatural power of God was at work in Christ's miracles and that he was primarily concerned that people see beyond the miracles to see their significance. If you were asked to select a miracle to stand as the "flag-ship" of all Christ's earthly miracles, which one would you choose? The raising of Lazarus? The feeding of the five thousand? Would you have chosen this simple incident of changing the water into wine? How, then, did this incident manifest His glory?

It showed His glory by showing that true spirituality is consistent with ordinary life. The miracle took place in a home at a simple country wedding. A lot of people think that true greatness and godliness can only be enjoyed in some cloister far away from the environment of ordinary life, far away from the everyday joys or hassle of human existence. It is not so. Christ did not wait for the great occasion. He made every occasion great. Let's be like Him. We must not make ourselves other than real human beings before we can be useful and dedicated Christians.

February eleventh

"On the third day there was a wedding in Cana of Galilee, and the mother of Jesus was there. Now both Jesus and His disciples were invited to the wedding. And when they ran out of wine, the mother of Jesus said to Him, 'They have no wine'. Jesus said to her, 'Woman, what does your concern have to do with Me. My hour has not yet come'" (John 2: 1-4).

At a Jewish festal occasion the whole festivities might be prolonged for a week. For the wine to run short before it was due to end was a very serious blow, particularly damaging to the reputation of the host. Mary saw that the host at the wedding in Cana was absolutely mortified and she knew her Son had the power to do something about it. When she asked Him He implied in His answer that there were limitations to her understanding of Him. She had to understand that He was waiting for "His hour" to come. He was not going to be pushed into a full manifestation of His glory. Yes, He did the miracle but it was not yet "His hour". He saw His life in terms, not of His wishes but in terms of His Father's purposes for Him.

Mary had to learn just about the hardest lesson in all Christian living. She had to learn how to wait for God. Have you learned it, yet? Are they shoving you to do something and you know it is not yet time. Then learn to wait. Hold back. "Like the tramping of a mighty army, so is the force of an idea whose time has come", wrote Victor Hugo. So, Christian, wait, I say, on the Lord. His timing is perfect.

February twelfth

"His mother said to the servants, 'Whatever He says to you, do it'" (John 2: 5).

Mary had approached the Lord Jesus as His mother and was reproached, now she responds as a believer and her faith is honoured. She asks the servants to do what He tells them. It was very good advice but have we taken it? You might say to me that you don't have the Lord physically present in your home to tell you what to do next. True, but you do have His Word, don't you? There are standing orders in the Bible that we should be getting on with. We should, for example, teach children spiritual truths, we should visit the sick, we should pay our debts, we should be kind to one another.

Have you every studied the "One- anothers" in the Bible? They are fascinating. The Bible tells us we should care for one another, be devoted to one another, encourage one another, have fellowship with one another, forbear one another, forgive one another, greet one another, honour one another, be hospitable to one another, pray for one another and be of the same mind with one another. That's enough to be going on with! Presidents of countries don't have to write to the citizens to ask them to pay their taxes every year, do they? It is a standing order. So, don't be always looking for a dramatic intervention in your circumstances to help you to know what to do. The Lord has said what He hates and what He loves. Those are your fences: you can decide and act between them.

February thirteenth

"Now there were set six waterpots of stone, according to the manner of purification of the Jews, containing twenty or thirty gallons apiece. Jesus said to them, 'Fill the waterpots with water'. And they filled them up to the brim" (John 2: 6-7).

As the feast continues there are six waterpots standing by to supply water for the rinsing of the guest's hands and for washing the various vessels required for the feast in accordance with old established traditions. Jesus transformed ceremonial and tradition into something far better! Be reminded that John's Gospel is an expansion of John' prologue and did not John's prologue state that, "The law was given through Moses but grace and truth came by Jesus Christ"? The law could point the way but it could give you no permanent relief of conscience. It could command you to do the things it asked because you had to. In Christ you do things He asks because you want to! In Christ things are always better than anything else. His wine for their water. His joy for their ceremony.

February fourteenth

"When the master of the feast had tasted the water that was made wine, and did not know where it came from (but the servants who had drawn the water knew), the master of the feast called the bridegroom. And he said to him, 'Every man at the beginning sets out the good wine, and when the guests have well drunk, then that which is inferior" (John 2: 9-10).

The Devil always gives his best first and his worst last. Adultery may appear to be as soft as down but in the end it is a flaming vulture. Drugs at what young people call an E-rave party may give a feeling of physical bliss but those same drugs can kill. A promiscuous Californian once turned to a Christian who worked in his office and explained his lifestyle. He had a beach house. His women came and went and brought him no hassle. "But why", he asked earnestly, "Do I have this great feeling of emptiness?" The answer is that the Devil lets you find out the end result of taking his gifts for yourself. He doesn't ever come up front with what is going to happen, does he? The more satisfied you try to be with the Devil's gifts, the more dissatisfied you will be. Selah.

February fifteenth

"... But you have kept the good wine until now" (John 2:10).

I sat recently at dinner with a Sri Lankan plant scientist. For eighteen years he had studied the cell wall of the runner bean. He told me that if fifty scientists studied the same cell wall for a hundred years they would not know fifty per cent of its secrets. And that was only the runner bean! The man had gained his Doctorate at Cambridge University studying the leaf of the strawberry plant. What a fascinating dinner I had!

If the very fine detail of creation is so fascinating, what must the Creator be like? One thing is for sure; His gifts are the opposite to Satan's. They come on an ascending scale. Those who trust Him as Saviour will sit one day at the marriage supper of the Lamb, not as guests but as His Bride and for ever they will enjoy fresh revelations of His glory and all of them will say, "Lord, you have kept the best wine until now."

February sixteenth

"When He had made a whip of cords, He drove them all out of the temple, with the sheep and the oxen, and poured out the changers money and overturned the tables. And He said to those who sold doves, 'Take these things away! Do not make my Father's house a house of merchandise'" (John 2: 15-16).

S heer skulduggery went on in the temple in the name of true religion. The people were being fleeced. A visit to the temple often meant a sacrifice and any animal presented must be unblemished. The temple authorities appointed inspectors to examine the victims which were being offered. The fee was 2p. If the inspectors thought an animal had been bought outside the temple you could nearly always be certain that they would reject it. They would then encourage you to buy an animal from them. The point was, for example, that a pair of doves cost 19p outside the temple but 180p inside! Two and a quarter million pilgrims sometimes came from all over the world to Jerusalem to keep the Passover. That meant a lot of money was made by extortion. The Saviour couldn't bear it and drove them out, His anger directed at the detractors from worship. Woe betide anyone who even in our generation detracts God's people from worship. Christ can still drive them out.

February seventeenth

"Then His disciples remembered that it was written, 'The zeal of your house has eaten Me up'. So the Jews answered and said to Him, 'What sign do you show to us, since you do these things'. Jesus answered and said to them, 'Destroy this temple, and in three days I will raise it up'. Then the Jews said, 'It has taken forty six years to build this temple, and will you raise it up in three days?' But he was speaking of the temple of His body" (John 2: 17-21).

The Jews asked the Saviour for a sign to legitimatise His action in order to show that He had authority to do what He did. He answered that the ultimate proof and demonstration of His authority would be His resurrection after crucifixion. Do I write today to someone in the grip of bereavement? Are you numb with sorrow? Does your heart ache? Here is the very heart of the Christian message which can be summed up in one word: Hope!

I stood one day in a sixty mile an hour gale at the graveside of a Christian lad. Long will I remember the heartbreaking sorrow of it all. As his father gazed into that grave he said to me over the sound of the howling wind, "Only the Lord could bring him out of it!" As the years of my life roll by I often think of those words. The father was right and because Christ lives we shall live also. Hope, Christian, hope. Not "Hope so" but hope as a death-conquering fact.

February eighteenth

"Therefore, when He had risen from the dead, His disciples remembered that He had said this to them; and they believed the Scripture and the word which Jesus had said" (John 2; 22).

When eventually Christ's disciple ran into the tomb ahead of Peter and saw Christ's grave clothes lying there we are told that "He saw and believed". It is obvious that he and the rest of the disciples did not believe or understand the truth of the resurrection until after the event. Pity, isn't it, that they hadn't believed it before the event? It would have saved them endless trouble. They wouldn't have fled from the Saviour in His hour of need for a start. Belief would have staved off panic and doubt and fear and it will do the very same for us. There is not an issue in our world that the Scriptures, the Lord's Word to us, do not have something to say about. Stop for a moment and ask yourself, "What does the Bible have to say about this issue that threatens to overwhelm me?" When you have identified it, believe it and face the issue. Let Biblical thinking overcome emotional thinking. You will be more than a conqueror even before the event. If the English say that the great battles of their history were first won on the playing fields at Eton, so your great battles can be conquered by believing God's Word before the event.

February nineteenth

"Now when He was in Jerusalem at the Passover, during the feast, many believed in His Name when they saw the signs which He did"
(John 2: 23).

 eople are very fickle. You and I would be well advised to remember that. Are you making a major decision in your life and basing it on public opinion? Be careful.

I know I may sound cynical and that using an incident from the life of Voltaire may not be the best example to use in a Christian book but sometimes, as Jesus pointed out, the children of darkness are wiser than the children of light. Voltaire was driving in a carriage to a theatre where one of his plays was being staged. "Look at the crowds queueing to see your play", said his companion. "The same crowd would come to see me hung", replied Voltaire. These people believed in Jesus because they loved the spectacular miracles which He did. They did not love Him. They were superficially impressed because they saw the bare signs of Christ's greatness but they had not grasped the truth that was signified by the signs. True faith that lasts and that transforms people is that which involves unreserved personal commitment to Jesus Christ as Lord. It is a tragedy to see the signs but not to see Him.

February twentieth

> *"But Jesus did not commit Himself to them, because He knew all men, and had no need that anyone should testify of man, for He knew what was in man" (John 2: 24-25).*

hese people may have believed in Christ's Name but He did not believe in them. They may have committed themselves to His Name but He did not commit Himself to them for He knew their heart. When the Lord searches the heart it is amazing what He finds. We judge things by appearances, the look in the eye, the clothes worn, the car driven, the house lived in, the school tie worn, the computer worked on, the holidays taken, the chic-ness or lack of it. We judge by sales achieved, exams passed, achievements gained. I was asked to take a Christian meeting a while back and to send to the organisers my "list of achievements so far". I couldn't believe it! The Lord looks on the heart, not your C.V. It is what is in your heart that determines what you become. If you determine in your heart to set the Lord always before you, true success will be yours. The Lord will commit Himself to you. Caught that? That will be a commitment that will have no end.

February twenty-first

> *"There was a man of the Pharisees named Nicodemus, a ruler of the Jews. This man came to Jesus by night ...." (John 3: 1-2).*

he Lord Jesus may not have committed Himself to certain people "because He knew what was in man" but there was a man at that time to whom Christ did commit Himself and his name was Nicodemus. Why? Because he was different. He was willing to learn more. I like to think that he came to Christ at night, not because he was scared of what others might think, but because he simply couldn't wait until the morning. The conversation he had with Christ was unquestionably one of the most profound in all history. It reached into the very heart of the eternal and displayed the heart of God to sinners like no conversation has ever done.

Do you have that willingness to learn more of God? Are you hungry and eager for truth in a world of moral chaos? It is that willingness that

Christ can perceive. He will meet you in your need and lead you into all truth. If you are willing He is able to open Heaven to you. There is, willing heart, a place for you.

February twenty-second

"This man came to Jesus by night and said to Him, 'Rabbi, we know that You are a teacher come from God; for no-one can do these signs that You do unless God is with him'. Jesus answered and said to him, 'Most assuredly I say to you, unless one is born again, he cannot see the Kingdom of God'" (John 3: 2-3).

Nicodemus, one of the seventy men who ran the religious affairs of the Jewish nation and who had religious authority over every Jew in the world, had come to hear the latest word from God. The Saviour, though, that great seeker of souls, bypassed Nicodemus' words of greeting and reached into his spiritual condition. He explained to Nicodemus that he needed a new birth, a new life before the Kingdom of God could be seen, let alone entered into. This truth of the importance of the new birth crashed across all human thinking, all human religion, all human philosophy and theology. It was a very revealing word.

Here is the greatest teacher of all, teaching another teacher that what he needed was not to graduate but to go back beyond babyhood! No wonder Nicodemus reeled at the very thought. He had never heard of a regeneration in the here and now. He never dreamt one could enter immediately into the life of the coming age. John, of course, is expounding his prologue which told of people receiving Christ and becoming children of God. Nicodemus thought his place was assured by virtue of his race and religion. He was now told there was a place for him on the grounds of a life given as a gift from above, alone.

"Why do you regularly preach on the text, 'You must be born again'" someone asked of the great George Whitfield? The great man replied, "I frequently preach on the text 'You must be born again' because you must be born again."

February twenty-third

"As Moses lifted up the serpent in the wilderness, evenso must the Son of Man be lifted up, that whoever believes in Him should not perish but have eternal life" (John 3: 14-15).

*N*icodemus desperately wants to know what process is involved in the new birth. The Lord Jesus answers him with an Old Testament illustration. He tells of the occasion when Moses held up a bronze serpent in the wilderness and when the people of Israel, who were suffering from poisonous snake bites, looked to the bronze serpent they lived. There was, though, no healing virtue in a bronze serpent. It was the saving grace of God that healed the Israelites. So it is that in the Saviour who was lifted up on the cross there resides infinite saving virtue. There is no saving virtue in a crucifix but there is everlasting life available to all who look to the Saviour. Young people all around us, when faced with complex moral issues, will ask, "Give me the answer in a sentence". Here then is the answer to the greatest question of all. What is that? It is, "What must a person do to be saved?". The answer can be summed up in three words, "Look and live."

February twenty-fourth

"For God so loved the world that He gave His only begotten Son, that whoever believes in Him should not perish but have everlasting life" (John 3:16).

*B*ob Hope used to crack a joke about passengers in a plane that was crashing. "Somebody do something religious", a terrified passenger shouted. "So", said Bob, "They lifted a collection". The crass joke did, though, have a ring of truth about it. For a lot of people religion is all about asking for money. Even in Christ's day, as we have seen earlier in this book, they were making money out of religion. It was all a cry of "Give us, give us, give us". John 3:16, possibly the best known text in the Bible, says nothing about money. It is all about God giving us a gift that we can cannot get by paying. It is the gift of eternal life. Notice how absolutely limitless the love of God is. It goes out to everyone. There is no distinction or exception. It doesn't matter what culture you are in, what race you belong to, or what times you are living through. You put your faith in Christ and you will be rescued from destruction and enjoy eternal life. And it doesn't cost you a penny.

February twenty-fifth

*"For God did not send His Son into the world to condemn the world,
but that the world through Him might be saved. He who believes in
Him is not condemned; but he does not believe is condemned
already, because he has not believed in the Name of the
only begotten Son of God" (John 3: 17-18).*

*T*he story is told of a visitor who was being shown around an art gallery by one of its attendants. The gallery contained masterpieces by artists of great genius. After the tour was over the visitor said, "Well, I don't think much of your old pictures". The attendant wisely and quietly answered, "Sir, I would remind you that these pictures are no longer on trial but those who look at them are". All the man had done was to condemn himself. Many people find no beauty in the person of Christ. They condemn Him outright but forget that they are, by doing so, condemning themselves. God, according to our text, hasn't condemned them. He has only loved them. The more they reject Christ the more they only confirm their condemnation

February twenty-sixth

*"After these things Jesus and His disciples came into the land of Judea,
and there He remained with them and baptised. Now John also was
baptising in Aenon near Salem, because there was much water there"
(John 3: 22-23).*

*W*e all get tested. We profess something, teach something and then the time comes when the Lord tests us on what we have professed and taught. None of us escape that testing. In the Greek temples of the past cracks would appear at times in the Doric columns. Sometimes instead of dealing with the foundations the temple authorities would fill in the cracks with wax which would look like marble. All looked fine until a fire broke out and, as the flames licked at the columns, the great time of testing came. The wax, of course, would melt and the columns would collapse bringing the great structure of the temple down with them.

Christ now moved into John the Baptist's domain and his time of testing came. How would he stand? Further, says Scripture, "No other foundation can anyone lay than that which is laid, which is Jesus Christ.

Now if anyone builds on this foundation with gold, silver, precious stones, wood, hay, straw, each one's work will become manifest; for the Day will declare it, because it will be revealed by fire; and the fire will test each one's work, of what sort it is. If anyone's work which he has built on it endures, he will receive a reward. If anyone's work is burned, he will suffer loss". Selah.

February twenty-seventh

" ...And they came to John and said to him, "Rabbi, He who was with you beyond the Jordan, to whom you have testified, behold, He is baptising and all are coming to Him!" John answered and said, "A man can receive nothing unless it has been given to him from Heaven. You yourselves bear me witness that I said, 'I am not the Christ', but 'I have been sent before Him'" (John 3: 26-28).

John's disciples are not pleased that John is losing his congregation to Christ. Notice it was not the burden of the teaching between John and Christ that concerned them but the measure of the success of each. Christ was obviously more successful than John and they didn't like it. John's time of testing had come and he came through it magnificently. Not a touch of jealousy blighted his soul; the negative, miserable, suspicous monster had no part in John's ministry. He simply replied that he had never expected anything else. He knew he was never to have the leading place. He was simply an announcer, a herald, a forerunner preparing the way for the great One who would follow. That was his work and he was content. Don't you think that what is wrong with us half the time is that we are so busy wanting other ministries for the Lord, which were never meant for us, we miss doing the work He has called us to do?

February twenty-eighth

"He who has the bride is the bridegroom; but the friend of the bridegroom, who stands and hears him, rejoices greatly because of the bridegroom's voice. Therefore this joy of mine is fulfilled" (John 3: 29).

How many a wedding I have been to in my life where the "best man" was in fact the "worst man". He was a thorn in the side of the bridegroom. Given "the floor" at a wedding reception there are few young men who can resist pushing themselves rather than helping the bride- groom. I have truly endured too many "best man" speeches.

In the ancient world the bridegroom's friend could introduce the bride to the bridegroom. He could put a word in for him. He arranged the invitations, he presided at the wedding feast. He even guarded the marriage quarters and would let no false lover in. He would only open the door when he heard the bridegroom's voice and recognised it. He would let him in and then went away rejoicing because his task had been completed. John the Baptist was Christ's friend. He willingly and gladly faded out of the centre of the picture when Christ was introduced by him to those who would trust Him. Are you such a friend to Christ?

February twenty-ninth

"He must increase, but I must decrease" (John 3:30).

I never read these final words of John without feeling their dignity and majesty. No greater words ever fell from human lips. "There was no unwarranted derogation of his own personality or work; but the content of the star at its lustre is best in the rising glory of the sun ...... such was the recessional," said G. Campbell Morgan. What does Dr. Morgan mean by "the recessional"? There are different opinions as to whether from John 3: 31-36 John is still speaking or whether John ends with the great words, "He must increase and I must decrease". Dr. Morgan believed John stopped speaking with these words. Arguably, he is right. The whole of the Old Testament has come to its climax. The last messenger of that Old Testament, John the Baptist, had done his work. So we find the final words of the Old Testament. It is, in other words, the great recessional, i.e. all that happened from the Garden of Eden until now is over. As it all recedes, John now turns to that which proceeds from it all, the person of Christ. The great recessional is followed by the great processional. Are you part of it? Then let the spirit of John the Baptist mark everything you do for Christ.

Wouldn't it be an honourable characteristic of your life if you always recognised gift and talent when you saw it, even in your own community, especially when you first see it begin to rise? A note of appreciation, a word of encouragement. A helping hand to open a door of opportunity. How much better a characteristic than always downing people's gifts and talent. You can afford to be generous in spirit, can you not? Has not God been generous in sending you a Saviour? Be a generous person in all aspects of your life in return.

MARCH

March first

"But He needed to go through Samaria" (John 4:4).

I have a friend who is not, as yet, a Christian. He knows little or nothing of the Bible and in fact he recently asked me what the difference was between the Old and New Testaments. I am deeply fond of him. As it happened, I had been rather surprised by a prominent Christian who had stated to me that he felt a journey to Northern Ireland to speak at one service was a "misuse of the Lord's time and money". Rather reeling from the statement I was having coffee with my friend and shared the statement with him. Never will I forget his reaction. "Is there", he asked, "anywhere in the Bible where it speaks of God making a long journey just for one person?" I reeled again and gladly referred him to today's text.

It is true that geographically the straightest way from Judea to Galilee was through Samaria but it was not the usual way. Jews held Samaritans in abhorrence and generally, if they had to go to Galilee from Judea, they crossed the Jordan and travelled up through Peraea and entered Galilee that way. But Christ chose a road they did not take. Why? Because he wanted to reach one person. You may have to make such a journey today. Do it gladly. The repercussions will be eternal.

March second

"So He came to a city of Samaria which is called Sychar, near the plot of ground that Jacob gave to his son Joseph" (John 4:5).

J ohn catches the great drama of the moment. Here comes the Messiah in the blazing heat of noon to an area where hundreds of years beforehand Jacob, when dying, had given a plot of ground to his son Joseph. Joseph, of course, before dying, had given instructions to his people that when they left Egypt they were to take his bones and bury them in the Promised Land. About 300 years later they did just that and Joseph had been buried close to where the Messiah now stood. Obviously Joseph had had his eye on the Promised Land long before it was possessed. He knew Egypt was not to be the final home for his people. So it is that for the Christian this world is not their final resting place. Because Christ lives we shall live also. Let's keep our eye on the Promised Land. As we go about our work today let's set our affection on things above, not on things on the earth. Let's treat the earthly as transient and it will put its cares in the right perspective. Remember, you are just passing through.

March third

"Now Jacob's well was there. Jesus therefore, being weary from His journey, sat thus by the well. It was about the sixth hour" (John 4:6).

D o not miss John's revealing touch. You will remember that in his prologue he had stated that "The Word became flesh". John is now further expounding his prologue by showing us that Christ experienced the limitations of human life. Here he is wearied with His journey. It is worth remembering that human life does have its limitations. We cannot, as human beings, be everywhere and do everything. Much better to understand that certain things in life are not for us and to concentrate in the things in life that are. Christ was weary in doing His Father's will but He was not weary of it. In coming to fulfil His Father's will He had put Himself under its limitation. So must we if we would know contentment. In Christian service you can feel weary and limited in what you can do but you can also know deep contentment that nothing else can bring.

March fourth

"A woman of Samaria came to draw water. Jesus said to her, "Give me to drink" (John 4:7).

W hat could this woman, who was cohabiting with a man after five failed marriages, have in common with the Son of God? How on earth could He who was harmless, sinless and undefiled begin to communicate spiritual truths to such a woman? Don't you think it is important to ask such a question? For Christians to witness to those who know not God is no easy thing. Where do they ever begin? The answer lies in following the example of the Lord Jesus. What did He do? He found a point of common interest. They were both thirsty and He asked her for a drink. From there He led her to a point where He gave her living water.

Recently I went to Washington with the Mayor of a town in Northern Ireland, called Ballymena. We had a great time together and he confirmed for me the following story. He was once a garage mechanic and was lying working underneath a car one day when he was approached by an evangelist called Matthew Boland. Now Matthew was inviting folk to evangelistic services he was conducting in the local district and Mr. Coulter, the Mayor, detested the Gospel. Matthew, though, leaned underneath the car and instead of handing him an invitation said, cheerily, "Would you like a peppermint?". How could you refuse a cheerful chap with a peppermint!? Mr. Coulter found Christ at Matthew's services and became a Christian minister and eventually was appointed Mayor of Ballymena three times.

March fifth

"Then the woman of Samaria said to Him, 'How is it that you, being a Jew, ask a drink from me, a Samaritan woman?' For Jews have no dealings with Samaritans. Jesus said to her, 'If you knew the gift of God, and who it is who says to you, 'Give me to drink', you would have asked Him and He would have given you living water'" (John 4:9-10).

We are back on a familiar scene. John loves to show that God loves to give. It is true that Christ was asking the woman here for a drink of water but He points out that if she really knew who He was and that if she had understood the character of God, she would have asked Him for living water and He would have gladly given it.

Half time, in life, we have not because we ask not. Do you need power for service? Ask for it. Do you need a restored joy in your soul? Ask for it. Do you need guidance in that decision? Ask for it. Of course our asking must be in His Name and consistent with His character and declared purposes and interest. It must have the motivation that God be glorified but such limitations are, in fact, the door to incredible freedom. So, ask, and it shall be given to you.

March sixth

"Jesus answered and said to her, 'Whoever drinks of this water will thirst again, but whoever drinks of the water that I shall give him will never thirst. The water that I shall give him will become in him a fountain of water springing up into everlasting life'" (John 4: 13-14).

T he water in the well is contrasted by Christ with the water that He gives. One was stagnant, the other constantly springs up. One had to be obtained by effort (the woman "came" to draw water) the other was contained within. Even at this moment of writing I look out my hotel window and see Edinburgh Castle on the skyline. It has been there a long time and the garrison has often been able to hold out against seige because it has its source of water supply inside and the invader cannot cut it off. Jacob's well would dwindle and choke up with debris but Christ's living water would keep on rising up in the lives of those to whom it is opened, summer, autumn, winter or spring. The water in the well would bring temporary relief but the water that Christ brings gives permanent relief. I care not what desolation or drought may afflict you today; if you have tasted of the water that Christ gives it will make a wilderness flower and a desert sing. Drink, reader, drink.

March seventh

"The woman said to Him, 'Sir, I perceive that you are a prophet. Our fathers worshipped on this mountain and you Jews say that in Jerusalem is the place where one ought to worship'. Jesus said to her .... 'The hour is coming, and now is, when the true worshippers will worship the Father in spirit and truth; for the Father is seeking such to worship Him'" (John 4:19-23).

I f there is one thing that has always sickened me it is the divisions within the Christian church. If the woman at the well had a problem with religious difference between Samaritans and Jews what would she have made of it had she walked down the street that I know in Belfast that has seventeen different church buildings on it? What about your city or town or village?

Still, divisions though there may be, Christ is not divided, is He? The important question, according to Christ, was not where people worshipped God but how. I have worshipped God in a converted cow byre in South Korea with eight believers sitting on the ground around a flagon of wine and a piece of bread on a plate. It was every bit was wonderful as worshipping God in some magnificent church building in the western world.

"Jesus, where Thy people meet,
There they behold Thy mercy seat,
Where they seek Thee, Thou art found.
And every place is hallowed ground."

March eighth

"I know that Messiah is coming" (Who is called Christ). "When He comes, He will tell us all things". Jesus said to her, "I who speak to you am He" (John 4: 25-26).

First she was flippant. When Jesus asked her to call her husband she evaded it, flippantly; "I have no husband", she said. She obviously thought that she was an emancipated woman. She couldn't, though, hide from Him. When He told her that she had had five husbands and the one that she now had was not her husband she moved from being flippant to being respectful. "I perceive you are a prophet", she said. But now, here was something. He told her that He was the Messiah. She was now moved from flippancy and respectfulness to sheer worship.

The result of all this was that she immediately began to introduce people to Christ. How could it be otherwise? A person who has living water welling up within them cannot but share their secret. It was so with the famous Cornish miner-preacher, Billy Bray. "Why can't you worship the Lord without making so much noise?" Billy was once asked. "It's not my fault," replied Billy, "I am only the vessel; my Heavenly Father is pouring down the water of life freely, and if you can't bear it, call to Him not to pour so much."

March ninth

"Jesus said to them, 'My food is to do the will of Him who sent Me, and to finish His work'" (John 4: 34).

There is food that the best gourmets in the world could not present to you. There is food that some of the best connoisseurs on this planet have never tasted. It is succulent and satisfying beyond all human description. It has been tasted by those who seek to do God's will in their lives. Nothing, no nothing, can be more satisfying.

Obviously it is a big subject but, to put it simply, the will of God is to do the legitimate duties of today, and for His Glory. He will lead us on from there. So, go out today and do those legitimate duties as to Him. If you could not put that essay into His hand, look Him straight in the eye with that deal, or, go to that place with His approval, then review it and get things right.

March tenth

"Do not say, 'There are still four months and then comes the harvest?' Behold, I say to you, lift up your eyes and look at the fields, for they are already white for harvest!" (John 4: 35).

Christ is speaking of a spiritual harvest. Sure, the immediate harvest in Samaria first needed ploughing and sowing and was still four months off, but the soul-harvest is always ripe for reaping, immediately. Ask the Lord to open your eyes to see the soul-harvest around you, today. That person at work, that neighbour, that individual who crosses your path. There is that student studying philosophy and drifting into an immoral situation. There is that victim of divorce or a broken home who trusts no-one. There is that "party-boy" across the hall who cares about nothing but himself. All have souls that need the Saviour and God may use you to reap a harvest this very day. Go on, put the sickle in!

March *eleventh*

"And he who reaps receives wages, and gathers fruit for eternal life, that both he who sows and he who reaps may rejoice together. For in this the saying is true: 'One sows and another reaps'" (John 4: 36-37).

C hristian work is all about sowing and reaping but everyone involved in Christian work is both a sower and a reaper. Everyone doing Christ's work reaps what was sown by others and sows what others will reap. So, both sower and reaper are not to be jealous of each other but are called to rejoice together. I often tell the story of a dissolute young university student who went to a small Bible study in a home in Germany. He got converted and eventually founded a very famous home for orphans in Bristol and wrote his life story. A young man in Ireland read his story and said, "If God can do this for George Muller He can do it for us". He and his friends met to pray every week in Kells in Co. Antrim and the Lord sent the mighty 1859 revival to Ireland in answer to their prayers. At least 100,000 people were converted in one year including my great- grandparents and I am writing today under the direct influence of that little Bible study in that home in Germany. See what I mean by sowing and reaping in Christian work?

March *twelfth*

"Now we believe, not because of what you did, for we have heard for ourselves and know that this is indeed the Christ, the Saviour of the world" (John 4: 42).

T he Saviour of the world! Don't you love that word "Saviour"? I often use it in my conversation and I can sometimes feel it gently touch lives. I constantly cross lives scarred by sin, ravaged by health problems, brutalised by violence or overcome by events beyond their control; don't you? All around us are people who are lonely, depressed, weary, ready to quit.

Governments ultimately fail because they cannot deliver on all their promises. The world's pleasures are so transitory and do not satisfy; they leave people empty. People go on to read another novel or see another film. Their lives are restless and unfulfilled. But, a Saviour? Who could claim such a title? Who could deliver on such a promise? The Samaritans heard of one through this woman but personal contact with Christ was necessary to make faith complete. They found Him to be all that she said He was. Have you?

March thirteenth

"Now after the two days He departed from there and went to Galilee. For Jesus Himself testified that a prophet has no honour in his own country. So when He came to Galilee the Galilaeans received Him, having seen all the things He did at Jerusalem at the feast, for He also had gone to the feast" (John 4: 43-45).

*T*he people in Galilee were no different to people anywhere at any time. They were slow to honour where honour was due in their own community. It has always been so. "We knew him in short trousers", people say, as if that were an attribute that ensures he never deserves to make it! Of course, when he does make it, bus loads of them suddenly come to be a friend of his!

Wouldn't it be an honourable characteristic of your life if you always recognised gift and talent when you saw it, even in your own community, especially when you first see it begin to rise? A note of appreciation, a word of encouragement. A helping hand to open a door of opportunity. How much better a characteristic than always downing people's gifts and talent. You can afford to be generous in spirit, can you not? Has not God been generous in sending you a Saviour? Be a generous person in all aspects of your life in return.

March fourteenth

"So Jesus came to Cana of Galilee where He had made the water wine. And there was a certain nobleman whose son was sick at Capernaum. When he heard that Jesus had come out of Judea into Galilee, he went to Him and implored Him to come down and heal his son, for he was at the point of death. Then Jesus said to him, 'Unless you people see signs and wonders, you will by no means believe'. The nobleman said to him, 'Sir, come down before my child dies!' Jesus said to him, 'Go your way; your son lives'" (John 4; 46-50).

*T*his royal official meant business. It takes a lot to leave a dying child but he was desperate and made a long journey to the One who could give him hope. Imagine his surprise when after pleading with Christ to come down and heal his child, Christ raises a point of theology about the whole question of people basing their beliefs upon signs and wonders. You can almost hear the nobleman say in reply, "Not theology now Lord, my child is dying!"

The Lord, though, was trying to comfort the man for He immediately told him that his child lived. He was basically telling him, "If it is signs and wonders you want before you believe, then you are in for a rough 24 hours!" If the man were to have peace of mind on his journey home then he must take the Lord's word for it that his child was healed. There would be eventual evidence for sure, but it would be delayed evidence. So, you may have no external evidence that all the things that are happening to you today are working together for good. Yet, you have the Lord's word for it that they are. Is the Lord's word not enough to be going on with?

March fifteenth

"So the man believed the word that Jesus spoke to him, and he went his way. And as he was now going down, his servants met him and told him, saying, 'Your son lives!' Then he enquired of them the hour he got better. And they said to him, 'Yesterday at the seventh hour the fever left him'. So the father knew it was at the same hour in which Jesus said to him, 'Your son lives'. And he himself believed, and his whole household" (John 4: 50-53).

Notice that this man believed twice. He first believed the Lord's word without immediate evidence and then he believed again when he saw the evidence. Every Christian experiences the same thing. Their faith first comes by hearing and hearing by the Word of God. They believe the Gospel because Jesus said it was true.

Life, though, soon begins to sweep over them. Disappointment knocks at their door, bereavement and grief edge into their experience, trouble rumbles across their days. In all sorts of ways they prove that Jesus Christ is who He says He is and that His word is true; evidence for it comes in all sorts of places and through all sorts of experiences. Tribulation produces perseverance; and perseverance character; and character, hope. They had hope when they first believed now they have the evidence for it they have even greater hope and believe again. Like the nobleman, they have believed twice.

March sixteenth

"Then he enquired of him the hour when he got better. And he said to him, 'Yesterday at the seventh hour the fever left him'" (John 4: 52).

We are, as human beings, constantly behind events. Things happen to our friends, neighbours or across the nations, and we are constantly trying to catch up on events. We have to concentrate on our immediate responsibilities and so are behind on what is happening elsewhere. Is it not so with God? Did not John say in his prologue, "In the beginning was the Word?" He is before all things. The Lord is never behind any event, He is always before it. He knew of the boy's condition long before his father got to him to see how he was. The Lord always covers the ground we will pass through long before we get there. So, don't be afraid to go around the corner. He is already there.

March seventeenth

"Jesus said to him, 'Rise, take up your bed and walk'. And immediately the man was made well, took up his bed and walked. And that day was the sabbath. The Jews therefore said to him who was cured, 'It is the sabbath; it is not lawful for you to carry your bed'. He answered them, 'He who made me well said to me, 'Take up your bed and walk'" (John 5: 8-11).

There is always some serpent to slime your Eden. The Pharisees, who are by no means dead even yet, are such serpents. They make a list of do's and don'ts which are not based on Scripture but on tradition or personal preference and they judge themselves and others on their performance. The Pharisee advice is that of exalting self by disparaging others which is a very cheap way of attaining moral superiority.

The Pharisees amplified the sabbath law by adding thirty-nine categories of unpermitted work along with a number of tedious restrictions. Some of the more ridiculous restrictions included not carrying a needle in your robe in the sabbath or not removing your fingernails by means of your nails or teeth, and not pulling out a hair of your head! They even had one restriction where they said that a woman dressing her head on the sabbath was working! They went for the healed man for carrying his bed on the sabbath but he had an answer for them. "The man who cured me told me to", he said. If the man had the power to cure, then surely He had the right to tell him to carry his bed. So if the Lord has told you to do it, do it and forget the Pharisees. If the paralysed man had listened to those fellows he could have sat by that pool to the day of his death for all they cared.

March eighteenth

"But Jesus answered them, 'My Father has been working until now, and I have been working'. Therefore the Jews sought all the more to kill Him because He not only broke the Sabbath, but also said that God was His Father, making Himself equal with God" (John 5: 17-18).

Christ's defence of what He had done for the paralysed man was wholly shattering. It moved those Pharisees into murderous hate for the Saviour. His defence was that God did not entirely stop working on the Sabbath and that neither did He. Sure, God rested on the Sabbath from His work of creation but He still had to uphold the world He had created. The rivers flow, the sun comes up, the grass grows, the crops flourish on the Sabbath just as much as any other day. So too do His higher works of judgment, mercy, kindness, love and compassion. If Christ healed a sick man on the Sabbath, He was no more breaking the fourth commandment than His Father broke it by making the world go round on the Sabbath.

Why did the Pharisees get so mad? Because Jesus was putting Himself on an equality with God. In days of syncretism many are tempted to lower Christ to an equality with the gods of this world rather than to stand for the Scriptural truth of Christ being in God. "All authority in Heaven and on earth," said the risen Saviour to His disciples, "Has been given to Me". That authority is not shared with anyone else no matter how praiseworthy that person might be. "Everyone who calls on the Name of the Lord will be saved", said Christ. That is not the Christ of soft modern thinking but it is the Christ of the Scripture. People still get mad at Christ claiming to be God to this very day. Don't give in to them.

March nineteenth

"Most assuredly, I say to you, he who hears my word and believes on Him who sent Me has everlasting life, and shall not come into judgment, but has passed from death into life. Most assuredly, I say to you, the hour is coming, and now is, when the dead will hear the voice of the Son of God; and those who hear will live" (John 5: 24-25).

Who determines our final destiny? Christ decides. He will be the central figure on the Judgment Day and the basis of the judgment will be people's attitude to Him and the nature of the judgment will be exclusion from His presence. And what will the Judge say about you and I? The fact is that we don't have to wait until His Judgment Seat to find out. Today's verse tells us that we can meet Him here and now and the word of the Judge is that anyone with a hearing ear and a believing heart who accepts the gift of eternal life by faith will never experience eternal separation from God. Notice that future judgement has already passed over; the word is that the believer has passed from death into life. Here then we have no long waiting to find out where we will be in eternity. Here is no torturous route through Purgatory. Conversion and possessing eternal life are synonymous; notice that it is not they that live shall hear but they that hear shall live. There is a glorious difference.

March twentieth

"For as the Father has life in Himself, so He has granted the Son to have Life in Himself" (John 5: 26).

Consider the power of the teaching in today's text. Christ is presented as the source of life. It does not say that as the Father has life so the Son has life. It says as the Father has life, in Himself, so He has granted the Son to have life "in Himself". So it is that Christ is not only alive, He is the central source of all life. Without Him was not anything made that was made.

For a lot of people status depends on their academic achievement or their home, their money, or their talent. Such things do not give you status in God's world. The major thing is; "He made me" and therefore all else is secondary. God is the source of my life. If that is so then I don't have to spend my life and energy chasing status symbols. The glory of God is the chief end of my life and He is my exceeding great reward. What a status!

March twenty-first

"If I bear witness of Myself, My witness is not true" (John 5: 31).

*T*he towering claims of Christ are stupendous. All of us have to face them and decide as to their authenticity. Christ now defends His claims by calling in some witnesses to verify them. He categorically states that His testimony alone would not be valid (See Deuteronomy 19; 15) and calls in the first witness to His Diety, namely God the Father.

Christ actually states in John 5;19 that the very words He spoke were not His own but His Fathers. He was relaying them. That God the Father was a witness to His Diety is vital. So, at His baptism a voice was heard from Heaven saying, "This is My Beloved Son, hear Him". At the Transfiguration His voice again broke through with the same message. At the Crucifixion the Father answered the Saviour's work by ripping the temple curtain from the top to the bottom opening up a new and living way into His presence. On the dark morning of the third day of Christ's burial, the Father raised Him from the dead. Christ's claims have been authenticated by the greatest authority of all. You can believe every word He says.

March twenty-second

"....Have borne witness to the truth ... He was the burning and shining lamp ..." (John 5: 33-35).

*I*t was not that John's career was signalised by a blaze of wonder for the Scripture expressly states that "John did no miracle". It is not that He was a master of superb eloquence but He was "a cry", a short, thrilling piercing cry ringing across a desert place. He was "the clasp", if you like, between the two Covenants. He was not a prairie fire but a burning and shining lamp. The lovely thing is that He was content to be just that. John did not live even to the age of 35; he did not even live to see the Resurrection of Christ. He was sent to clear the way, to prepare the way and to get out of the way. He was one of God's hidden ones. While the world has been rent by faction and war, ravaged by fire and sword, bomb and bullet and trouble, God always has His hidden ones who will hear His call and do what He asks of them. Are you one?

*M*arch *twenty-third*

"You search the Scriptures, for in them you think you have eternal life; and these are they which testify of Me" (John 5: 39).

I don't know what situation you might face today. It may be very frightening. I do know, though, that the words of Christ are comforting. I know that His Father's witness to His power underlines our belief in Him above other witnesses. I know that John the Baptist's witness was singular and unique. Christ's works, though, are also a permanent witness to what He can do for you, even to this very day. Do you not think it helps to know that you can put your hand in the hand of the Man who stilled the water? Does it not calm you down when you think that whatever may hassle you today can be handled by One who heals the sick, gives sight to the blind, chases demons, feeds multitudes? There is nothing too hard for the Lord; nothing. Not even your situation. Interviewing the Chaplain to the United States Senate one snowy afternoon in Washington, he told me of a motto he had. I pass it on to you on this difficult day in your life. Learn it well. "Without God we cannot; without us He won't". With the witness of His mighty works behind you He will give you grace this day to play your part.

*M*arch *twenty-fourth*

"The Scriptures ..... are they which testify of Me" (John 5: 39).

*I*n Genesis He is the seed of the woman, in Exodus the Passover Lamb, in Leviticus, the High Priest, in Numbers the City of Refuge, in Deuteronomy, the Prophet like Moses, in Joshua, the Captain of our Salvation and in Judges the Deliverer. In Ruth, He is the Redeemer, in I and II Samuel, David's Greater Son, in Kings and Chronicles, the Reigning King, in Ezra, our Faithful Scribe, in Nehemiah, the

Rebuilder, in Esther, our Mordecai. In Job He is the True Comforter, in the Psalms, our Shepherd, in the Proverbs, our wisdom, in Solomon, the Bridegroom, in Isaiah, the Prince of Peace, in Jeremiah, the Righteous Branch. In Lamentations He is the Weeping Prophet, in Ezekiel, the Four Faced Man, in Joel, the Baptiser, in Amos, our Burden Bearer, in Obadiah He is the One mighty to save. In Jonah He is the Compassionate One, in Micah, the Messenger with beautiful feet, in Nahum, the Avenger. In Habakkuk, He is the Reviver, In Zephaniah, the Saviour, in Haggai, the Restorer. In Zechariah, the Opened Fountain, in Malachi, the Son of Righteousness. And that's only the Old Testament!

March twenty-fifth

"Now the Passover, a feast of the Jews, was near ... and Jesus took the loaves and when He had given thanks He distributed them to the disciples, and the disciples to those sitting down; and likewise also fish, as much as they wanted" (John 6: 4,11).

The Passover feast was first held when the Israelites had just been spared the devastating work of the avenging angel in Egypt. They had to eat the feast with a belt on their waist, their sandals on their feet and their staff in their hand. They were to eat it in haste. It was a feast related to journeying. Now, suddenly, a huge journeying crowd arrive at the mountain in Galilee where the Passover Lamb Himself was seated with His disciples. He fed them by a miracle. Interesting, isn't it, at the way the Passover Lamb spreads the feast for His people and finds that they are interested in the food and not interested in Him? Indeed they wanted to make Him King on the spot but He would have none of it because He refused to have His Kingdom filled with people who wanted what He could give without wanting Him. If I arrived at your home and you gave me a meal and I was not the slightest bit interested in you, would you give me a meal again? So it is that Christ refused to repeat the miracle for the crowds the next day. We trust Christ for who He is, not just for what He gives.

March twenty-sixth

*"Do not labour for the food which perishes, but for the food which
endures to everlasting life, which the Son of Man will give you, because
God the Father has set His seal on Him" (John 5: 27).*

What is the first duty of the Christian? Some would tell us that
it is to care for the poor. They would insist that we stop
preaching the need for repentance toward God and faith in
our Lord Jesus Christ. They would accuse us of merely using words.

That we should care for the poor is vital because our Saviour certainly did, but it is not the primary duty of the Church. The primary
duty of the Church is to witness to the Gospel, for, as Professor David
Gooding has said, "For people to take God's physical food and not be
interested in the hand that gave it is such a disaster it not only removes
the highest level of significance from our daily bread, but it brings us in
danger of perishing eternally. Life is a journey and bread and fish will
certainly keep you going for your allotted span but what then? To go
through life dismissing the Giver of your daily bread and then to go out
into it would mean an eternity of eternal famine. To eat physical bread
and deny spiritual bread is a disaster. It is such a ruination of God's
purpose for mankind that our Lord will not be party to maintaining the
idea that so long as people are physically fed that is the main thing in
Christianity."

March twenty-seventh

*"And Jesus said to them, 'I am the Bread of Life. He who comes to me
shall never hunger, and he who believes in Me shall never thirst'"
(John 3: 35).*

As the Israelites were on a journey to their inheritance, God
rained down manna, or bread, from Heaven upon them in the
wilderness. So we too are on a journey to an inheritance,
incorruptibile and undefiled reserved in Heaven for us. On the way we
will need sustenance and so we have Christ the Bread of Life. As bread
is all sufficient for life and contains all the elements needed for nutri-
tion, so in Christ we have everything we need for life and godliness. He

is our hiding place in the storm, our water in drought, the shadow of a great rock in a weary land. For the polluted He is purity. For the irritable, He is patience. For the fearful, He is courage. For the weak, He is strength. For the ignorant, He is wisdom. He is enough.

March twenty-eighth

"And when evening came His disciples went down to the sea, got into a boat, and went over the sea towards Capernaum" (John 6: 16-17).

The men knew how to manage a boat from their long experience. If the wind is contrary there is only one thing to do, as any skilled sailor will tell you; put the boat about. It is a dangerous manoeuvre but if successful the contrary wind will now blow the boat back to safety. Why did they not go back? Because, according to Mark 6 the Lord had sent them on a mission and they never dreamed of going back. Put all the references in the Gospels together and you will see that these men struggled for nine to ten hours and covered only about three miles. So it is that as you struggle on, Christian, and the winds are contrary and we are trying to obey a calling and we feel swamped, how easy it would be to go back. But they kept on and then the sign was given. So it will be for you and I. Keep on going on today. The sign, which is a miracle, will come.

March twenty-ninth

"And it was now dark and Jesus had not come to them" (John 6: 17).

Is it dark in your life? Have you been praying and longing for an answer to prayer? Are the delays of God puzzling you? You have heard it before but let me repeat it again; God's delays always end up in being God's delights. These men, by Christ's delay, were about to discover that the Lord had power over nature. Jairus, the Jewish leader, had asked Christ to come to his dying child. Christ stopped to talk and heal a woman who was ill and they told him, in the interim, that his child had died. Christ, of course, could have healed his child and he would have discovered that Christ had power over disease. By His delay Christ soon showed Jairus that He had power over death. Sometime later Mary and Martha scolded Christ for what they thought was a very serious delay on His part.

"If you had been here our brother would not have died", they said. By that delay they discovered that Christ had not only power over nature, disease and death, but they discovered that He actually had power over decomposition. Christ raised Lazarus from the tomb! Don't get mad at those delays of the Saviour. You will yet delight in them.

March thirtieth

"So when they had rode about three or four miles they saw Jesus walking on the sea and drawing near the boat" (John 6:19).

They saw a figure approaching them, walking, head against the contrary wind because He was overtaking them. The wind which was holding them back was not holding back that approaching figure. They were almost sinking but He wasn't. He who had refused to be crowned King upon the basis of bread was, make no mistake, King in every realm. The tossing sea could not overwhelm Him.

I was once sitting in a little cafe at the southernmost tip of the world in a place called Bluff in the South Island of New Zealand. I was watching a huge ship being taken out into the ocean when suddenly the pilot was taken off. "He doesn't go all the way, you know", said the waitress in the cafe. I thought long thoughts about the pilot of my soul who has promised through calm or storm to never leave me or forsake me. Selah.

March thirty-first

"He said to them, 'It is I; do not be afraid'. Then they willingly received Him into the boat, and immediately the boat was at the land where they were going" (John 6; 20-21).

Mysterious, isn't it? All that wind and wave and terror. All that rowing and fright. All that frustration and delay. All that sticking to a calling with no turning back. And then? The Lord comes on board and a mysterious journey takes them to their desired haven, immediately. That's what it says, doesn't it? "Immediately the boat was at the land where they were going".

They obviously weren't at the land when the Lord got in the boat. Far from it. But they were now. The Ulster writer C. S. Lewis was talking about the same thing, wasn't he, when the children suddenly found themselves in Narnia through a cupboard they were hiding in?

One minute they were in an everyday world, the next, Narnia. The message is clear. As you toil, Christian, towards your desired haven, Christ will suddenly appear and take you there. Immediately. Perhaps today.

ook around you, Christian. How do the vast majority of people make their plans? They make them to please themselves. They have no awareness of living from moment to moment in sensitive rapport with God's directing will. One time is as good as another with them. Their time is always ready to follow their whims and desires. They don't care to ask the Lord as to what He wants, do they?

APRIL

April first

"Then Jesus said to them, 'Most assuredly I say to you, unless you eat the flesh of the Son of Man and drink His blood, you have no life in you. Whoever eats my flesh and drinks my blood has eternal life, and I will raise him up at the last day'" (John 6: 53-54).

I t is important to remember that today's texts are not speaking about the Lord's table. To take that view would mean that a vast number of people who have been converted but who have not yet broken bread or drunk wine in remembrance of the Lord Jesus would not be the possessors of eternal life. Apart from this the bread and wine are not literally the body and blood of Christ. If they were it would mean that when Christ said, 'This is My body' while holding the bread, He would then have been speaking of two bodies, wouldn't He?

Today's texts are an analogy telling us that just as we must ingest food and let it become part of us if we want it to maintain us, so Christ in us is the hope of glory. That's why the disciples were told to gather up all the fragments which were left after Christ had fed the five thousand.

It represents Him as the Living Bread. If that Living Bread is within you it will never be lost. And, with all my heart, I believe neither will any true believer. "He who eats this bread", said Christ, will live for ever. How very saddening it is to find many Christians across the world who have no assurance of their salvation. Meditate long in your heart upon the promise of today's texts that those who have feasted on Christ He will raise up at the last day. In such an assurance we can not only face the terror of death but we can face the fury of life.

April second

"Therefore many of His disciples, when they heard this, said, 'This is a hard saying; who can understand it?'. When Jesus knew in Himself that His disciples murmered about this, He said to them, 'Does this offend you?'" (John 6: 60-61).

I t was not just the disciples who found the saying about eating Christ's flesh and drinking His blood offensive. Christians have often been accused in history of cannabalism because of a misunderstanding of this verse. It is important to notice that instead of softening His statement to accommodate the disciples, Christ strengthened it by pointing out that He didn't just come into the world to lead a good life but He came in order to bring us on our journey to the next. He is the means to maintain us on our journey. We feed upon Him as we go. He refuses to take back the statement He has made, praise His Name. If others are offended by the statement, why should we?

There is, often, a very dangerous imbalance that creeps into Christian's lives. They begin to look to public Christian activity as the means for maintaining their Christian life rather than enjoying and feasting upon Christ. When suddenly that public activity is, for various reasons, no longer possible they then hit a really dangerous situation. Feast upon Christ in your heart and soul and mind daily. No matter what your circumstances you will have a healthy balance to your Christian living. Mark this truth well for you know not what this day may bring.

April third

"The words that I speak to you are Spirit, and they are life"
(John 6: 63).

Bread is made of fine flour and even in the grinding of the flour the life germs of the wheat are not destroyed. It is the presence of life and bread which causes it to sustain life in us. It is also the presence of life in the words of the Bible which makes it for every generation a book which is more relevant than tomorrow's newspaper.

I shall always remember one evening speaking at an evangelistic service. When it was over a man approached me to tell me that he had been coverted to Christ during the service. I asked him what had reached him. "The Bible text on the wall behind you", he said with a smile! When God spoke the universe came into being. When He takes His Word and speaks it to our hearts, it contains life.It builds life. It joins us all the more securely to that eternal, spiritual realm. One way of feeding on Christ is to cherish and obey His Words. They are, spiritual, life-giving food. As Jeremiah put it long ago, "Your words were found, and I ate them, and your words became to me a joy and the delight of my heart". Christ spoke as no-one has ever done. Let His words meet with faith in your heart and they will do you immense good today.

April fourth

"Then Jesus said to the twelve, 'Do you also want to go away?' Then Simon Peter answered Him, 'Lord to whom shall we go? You have the words of eternal life'" (John 6: 67-68).

Gracious words: words that lift the weary, heal the brokenhearted, comfort the bereaved, forgive the sinner, draw back the backslider; encourage those who feel like quitting. No words like His. Authoritative words; not folksy, not gallery-pleasing, but self- evident. They can stand up anywhere, in any clime or culture on the face of the earth, speaking to hearts in whatever circumstance. Relevant words; wrapped in metaphor or parables they are limitless. The Good Samaritan, the rich fool, the barren fig tree, the lost coin, the great supper, the drag-net, etc. As F. B. Meyer put it, "Thousands would gather in the desert or on the hills, forgetful of all beside, and willing to stand the live-long day to listen to lips which dropped with honey. His words swayed the multitudes as vines swing in the autumn air". Like Peter, to whom else would we turn in these days? He has the words of eternal life. Worship Him, today.

April fifth

"His brothers therefore said to Him, 'Depart from here and go into Judea, that your disciples also may see the works that you are doing. For no-one does anything in secret while he himself seeks to be known openly. If you do these things, show yourself to the world'. For even His brothers did not believe in Him. Then Jesus said to them, 'My time has not yet come, but your time is always ready'" (John 7: 3-6).

Look around you, Christian. How do the vast majority of people make their plans? They make them to please themselves. They have no awareness of living from moment to moment in sensitive rapport with God's directing will. One time is as good as another with them. Their time is always ready to follow their whims and desires. They don't care to ask the Lord as to what He wants, do they?

Christ's unbelieving brothers urged Him to go up to the Feast at Jerusalem and do some spectacular miracles and show Himself to the world. But Christ refused. His time is regulated by His Father. He refuses to go anywhere until that will is shown. His hour has not yet come. His public entry into Jerusalem was still six months down the line. Are you planning something? Then trust in the Lord with all your heart. Lean not to your own understanding. In all your ways acknowledge Him and He shall direct your path. Don't let your family or anyone else push you out of first seeking the Lord about your plans. Remember, when God opens a door, no-one can shut it.

$\mathcal{A}$pril   sixth

"Now about the middle of the Feast Jesus went up into the Temple and taught. And the Jews marvelled, saying, 'How does this Man know letters, having never studied?'" (John 7: 14-15).

$\mathcal{A}$re you just a little bit ashamed to stand up as a Christian at this time in your life? You may be surrounded by the intellectually brilliant and by people who are exceptionally well read. You may be very reticent to declare that you are a follower of the Lord Jesus. The philosophers and scientists, the academics and teachers of your day, they appear to have a lot of answers and your faith in Christ may be sneared at by many of them. Note, then, today's text. Christ was surrounded by prejudice and hatred so His Father now signals that He should go incognito to the temple to teach (see John 7: 10).

The people listening hadn't a clue as to who He was and He didn't tell them. The emphasis was on His teaching. How did the people react? They immediately knew that His teaching was magnificent. "How does this Man know letters having never studied?", they asked. We need never, ever, be ashamed of the teaching of the Lord Jesus. It will stand up anywhere. Plato, Aristotle, Socrates, Kant, Floyd, J. S. Mills, Jean Paul Satre, Marks, Angles, Ayer, you name them, Christ is the highest problem in philosophy. His morals and ethics tower on their own merit above any other teaching. Hold to it. Remember that even when the people didn't know who the teacher was, the teaching stood out. It still does.

April seventh

"If anyone wants to do His will, he shall know concerning the doctrine,
whether it is from God or whether I speak on my own authority"
(John 7: 17).

Interesting, isn't it? Christ calls upon everyone to test His teaching by an experiment. If you are ready to do the will of God the capacity for discerning that Christ's teaching and its messages are of God will follow. If you say to God, "Show me if Jesus Christ is the Son of God and if you don't I am not prepared to do Your will", you might as well quit. Here we see an attitude which brings detection of final authority. If you are ready to do God's will you will come to know the truth. Trust is self-authenticating.

Don't you think that Christ's challenge to carry out this experiment is worth taking up? No-one who ever said, "Lord, I am willing to do Your will" was left in the dark as to what it was.It's all down to an attitude. Aren't most things?

April eighth

"Do not judge according to appearance, but judge with righteous
judgment" (John 7: 23-24).

We judge most things by appearance. Try, oh try, in your life to see below the surface of things and to judge things fairly. We are living in a world which places great emphasis on outward image. We live in a world of spin-doctors who "package" politicians, or celebrities, or authors or whatever. They could present virtually anything and make some feature of it appear attractive.

If you were to walk in Highgate Cemetery in London and read a headstone there you would find the words, "M. Faraday, 1791-1867". There is no epitaph and nothing to tell you that your life in a modern world has been deeply affected by the things that this great scientist discovered in the world of refrigeration, electricity,glass, etc. On and on the list goes but with a direct line back to this son of a Yorkshire blacksmith. He was a wonderful Christian and lived a life to God's glory which is inspiring, even to this day. You would never know it, though, from his headstone. If you judge according to appearance you will miss gems. A second look, even a third or a fourth will reveal things that you missed. Are you ready to throw in the towel on some work or other in which you are involved? Be careful. It may not yet be over. You may be on the verge of something great. Your input may, under God, be of far greater importance than you imagine. Take another look before you do something you may regret for the rest of your life.

April ninth

"The Pharisees heard the crowd murmuring these things concerning Him, and the Pharisees and the chief priests sent officers to take Him. Then Jesus said to them, 'I shall be with you a little while longer, and then I go to Him who sent Me. You will seek Me and will not find Me, and where I am you cannot come'. Then the Jews said among themselves, 'Where does He intend to go that we will not find Him? Does He intend to go to the Dispersion among the Greeks and teach the Greeks?'" (John 7: 32-35).

When the Lord Jesus spoke of going away many around Him thought He was going to Greece. But no, He was going to the cross. The manner of Christ's going away was a very important part of the divine strategy. His teaching would earn Him a cross and He being lifted up would draw the people to Himself. His resurrection would prove what His Father thought of His works.

It is a tender point but one we must never forget. All of the Saviour's earthly life was foreshadowed by the cross. At every point, at every turn, through every domestic and public scene, the darkness and horror of it all awaited Him. He never flinched. He never wavered. All the joys that the Christian possesses came because of His sorrow. Our sins are forgiven, we have peace with God, we enjoy assurance of Heaven and the presence of the Comforter and the anticipation of crossing that final river and meeting the Lord on a celestial shore. It was all bought at an incalculable price. Let's not forget to thank Him, today, for His love.

April tenth

"On the last day, that great day of the Feast, Jesus stood and cried out, 'If anyone thirsts let him come to Me and drink'" (John 7: 37).

At the Feast of Tabernacles the people lived for a whole week in tents. It was to serve as a reminder of their pilgrimage days. The Jews also added some ceremonies to the Feast. Not only did they live in booths but they went down to the pool of Siloam with a golden pitcher, daily, filled it with water and the water was ceremoniously poured at the base of the altar. This was done twice on the last day of the Feast. It was a reminder that when they had run out of water in the wilderness, the Lord had provided it for them, miracuously, twice. It was also an unspoken prayer for more rain.

But the prophets spoke of a day when God would pour, not just water, but His Holy Spirit on all flesh. And there would be more, much more (see Isaiah 60; 1-3, 25; 6-8, Zechariah 14; 4-9, 7-20). God, you know, has not just given us joys in life to mock us but they point to a bigger joy. That's what the Feast of Tabernacles taught; the best is yet to be. Do you believe that? Then live as if you do.

April eleventh

"On the last day, that great day of the Feast, Jesus stood and cried out, saying, 'If anyone thirsts let him come to Me and drink' ..... Now some of them wanted to take Him, but no-one laid hands on Him"
(John 7: 37,44).

The water had just been poured at the base of the altar at the great Feast of Tabernacles ceremony in Jerusalem in the presence of thousands for the second time when a lone voice cried, 'If anyone thirsts, let him come to Me and drink'. Some wanted to seize Him right away. Why did they so detest Christ? It was because they liked the ceremony of the Feast of Tabernacles with their High Priest in all his glory and the symbolism that went with it all. What they didn't want was the reality. The speaker dressed in the simple homespun clothes of a countryman, not having where to lay His head and often hungry and thirsty Himself, spoke of Himself as the great thirst-quencher. They simply wouldn't have it. Will you? Christ is Christianity. Other teachers talk about truth and set themselves to invent vast systems of philosophy which people must read and understand. But our Lord has one cure for all woes, all needs, and all wants - "If anyone thirsts let Him come to Me and drink", He says. So drink, my reader, drink of Him. You are not big enough to be the goal of your own existence. Make Him your goal.

April   twelfth

"He who believes in Me, as the Scripture has said, out of his heart will flow rivers of living water" (John 7: 37).

et me tell you a story. One evening in May during the Presidency of Richard Nixon, Washington resembled an armed camp of troops and policemen surrounding the principal buildings and institutions of Government. President Nixon was restless. The large student demonstration against his South-East Asian policy was due in the capital the next day and the White House logged 51 telephone calls from the President to his friends and staff round the country between 10.35 a.m. and 3.50 a.m. At 4.30 a.m. he went out of the White House with his valet Sanchez and went to Capitol Hill and into the House Chamber.

A surprised custodian unlocked the Chamber doors after a five minute hunt for the keys. As the President showed his valet around (Sanchez had never been there before) he was approached by a group of cleaning ladies. One of them, a black woman called Mrs. Kerry Moore, asked him to sign her Bible. Nixon said he was glad to see that she carried her Bible with her, adding as he signed it, "The trouble is that most of us these days don't read it enough". "Mr. President", said Mrs. Moore, "I read it all the time!" There then followed a very moving conversation that took the President right back in his memory to his days as a child with his mother. She had been a very godly lady. What moves me about the story is the fact that in all of the United States on that momentous night the one person who really got to the President's heart was a Bible carrying cleaning lady. Selah.

April   thirteenth

"This He spoke concerning the Spirit, whom those believing in Him would receive; for the Holy Spirit was not yet given, because Jesus was not yet glorified" (John 7: 39).

he supply of rivers of living water that Christ referred to was the gift of the Holy Spirit. When Christ ascended He received of the Father the promise of the Holy Spirit. Then a new era broke on the world. Before the Ascension the Son of God had rested "upon" people fitting them for service; from Pentecost onwards the Son of God was to be "in" them.

What are the practical effects in people's lives of the Holy Spirit dwelling within them? Among other things it gives them the opportunity to change the world they live in. This group of men that made up the Pre-Ascension disciples were the same group of men that made up the Post-Ascension group who were transformed by the Holy Spirit's power. It was said of them that they turned the world upside down. We are told that J.S. Sully left his post at Pepsico to become President of a little known, unproven company called Apple Computer in 1993. The co-founder of Apple, Steve Jobs, goaded him to do it with the question; "Do you want to spend the rest of your life selling sugared water or do you want a chance to change the world?!" Sully opted for changing the world. Have you, Christian, have you?

April fourteenth

".... But some said, 'Will the Christ come out of Galilee? Has not the Scriptures said that the Christ comes from the seed of David and from the town of Bethlehem where David was?" (John 7: 41-42).

Here John is speaking ironically. He knew that Christ was "born of the "seed of David" (See Romans 1; 3). He knew that Christ had been born in Judea in Bethlehem. He knew that Christianity was not a philosophy that any bright mind could think up if they were intelligent enough. He knew that God's unspeakable gift to us, the gift of Christ, was wrapped in the process of history.

What John is doing is showing that people were right to expect a historical Christ but that the problem lay in the fact that they never asked Him of His birth and ancestry. They were so hostile to Him that their own hostility cut them off from the evidence they needed. That is often a problem with us in life in general, isn't it? We get so hostile to something or somebody without first checking it out and our hostility cuts us off from incalculable blessing. It is called prejudice and prejudice is the greatest enemy of truth. Watch your prejudices.

April   fifteenth

"Then the officers came to the Chief Priests and Pharisees who said to them, 'Why have you not brought Him?' The officers answered, 'No man ever spoke like this Man!'" (John 7: 45-46).

The truth was that these officers did not arrest Christ for the simple reason that He had arrested them! Their testimony of Him was that no-one had ever spoken like Him. In the Garden of Eden God spoke with Adam every eventide. That is what God wants to do; He wants to communicate with us. Satan, of course, slithered into the Garden and tempted man and he fell. Satan really convinced man that talking to God and obeying God was a waste of time; be a God yourself was his idea! And silence reigned.

Notice, though, that when Jesus was a lad of twelve the spiritual leaders talked with Him. When He entered His public ministry sinners of various hues constantly interrupted His meals wanting to talk with Him. He even took little children on His knees and talked with them. Christ restored the communication that Satan had broken. People basically began saying, "We never thought God was like this. He loves us". He had not come to condemn the world but to save it. That was His message. Even the men sent to arrest Him owned up to its power. Have you talked with Him today. He wants to talk with you.

April   sixteenth

"Then Jesus spoke to them again, saying, 'I am the Light of the world. He who follows Me shall not walk in darkness, but shall have the Light of Life'" (John 8: 12).

In their journey across the wilderness the children of Israel were fed with manna, supplied with water and guided by a pillar of fire by night and a cloud by day. This cloud was obviously white, like one of those cumulus clouds which sail slowly across the blue of a summer sky. The fire at the heart of the cloud was only visible when the daylight was gone. When it moved, those two and a half million people had to move. That same cloud gave light in darkness every night of their wilderness lives. We too are pilgrims in this world and we have in Christ, living bread, living water and incredible light. Just as the cloud

71

was a guide by day and a light by night, so the Lord Jesus will be such a light and guide to us. But we must follow Him. We must put Him first. If we do this then confusion, perplexity and joylessness will be replaced with the light of life.

April seventeenth

"Then Jesus said to them, 'When you lift up the Son of Man, then you will know that I am He, and that I do nothing of Myself; but as My Father taught Me, I speak these things'" (John 8: 28).

There is a playlet which always challenges me. It is called, "The Long Silence" and has individuals challenging God as to His right to judge people. A victim of a nasty concentration camp says, "We endured terror, torture and death". A black boy shows an ugly rope burn and says his crime was being black. A pregnant school-girl says, "It wasn't my fault". A victim of Hiroshima speaks up. A thalidomide child protests. They all say that before God can be qualified to be their judge, He must endure what they endured. Their decision was that God should be sentenced to live on earth as a man. "Let Him be born a Jew", they say. "Let the legitimacy of His birth be doubted. Let His family think Him out of His mind. Let Him be betrayed by His closest friends. Let Him face false charges, be tried by a prejudiced jury and convicted by a cowardly judge. Let Him be believed. Let Him see what it means to be alone. Then let Him die. Let there be a great host of witnesses to verify it". There was a long silence when they all had finished pronouncing sentence. Suddenly all knew that God had already been through all that they were demanding. Selah.

April eighteenth

" .... for I always do those things that please Him" (John 8: 29).

Wouldn't today's text make a superb motto for your life and mine? Watch our Lord Jesus in His life. At the age of twelve He tells His parents, Joseph and Mary, that He must be about His Father's business. He submits Himself to baptism that He might fulfil what His Father requires of Him. He says that to do His Father's will is His meat and drink. To glorify His Father's name and to divert the attention of people to Him was the passion of His life. What is yours?

Is it to die to self and be alive to God? To do those things that please Him would, instead of narrowing your life, widen it. It would soon be said of you, should you work on a factory floor, lecture in a university lecture theatre, run a farm, or work in the City, that wherever you went you brought a sense of God with you. It can be done. So get out there today and do everything to the glory of God.

April nineteenth

"Then Jesus said to those Jews who believed in Him, 'If you abide in My Word, you are My disciples indeed'" (John 8: 31).

T he word disciple means "learner". All your life as a Christian you should be learning more and more about the Lord Jesus. He is the root by which a Christian grows and the rule by which a Christian lives. They do not love Christ who love anything more than Christ. Tomorrow's history has already been written; at the Name of Jesus every knee must bow.

The mark of true disciples of Christ is that they remain in the Word of Christ. That means they listen to it and seek by the Spirit to penetrate into the truth it contains. Disciples adhere to Christ's teaching and direct their lives by it. How many books do you read twice? Yet in Christ's words contained in Scripture are verbal vaults which you can turn to a million times and still find more and more treasure. Discipleship also involves obeying the words of Christ. His word is not simply for academic satisfaction or for intellectual appreciation. It is given so that we might find out what God wishes us to do and then to do it. It is the way to true happiness.

April twentieth

"You are of your father the Devil, and the desires of your father you want to do. He was a murderer from the beginning, and does not stand in the truth, because there is no truth in him. When he speaks a lie, he speaks from his own resources, for he is a liar and the father of it" (John 8: 44).

C hildren always bear a resemblance to their father. It is inescapable. Just as those who follow Christ bear the marks of being Christ's disciples, so those who follow Satan do the same. What were the two characteristics of Satan that Christ highlighted? First, He highlighted that Satan is a murderer. He brought sin into the world and death by sin. Second, he highlighted the fact that Satan loves falsehood. Every lie that human beings ever spoke came from him.

Look around the world today. In this past year in which I have lived hundreds of people have been killed by terrorist bombs. In Vienna, in Austria, in Israel, in the U.S.A., in Greece, in England, in Turkey, in Pakistan. Corsica had twenty-seven bombs in one night this year. On and on it goes. In the Republic of Ireland this year the fact emerged that men can be hired for £5,000 to kill someone. It is all Satan-inspired, and what Satan is determines his stand. Though when the false, Satan, met the true, Christ, the false tried to destroy it. The haunting question is, though, whose fatherhood does my life portray?

April   twenty-first

"Which of you convinces Me of sin? And if I tell the truth, why do you not believe Me?" (John 8: 46).

A colleague of mine quite recently heard a Pastor say he hadn't committed a sin for some considerable length of time. My colleague, though, noted that the Pastor happened to be breaking the speed limit at the time he made his claim!

Can you imagine the reaction of the crowd to the Saviour's question? There was absolute silence. There is no-one who could have convicted Him of any sin whatsoever. They could neither bring a charge nor prove one. Why? Because He was sinless. He knew no sin. He did no sin, neither was any deceit found in His mouth. What does that imply? It implies that if He was sinless, then He always speaks the truth. It means I have a perfect Mediator and Saviour. He is just what my sinful heart needs and I as a sinner gladly hide in Him, the sinless. Do you?

"Touch my blest Saviour first,
Take Him from God's esteem,
Prove that He has one spot of sin,
Then tell me I'm unclean."

April   twenty-second

"I do not seek My own glory" (John 8: 50).

So what's he after?" we ask. We are suspicious of people and their motives. We take few at face value. We feel there is always some catch. Even our mail has become junk mail; it is full of glossy promises with subtle almost hidden agendas. Selfishness and skulduggery is all around us. The test of time has thrown up few free lunches.

See, though, the Christ of God. What was He after? His Father's glory. Before the pitiless onslaught of the Pharisees and Sadducees, He never flinched. In the subtle temptation of Satan under a blazing sun in the wilderness, He never relents. In the face of well-meaning but blundering disciples and their ideas, He never lowered His sole purpose. The crowd didn't sway Him, the long days of fasting didn't divert Him. Never, ever, day or night did He seek His own glory. He simply sought His Father's.

We live in days of Me-ism and greed. We live in times when life for millions is a competition and their neighbours are their rivals. We live in days when people boost their self-worth by status symbols and boost their self-esteem by diminishing everyone else's. Is it any wonder that the result is pandemic discontent? Let us heed Paul's words; "Do nothing out of selfish ambition". To seek God's glory alone is true contentment.

April   twenty-third

"Most assuredly, I say to you, if anyone keeps My word he shall never see death" (John 8: 51).

In this conversation of Christ we are following day after day, one astonishing claim of Christ tumbles out after another. This one towers very high. What does He now mean by saying that anyone who kept His words would never see death?

One thing is for sure; Christ was not saying that believers will not see dying. He means that believers will never have to confront death in its terror as the occasion leading to final separation from God. The worst part of death will not touch them. The person who enters into fellowship with the Lord Jesus has entered into a fellowship which is independent of time. It is a relationship with God which neither time nor eternity can sever. Such a person goes not from life to death but from life to life.Here then is freedom from bondage to the fear of death.

At the end of this conversation the Jews picked up stones to stone the Saviour. Today's text proves that Christ never claimed to be a mere moral teacher. He is either the Son of God or else He is a lunatic or a devil. We must make our choice as to what we think of Him. We cannot remain neutral.

April   *twenty-fourth*

> *"Jesus said to them, 'Most assuredly, I say to you, before Abraham was, I Am'" (John 8: 58).*

"We are", said the famous Lucasian Professor of Mathematics at Cambridge University, Stephen Hawking in a B.B.C. broadcast, "Such insignificant creatures on a minor planet in the outer suburbs of a hundred thousand million galaxies so it is difficult to believe in a God that would care about us or even notice our existence".

Not so, if you know Jesus Christ. Before Abraham was, He existed. Before the stars existed, He existed. Before the earth existed, He existed. He is the Eternal "I Am". And does He care about us? He cares not only about us but if a little sparrow falls to the ground, it is noticed by Him. He has the very hairs of our heads numbered. "Say to the cities", writes Isaiah, "Behold your God". All eyes turned to look at the entrance on the scene of the Lord God, the mighty One. And how does He come? He comes as a shepherd! "He will gather the lambs with His arms, and carry them in His bosom, and gently lead those who are with young". The Eternal "I Am" is a shepherd. He will lead you in paths of righteousness and by quiet waters, He will restore your soul. Follow Him closely. Remember; He cares about you.

April   *twenty-fifth*

> *"Now as Jesus passed by, He saw a man who was blind from birth" (John 9: 1).*

Blind from birth! The blind beggar was an emblem of what mankind is like. Mankind is spiritually blind from birth and it needs light. Mankind says, "Give me! Give me! Give me!" almost from its first breath. Here though comes the Light of the World who sees man in all his need. The problem posed is, "How can Christ give a person sight who hasn't got the faculty of sight?" It is like the Lord's question to Peter; "Whom do you say that I am?" and Peter replies, "You are the Christ, the Son of the Living God". The Lord replied, "Flesh and blood has not revealed this to you but My Father which is inHeaven!" Nobody can work out that Christ is the Son of God through purely theological reasoning. It will take more than rational thought. It will take a divine revelation.

This point is worth remembering when you are witnessing to others. Should you give them all the answers to all of their questions it would still not convince them that the message is true. It will take the Light of the World to reveal Himself. The lovely thing is that in this story Christ uses means to reveal Himself. He didn't use means with the paralytic man but He does with this blind man. He didn't use means in the actual creation of the world. He spoke to nothing and it became something. The challenging fact is that the means He may choose to reveal Himself through today may be you.

April   twenty-sixth

"Jesus answered, 'Neither this man nor his parents sinned, but that the works of God should be revealed in Him. I must work the works of Him who sent Me while it is day; the night is coming when no-one can work'" (John 9: 3-4).

To many people in Jesus' day, and also in ours, special suffering is always a sign of special sin. While it certainly is true that sin sets in motion a whole train of consequences, it is not always true that present suffering in our lives is due to sin. This blind man is a perfect example of personal suffering being a means by which the grace and power of God can be manifest. His suffering was not due to sin but was in fact a conduit for showing what God can do. He was about to become a legend for the glory of God.

I do not know where you are today. Your circumstances may be dire; your health may be failing, your business may be collapsing, your plans wrecked, your finances stretched and your cupboard bare. You may be ready to quit. Don't. Why? Because this circumstance you are in is not because you have done wrong but because God is about to reveal His works in you. Hang on in there.

April twenty-seventh

"I must work the works of Him who sent Me while it is day; the night is coming when no-one can work" (John 9: 4).

The Lord Jesus knew that His time was limited. There were only a few months left now. The day of His earthly ministry would soon close and the night would settle in. He must fulfil His ministry, He must reach the blind man and manifest through him that He was the Light of the World.

You too, Christian, need to keep your eye on the dial for soon "The shadows will steadily creep far across the grass, the air will become chill and the moon will be up". Do you think you have many years in which to fulfil your ministry? You may not. This is your hour. It is your turn now. You must get on with it. As F. B. Meyer put it, "The unique work of healing blindness and enriching is confined to earth; and we must hasten to do all of this alloted to us before the nightfall". Your ministry will soon be over. Mark that word "soon". The longest life is but a day. Up! Be doing! Don't be like Coldridge who had lots of books in his head but never got down to writing them. Don't let the critics stop you. Don't let pride stop you. Don't let sloth stop you. None of these will stop the clock. Whatever the Lord has told you to do, do it with all your might; today. Now.

April twenty-eighth

"As long as I am in the world, I am the Light of the World" (John 9: 5).

The networking of the Bible is awesome. The blind man is sent to wash in the pool of Siloam (in Greek) Shiloagh (in Hebrew). The symbolism in the act reverberates back through the centuries. The time was 753 BC and Judah was threatened by the allied forces of Syria and Israel who were trying to compel it to form an alliance with them against the Syrians who were led by a fiend of a man who was trying to bring the whole of Western Asia under his sway. Ahaz and all Israel, when they heard what was happening, were "moved as the trees of the woods are moved with the wind". In other words they shook like a leaf! The Lord sent a word to Ahab to "Be quiet; do not fear or be faint hearted" but Ahaz decided to go to Asyria for help and couldn't see that Asyria would swallow the Lord's people and take them captive. The Lord then sent a message through Isaiah saying; "Inasmuch as these people refused the waters of Shiloah (meaning "the sent one") that flows softly.... the waters of the Euphrates, strong and mighty .... will go up over his channels and go over all his banks". The message is clear; choose the Lord's way today, for His river flows softly. The alternative is to be overwhelmed by the flood of evil which can so easily sweep you away.

April   twenty-ninth

"So he went and washed, and came back seeing" (John 9: 7).

The blind man soaked his eyes in the waters of "the sent one", the Pool of Siloam. The result was a total transformation of his darkness. He came back seeing for the first time in his life. Just as the water of the Pool of Siloam received the water which was carried or "sent" through a channel from the spring of Gehion in the Kidron Valley, so the Scriptures are a fountain of life originally written by men who were "carried along" by the Spirit of God. Every word of Scripture as originally written has been divinely sent. Soak yourself in its waters. Draw from the source that never will run dry. Live by its precepts, lean on its promises, drink in its freshness, nourish your soul on its nutrients, do not forsake it. There are other waters which will poison you, other sources which do not rise and come to you from the heart of God. Check your sources. Remember what John Wesley said; "Sin will keep me from this book but this book will keep me from sin."

April   thirtieth

"They brought him who formerly was blind to the Pharisees .... but the Jews did not believe concerning him that he had been blind and received his sight until they called the parents of him who had received his sight"
(John 9: 13-18).

The blind man could now see physically but he had not yet come to full spiritual sight, had he? John now records for us the fascinating contact between the man and the Pharisees and there is a good deal of material in the encounter to help us in our witnessing.

The blind man told them he reckoned that Christ was a prophet, a sent one. He had made a very good start seeking to identify Christ. They then called in his parents and, would you believe it, they started to argue with them that their son had never been blind to start with! "They", says the Scripture, "Did not believe concerning him that he had been blind and received his sight".

That's the way many folk still argue today. When you tell them that you were once in spiritual darkness but that now you can see they will argue that you were never spiritually blind to begin with! They will question the whole reality of revelation or even the need for it. They will argue that we are all "the children of God" whereas Scripture teaches that we are by nature "children of wrath" (Ephesians 2; 3) and need to be born again.

Recently, in Washington, I heard an Afro-American singer sing a beautiful hymn to five thousand people at a breakfast. When he had finished the audience responded with thunderous applause and the United States President, who had been sitting close to the singer, stood up and hugged him. My mind immediately flashed back to the author of the hymn. He was an atheist and captain of a slave-ship, travelling between Africa and the American continent. His name was John Newton and he was converted to Christ in the middle of a storm in the Atlantic and gave up the slave trade to become a humble preacher of the Gospel. If he had seen it I am sure he would have smiled to see the U.S. President and the Afro-American singer hug over his hymn several hundred years after it was written. The words of his hymn are still as relevant as ever;

"Amazing grace, how sweet the sound,
That saved a wretch like me,
I once was lost but now I'm found,
Was blind but now I see".

We want the Lord to immediately respond to our calls, don't we? When will we ever learn that not only does prayer change things, prayer changes us! It teaches us to be patient. It teaches us over and over again that things are not always what they seem. You may be on the verge of the greatest time of your life but at this precise moment you would argue that this is the worst time of your life. Take heart. What often seems worst is best.

MAY

May first

"He answered and said, 'Whether he is a sinner or not I do not know. One thing I know: that though I was blind, now I see.' Then they reviled Him and said, 'You are His disciple, but we are Moses' disciples. We know that God spoke to Moses: as for this fellow, we do not know where He is from'" (John 9: 25-29).

There's a lot of knowing and not knowing in this dialogue, isn't there? The Greek word for "not knowing" is agnosticism. It is a humble word. It is a humbler word than athiest, isn't it? Often when people are pressed with Christ's claims they simply say that they don't know whether He is the Son of God or not. Yet, the question is whether they are saying they don't know or if they are saying they couldn't know. For, if they don't know but could, they are lazy and that is not a very respectable intellectual position, is it? On the other hand, are they saying they don't know because it can't be known, because there isn't enough evidence?

Christ is saying you can know. He claims that He can give you the sight to see with. As Professor David Gooding has put it; "Thorough going agnosticism is a very difficult position to hold unless you know that Christ is wrong. To say you know that Jesus Christ is wrong, you know a lot, don't you?". Don't be persuaded of the seeming humility and smoothness of agnosticism. It is a subtle giant which you could link arms with and continue in spiritual blindness forever. If you want to know Christ, the Light of the World, my reader, you can.

May second

"Then he said, 'Lord, I believe!' and he worshipped Him. " (John 9:38).

It had been slowly dawning on this man that amidst the mudpack and the pool and the religious arguments that the One who had healed him was no ordinary person. In all history, he reminded the Pharisees no-one had ever been healed of congenital blindness (that is blindness from birth). He began to realise that what had happened to him was a miracle from God and that the man who had done the miracle must be from God. He also realised that since God does not answer the prayers of unrepentant people, then this man could not be the unrepentant sinner the Pharisees accused him of being!

The truth was that the man's spiritual sight was now dawning. He refuted the Pharisees on their own ground but they threw him out of the synagogue. They literally excommunicated him. But Jesus found him. What a moment! Being excommunicated from dead religion and being found by the living Saviour is no mean swap. "Do you believe in the Son of God?" asked Christ. "Who is He, Lord, that I might believe in Him?" said the man. "You have both seen Him and it is He who is talking with you," said Christ. Immediately the man said, "Lord, I believe!" and worshipped Him.

Have you left moribund, decadent, dead, organised religion for a living Saviour? There is no comparison, is there?

May third

"And Jesus said, 'For judgment I have come into this world, that those who do not see may see, and that those who see may be made blind'"
(John 9: 39).

Today's verse seems to be categorically denying Christ's earlier claim that "God did not send His Son into the world to condemn the world, but that the world through Him might be saved". Think about it, though, and you will find that this verse is no discrepancy. The Saviour is not saying that He has come to execute judgment. He is simply saying that His presence in the world constitutes a judgment in that it compels people to declare themselves for or against Him. If they are against Him they are judged already (see John 3; 18). He didn't pass the judgment, they passed it on themselves.

Do people have a choice regarding Christ? Certainly. Christ stood and wept over Jerusalem and said He would have gathered gladly them as a hen gathers her chickens under her wings but they would not. Notice that, He would but they wouldn't. If people are spiritually blind

God is not condemning them for it. If you are blind you couldn't be blamed for not seeing. God will never condemn anybody for not seeing what they could not see. But God will condemn people for not seeing what they could see. If you reject the Light of the World you must take responsibility for it and as long as you do your guilt remains. The blind man, though, went on his way and we do not read that he ever begged again. When you come to know the Lord you no longer go around saying, "Give me! Give me! Give me!" Rather you set out on a life of service where you do the giving.

May fourth

"Most assuredly, I say to you, he who does not enter the sheepfold by the door, but climbs up some other way, the same is a thief and a robber. But he who enters the door is the shepherd of the sheep. To him the doorkeeper opens" (John 10:1-3).

John now turns to a question which is fascinating. The question he wants us to think about is: "How do sheep come to see and know who the true shepherd is?" There can be, ultimately, no more important question. The first part of the answer to John's question is given in the metaphor of a communal fold. This was a fold in a town where shepherds would bring their flocks of a weekend and while they went into town they would leave a doorkeeper at the door to guard the sheep, seeking to ensure that no thief stole them. The fold held sheep belonging to several different shepherds. When the shepherd came back he would come to the doorkeeper to claim his sheep and would lead them out and take them up to the hills.

John the Baptist is, of course, the doorkeeper in the metaphor. Christ now approaches to take His flock out. All who claimed to be the Messiah but did not come through John were but thieves and robbers. John gladly opened the door to Him and he began calling His sheep by name. "Anna! Simeon! Nathaniel! Peter! Mary! Martha! Lazarus! Mary Magdalene! Blind Bartimaeus!" And a host of others. They all recognised His voice as the voice of the true shepherd and He led them out. He called each one by name then and He calls each one by name still. That's how personal it is. He calls you by name, too. Have you heard His voice?

May fifth

"And when he brings out His own sheep, He goes before them"
(John 10: 4).

I

t is not easy to follow Christ. The communal fold, of the metaphor, is a very comfortable place. It is warm and sheltered. We do not like change, we do not like to be moved to a strange place. The familiar is easier. Yet, the penetrating but gentle voice stirs us to draw us to the hills where fresh, luscious grass grows, where fresh breezes blow and the dew descends. Notice, though, that He does not ask you to go along a path that He has not covered Himself. He goes before you. He doesn't drive you, either. He leads you beside still waters, He leads you in paths of righteousness. Even if you should have to walk through the valley of the shadow of death, He has been there Himself and has conquered your predators. Anyway, shadows cannot hurt you, can they? There must be a light in the valley, else there would be no shadow. That light is the Light of the World.

Are you timid to enter a crowded formal gathering without someone to lead you? Do you fear to meet certain people indirectly without a "go-between"? Are you facing certain circumstances that you find so overwhelming you do not wish to go forward in your life? Then try to remember; "He goes before".   He is between you and whatever lies ahead. Comforting, isn't it?

May sixth

"Then Jesus said to them again, "Most assuredly, I say to you, I am the door of the sheep. All who ever came before me are thieves and robbers, but the sheep did not hear them. I am the door. If anyone enters by Me, he will be saved, and will go in and out and find pasture" (John 10: 7-9).

T

his is a short parable inserted into a longer parable. In the longer parable Christ is likened to the shepherd, in the shorter parable He is referred to as the door or the way of salvation. The Saviour is claiming that He is the way into the true order of life. All who had made such a claim before were thieves and robbers; they were false Christs. They still are. They offer a golden age through revolution of one kind and another and bring no peace. Christ brings perfect liberty; they shall go "in and out". Christ also brings perfect sustenance; "they shall find pasture".

What are you feeding on in your mind and soul? Ultimately you will find that there is only one source which can unfailingly satisfy the deepest cravings of your mind and soul. It is Christ and the pasture He feeds His sheep on. The grass might, of course, look greener on the other side of the fence but remember that that grass is under another's management. It is a fact that under bad management sheep can turn an area of good and luscious pasture into an area devastated by erosion. Under whose management are you? Make sure it's ingress to rest and egress to pasture through Him.

May seventh

"The thief does not come except to steal, and to kill, and to destroy. I have come that they may have life, and that they may have it more abundantly. I am the Good Shepherd. The Good Shepherd gives His life for the sheep" (John 10:10-11).

Why do you trust the Good Shepherd? Merely because He gives you security, freedom, and good pasture? Surely the reason for your trust is deeper than that?

The scene is, say, the evening time. The shepherd is coming down the mountain side with his flock to his fold. The gorge they are descending together is dark and densely shadowed by foliage. Suddenly there is a snarl and a scream telling that a wolf has seized a tender lamb. The shepherd rushes to the rear of his flock and faces the wolf. A great struggle ensues and soon the shepherd lies dead, slain by the wolf. The little lamb limps away, scared to death, but free.

Why do you trust the Good Shepherd? Supremely because when the wolf came "This shepherd by pity was led, to stand between us and the foe and willingly die in our stead". He laid down His life for us in order that He might give His life to us. We love Him because He first loved us.

May eighth

"But he who is a hireling and not the shepherd, one who does not own the sheep, sees the wolf coming and leaves the sheep and flees; and the wolf catches the sheep and scatters them. The hireling flees because he is a hireling and does not care about the sheep" (John 10: 12-13).

I stood gazing at the painting, transfixed. It was entitled "The Hireling" and it had been painted by Holman Hunt. Beneath the painting were some letters in a glass case. The letters had been written by Hunt to a curator of the gallery explaining the meaning behind his painting. The young man, for example, sitting on the grass bank talking to a girl was a hireling brought in for a day to look after the flock. He was sitting chatting to the girl with a deathhead moth in his hand which was, in Victorian days, a bad omen. He didn't care for the flock. While he discussed superstition two sheep were in the corn. The sheep were as good as dead for corn causes a sheep's stomach to be blown. Some other sheep are standing on marshy ground where, notes Hunt, the little marshmallow flower grows. The hireling has some sheep on the wrong ground and they will get footrot and die. Only two sheep are lying down and they are sick. Sheep normally only lie down when they feel secure, so all the rest of the sheep in the painting are standing.

Hunt explained that his painting was representative of what he felt the state of the church was in his day. He felt that many Christian leaders were hirelings and while they spoke of superstitious nonsense in the pulpits of his day, their flocks were eating the wrong food, were on the wrong ground, many were sick, others were frightened and quite a few were in danger of perishing. I went home, chastened.

May ninth

"I am the good shepherd; and I know My sheep, and am known by My own." John 10: 14.

This verse tells us that Christ knows His sheep. How does this apply to us? For a start He knows the number of hairs on our head. For another, He knows every time we sit down and every time we get up. He knows our every thought. He knows our joys and our sorrows, our highs and our lows. He knows our sins and died for them. He knows our aspirations and gives us the Holy Spirit to help us achieve them. No-one knows like He knows.

His sheep, though, also know their shepherd. Christians are often asked how they know Christ. Safer ask a baby how it knows its mother. Why? Since birth it has been in constant contact with its mother. It has heard the very thumping of its mother's heart. Instinctively, the baby knows its mother. So the Good Shepherd encloses the Christian from the moment of new birth and through Him the Christian can hear the very heartbeat of God.

Buddhists never speak of knowing the Buddha. Muslims never speak of knowing Mohammed. Communists do not speak of knowing Lenin or Marx. Christians, though, the world over, will tell you that they know Jesus Christ. That is what makes them Christians.

May tenth

"Other sheep I have which are not of this fold; them also I must bring, and they will hear my voice; and there will be one flock and one shepherd" (John 10:16).

All over the world you will find them. I met one in the corridors of Capitol Hill in Washington one afternoon when I asked a gentleman the way to a House of Representatives Debate. "Tell them, when you get to the door", he said, "That you were talking to the Chaplain". Dr. Lloyd Ogilvy and I became friends and I spent a few hours with him the next day speaking of Christ and His Kingdom. I found a Joseph in Pharoah's court.

I shall never forget spending time in the Palace of Nations where the U.N. has its European headquarters in Geneva. I was in the Reuters Room and found that their Swiss correspondent was a humble and dedicated follower of Jesus Christ. I also met one in a converted cow byre in the heart of South Korea one day as eight of us broke bread in remembrance of Jesus Christ sitting on a stone floor. She had been born blind. On and on I could go through my life speaking of people I have met who by all sorts of fascinating ways have come into the Kingdom of God. There is no telling where you will meet them. I love the story Dr. Billy Graham told of going on board the Royal Yacht Britannia with President Regan and his wife and Queen Elizabeth II. As Dr. Graham passed the officer at the gangway, the officer saluted him and whispered, "Wembley '55, Sir!" The man had been won to Christ at one of Dr. Graham's services years before.

I am sure that you too, Christian, could speak of believers you have met in the rarest places and circumstances. What unites them all? A denomination? A particular form of ecclesiastical structure? No. The thing that unites them is a loyalty to the Lord Jesus. That is the flock that is indestructible. Christ is the Shepherd who gave His life for and to the sheep.

May eleventh

"I lay down My life that I may take it again. No-one takes it from Me, but I lay it down of Myself. I have power to lay it down, and I have power to take it again. This command I have received from My Father".
(John 10: 18).

No earthly shepherd could ever do what this shepherd did. An earthly shepherd has certainly given his life for his flock, but this shepherd gave His life that He might take it again! See the emphasis. Had He resisted death He could never have taken His life again. The emphasis is on the giving. It is, in fact, inaccurate to say that the Saviour was dying on the cross. He wasn't. Crucify Him, they did, but take His life, they couldn't. He gave His life, voluntarily. When people die they drop their heads in death. He, notice, bowed His head, first, and then gave His life. It was an act, a deed, not merely an experience. In all of John's Gospel this is the only thing that Jesus claims to have done Himself. "I lay it down of Myself", He said. The authority for the action He received from His Father, the act He did himself. Is it any wonder that we love Him because He first loved us?

May twelfth

"And I give them eternal life, and they shall never perish; neither shall anyone snatch them out of My hand". (John 10: 28).

I approached St. Peter's Church in Dundee with awe. This was where the great Robert Murray McCheyne, whose grave lies just by the front door, had preached with incredible power and saw incredible blessing following. He died at 29 years of age. People, I'm told, used to be deeply affected even by his godly demeanour never to speak of his wonderful preaching.

The caretaker showed me the grandfather clock that McCheyne's young people had bought him, she also showed me his pulpit kept in a back room, where he had preached. "I have to make my husband's tea," she said, "Would you like to see his (McCheyne's) Bible?" She brought it out wrapped in brown paper and handed it to me, excusing herself. She might as well have left me with the crown jewels!

I looked up today's text in McCheyne's Bible and in the margin he had written, in his beautiful handwriting, these words; "No-one can force them out". This means that the believer is eternally, unconditionally and absolutely saved. It is not saying that once a person is baptised they are always saved. It is not saying once a person has joined a local church that they are always saved. It is not even saying that people once having made a profession of faith are always saved. But it is saying, once saved, always saved. The true believer is eternally secure. There is no more precious assurance. Enjoy it .

May thirteenth

"If I do not do the works of My Father, do not believe Me; but if I do, though you do not believe Me, believe the works,that you may know and believe that the Father is in Me, and I in Him" (John 10: 37-38).

That's it", you say, "Christ's sheep know Him and enjoy the tremendous security that comes from knowing Him. This crowd didn't believe because they were not Christ's sheep. So God, from all eternity, chose some to be His sheep and others not to be His sheep. The ones that weren't His sheep, never would be His sheep, it was never ever intended that they would be and God doesn't want them to be".

Not so fast. Christ didn't say "What's the point of arguing with you lot for you are not My sheep and you never will be, anyway you are not elect. Goodbye". No. He says that though they don't believe in Him, they could. How? By starting somewhere easier. "Though you do not believe Me, believe the works that you may know and believe that the Father is in Me and I in Him", he says. The implication is, "How was I able to do such works?" If they consider this it will lead them to understand who He is and to believe Him. They were not His sheep, yet.

All sheep have the faculty of getting to know their shepherd, don't they? They are not born without that faculty. If you are seeking the Lord, He may be found of you. Start with His works, study them. See what they imply. It can lead you to faith in Him as Saviour and Lord.

May fourteenth

"Now a certain man was sick, Lazarus of Bethany, the town of Mary and her sister Martha. It was that Mary who anointed the Lord with fragrant oil and wiped His feet with her hair, whose brother Lazarus was sick. Therefore the sisters sent to Him saying, 'Lord, behold, he whom you love is sick'. When Jesus heard that, He said, 'This sickness is not unto death, but for the glory of God, that the Son of God may be glorified through it'" (John 11: 1-4).

There are eleven chapters now given by John to this, the last journey of Christ. Why the emphasis? Because they deal with life's ultimate problem which is death. Who is not afraid of death? It is life's last great enemy. It is usually the last thing we talk about. It makes us feel uncomfortable, awkward. We recoil when someone brings the subject up.

These last chapters of John, though, bring incredible hope. The Lord Jesus was on His way to the most significant event in all human history, namely, His death, burial and resurrection. He was going to render ineffectual Him who had the power of death, that is the Devil and thereby deliver them who through fear of death were all their lifetime subject to bondage. Even if we have to go through death, barring the second coming of Christ, the Lord Jesus can change our attitude to it. The next time Lazarus died it was with a very different attitude to the first time. The rest of His life was not spent in fear of death but was spent in view of a glorious resurrection and eternity that lies beyond. Through what we learn here our whole attitude to death can be transformed. The raising of Lazarus was Christ's greatest miracle.

May fifteenth

"Now Jesus loved Martha and her sister and Lazarus. So, when He heard he was sick, he stayed two more days in the place where He was" (John 11: 5-6).

The ways of God are strange and mysterious. Being thrown in an empty well leads to Joseph becoming Governor of Egypt. Being good-looking leads Esther to save the Hebrew people from genocide. Being blind leads Samson to his greatest victory over his enemies. Being rich leads Joseph of Armithea to give his sepulchre to the crucified Christ. Being poor leads the widow by the treasury in the temple to becoming the epitomy of how God views giving. Christ's refusing to immediately respond to Mary and Martha's call to come and see their sick brother leads to the greatest of Christ's miracles.

We want the Lord to immediately respond to our calls, don't we? When will we ever learn that not only does prayer change things, prayer changes us! It teaches us to be patient. It teaches us over and over again that things are not always what they seem. You may be on the verge of the greatest time of your life but at this precise moment you would argue that this is the worst time of your life. Take heart. What often seems worst is best.

May sixteenth

"Then after this He said to the disciples, 'Let us go to Judea again ..... Lazarus is dead'" (John 11 : 7-14).

Why did our Lord have to go to Bethany in person to raise Lazarus from the dead? Did not the Saviour save the nobleman's son by healing him from a distance? In this miracle the Lord deliberately stayed where He was until Lazarus dies and then says to His disciples, "And I am glad for your sakes that I was not there, that you may believe. Nevertheless let us go to him".

Why, then, did He have to go to Bethany in person? Because the rest of the New Testament teaches that when it comes to the resurrection of the dead our Lord will not remain on His throne and speak the word and summon the dead to arise. Note carefully the words of Paul in 1 Thessalonians 4: 16; "For the Lord Himself will descend from Heaven with a shout, with the voice of the archangel, and with the trumpet of God, and the dead in Christ will rise first". Every move Christ made in the miracle of the raising of Lazarus from the dead was filled with signs for us all. Again, note that the sign of Christ to believers in the raising of Lazarus is teaching us that if we die in Christ He will, at His second coming, raise our bodies in person. Coming to Bethany in person was the portent of the next great event that millions of Christians are waiting for. Even so come Lord Jesus!

May seventeenth

"Jesus answered, "Are there not twelve hours in the day? If anyone walks in the day, he does not stumble, because he sees the light of this world. But if one walks in the night, he stumbles, because the light is not in him"" (John 11: 9-10).

*A*re there not twelve hours in the day?", the Saviour asked. The answer is that there certainly are twelve hours of daylight in Israel. I have, though, just rung my good friend, Mr. George Peterson, the Honorary Sheriff of Lerwick, whose "Who's Who" entry states that his relaxation is "reading theology"! How did he think this verse applied in Shetland? "In Shetland", he replied, "We can read the newspaper in our gardens at 12 o'clock midnight in the summer". So, they certainly have more than twelve hours of daylight in Shetland. "Yes, but in winter we have only around six", he emphasised.

What then is the Saviour saying? He is saying that we all have only a limited time in which to do God's will wherever we live in the world. He is also saying that though it may be the eleventh hour of daylight in Shetland or Tel Aviv, that is no reason for retiring from it. He was moving on to do this great miracle, even at the eleventh hour of His ministry.

Every year my friend Steve Pullin and I visit Chester Cathedral where the worship of God has been offered for over one thousand years. We always stop by the famous clock within the cathedral precincts. A very memorable verse written by Henry Twells is placed beneath the clock. In the light of the fact that each one of us have sixty diamond studded minutes in each golden hour, with each one of them being a gift if we handle them with care, I ask you to meditate on Henry Twell's little verse.

"When as I child I laughed and wept
Time crept.
When as a youth I waxed more bold
Time strolled,
When I became a full grown man
Time ran
When older still I daily grew
Time flew
Soon I shall find, in passing on
Time gone."

May eighteenth

"Then Martha, as soon as she heard that Jesus was coming, went and met Him .... Then Martha said to Jesus, 'Lord, if You had been here, my brother would not have died.... Then when Mary came where Jesus was, and saw Him, she fell down at His feet, saying to Him, 'Lord, if you had been here, my brother would not have died'" (John 11: 20-21, 32).

There is a strange mixture of emotions in Mary and Martha's statements. There is a touch of scolding that seems to blame the Lord for being late. There is very deep faith that believed that Christ could certainly heal. There is absolute confidence that if Jesus asks His Father to raise Lazarus from the dead, prayer would be answered. There is a touch of forgetfulness that forgot that Christ did not need to be present to heal. There is also a touch of deep love and awe for Christ because both Mary and Martha call him Lord.

Are you having a day of mixed emotions? You are perhaps frustrated, even angry. You are, nevertheless, deeply devoted to the Lord but are forgetful that He has, as the man said, "Not brought you across the Atlantic to drown you in a ditch". So, in the flood of mixed emotions swamping you today try not to fall into a pining for what might have been. What good does it do? If God's will has been done, submit to it. In acceptance lies peace.

May nineteenth

"Jesus said to her, 'Your brother will rise again'. Martha said to Him, 'I know that he will rise again in the resurrection at the last day'. Jesus said to her, 'I am the Resurrection and the Life. He who believes in Me, even though he dies, he shall live. And whoever lives and believes in Me shall never die. Do you believe this?" (John 11: 23-26).

Here is another sign tucked into the miracle of the resurrection of Lazarus. There are two groups of people mentioned in this stupendous statement of Christ's. Those who may die and those who won't. As Lazarus has died in Christ and Mary and Martha were alive and remaining and living for Christ at the time of His coming to Bethany, so there will be two similar groups when the

Lord returns for the second time. If you and I must go through death we must not let this fact swamp our faith. If, on the other hand, we are left to be alive and remaining at His coming, that is His decision. As Jesus said to Peter when He asked what John would do, Jesus replied, "If I will that he remain until I come, what is that to you?" If we must die, we will get grace to die. If we must live, we will get grace to live. The truth is we often need more of the second than we do of the first. It is often easier to die for a cause than to live for it. Selah.

May twentieth

"She said to Him, 'Yes, Lord, I believe that You are the Christ, the Son of God, who is to come into the world'. And when she had said these things, she went her way and secretly called Mary her sister ..... when Mary came where Jesus was, and saw Him, she fell down at His feet ..... Jesus saw her weeping" (John 11: 27-28, 32-33).

Martha, in the depth of the crisis of the death of her brother, held a deep theological discussion with the Lord. Mary, in the depth of the same crisis, fell at His feet and wept. Neither were wrong. Some people are not overwhelmed with tears in the face of grief, others are. We must be very careful not to criticise those who weep uncontrollably in times of grief.

I was once approached by a lady who told me that some Christians had told her she had wept too much at the death of her husband and was letting the Lord down. How cruel! In this very same story we are told that "Jesus wept". Christians are not stoics. Stoicism was a heathen philosophy that praised those who showed no emotion in whatever circumstance. If the author and finisher of our faith wept openly in the face of grief, so can we. It is no sign of weakness. If in your present circumstances you are like Mary and feel like weeping, then weep. If you in your present circumstances feel like talking of spiritual things, like Martha, talk of them. Either way the Lord will comfort you as no-one else can.

May twenty-first

"Therefore, when Jesus saw her weeping, and the Jews who came with her weeping, He groaned in the spirit and was troubled. And He said, 'Where have you laid Him?' They said to Him, 'Lord, come and see'"
(John 11: 33-34).

Why did the Saviour groan in spirit? Some say it was because Mary and Martha and the crowd were forcing a miracle on Him. Not true. Jesus had already said He was going to perform a miracle (Verse 11). Some think it was because of unbelief, because of people weeping as if there was no resurrection. Others have suggested it was at the thought of the sorrow Lazarus would go through by returning to this sinful world.

It is true that to have grief without a sense of outrage at what sin has brought about would be mere sentiment while outrage without grief would be self righteous arrogance. Yet, surely, at the heart of Christ's grief and weeping is proof that He has empathy with us and for us when we face grief. The Greeks reckoned that if someone can cause us to weep then they have power over us. The Greek reader would have found Christ's weeping and groaning the most difficult thing to handle in this story. To the believer it is one of the most wonderful things in the story for it proves we have a High Priest who can be touched with the feelings of our infirmities. Lean hard on Him today

May twenty-second

"Then they took away the stone from the place where the dead man was lying. And Jesus lifted up His eyes and said, 'Father, I thank you that you have heard Me. And I know that you always hear Me, but because of the people who are standing by I said this, that they may believe that You sent Me'" (John 11: 41-42).

Christ comes to the tomb and orders the stone which sealed it to be taken away. Martha protests at the propriety of the Lord's demand. He then prays out loud. The prayer assumes that Christ had already prayed for the resurrection of Lazarus and had been granted His request. Why then must He pray out loud? Because the public must be reminded that He does nothing of Himself, that every move He makes is for the glory of God. Every single move. He wants them to know that when the Son asks, the Father grants. He also wants them to come to believe that the Father has sent Him and that this miracle will prove it.

This public prayer of the Saviour raises a very interesting point. Public prayers and private prayers are both addressed to God but it is vital that public prayers keep the public in mind. I am often given requests for public prayer but some of them that name names could have a very embarrassing and damaging effect on the privacy and dignity of some lives. In such circumstances we must be very careful. Public prayer should always keep the public in mind.

May twenty-third

"Now when He had said these things, He cried with a loud voice, 'Lazarus, come forth!'" (John 11: 43).

Why the loud voice? Was it so that Lazarus could hear Him? Certainly not. He spoke as to somebody who could hear Him. He had already said; "The hour .... now is when the dead will hear the voice of the Son of God, and those that hear will live". Note that it is not the living will hear and live, but the dead! "Little lamb" (correct rendering), said Christ to Jairus' dead daughter, "Arise." He knew she could hear Him just as He knew Lazarus could now hear him. His voice was not raised for the benefit of Lazarus but for the benefit of the crowd. Here was no muttering of a medium trying to communicate with the dead by incantations that only he or she can understand. It was, rather, a clear, loud call so that everybody around might know what was happening. Interesting, isn't it, that at the second coming the Lord will descend from Heaven with a shout and the dead in Christ shall rise first? This miracle is packed with signs for that great coming event.

Are you a discouraged Christian worker? All around you as you communicate the Word of God are people who are dead in their trespasses and sins and you wonder if they will ever respond to the call of Christ. Take courage from this story. Christ has all power in Heaven and earth and is mighty to save. No-one is too far gone for Christ to raise and comfort. Keep on giving out His Word.

May *twenty-fourth*

"And he who had died came out bound hand and foot with grave clothes, and his face was wrapped with a cloth. Jesus said to them, 'Loose him, and let him go'" (John 11: 43-44).

T he greatness of this miracle cannot possibly be exaggerated. Here is a man four days dead who is restored to life in a second. Here is a Christ who not only has absolute power over the world of spirits in that He calls a soul back from Paradise to join it again to its owner's body, not only has power over death itself, but, has power over decomposition. No matter where bodies are buried or cremated, no matter in how many far flung places, no matter under what conditions, the voice that called Lazarus will call them and put their bodies and souls together. No corruption or flame can finally separate them from resurrection. The resurrection of Lazarus is but a pale reflection of that coming resurrection. Lazarus was raised to face further sorrow but believers will be raised "incorruptible and we shall be changed" (1 Corinthians 15; 52). Our friends may bring us to the grave and leave us there, but God will not.

May *twenty-fifth*

"Then many of the Jews who had come to Mary, and had seen the things Jesus did, believed in Him ..... Then the chief priests and the Pharisees gathered a council and said, 'What shall we do? For this man works many signs' .... Then from that day on they plotted to put Him to death" (John 11: 45, 47,53).

S trange, isn't it how good news blesses some and hardens others? The most stupendous event ever yet seen, which is still having reverberations around the world drives some to believe in Christ and others to want to crucify Him. The very same miracle, done under the same circumstances, with the same evidence draws hugely diverse reactions.

It is fascinating to notice how Christ's enemies recognise that He had worked many miracles but that miracles alone have not converted them. Even the raising of a man who had been dead four days did nothing whatsoever to touch their hearts of stone. Don't believe anybody who tells you that if only Christ could do a great miracle before their eyes they would believe in Him. It isn't true. Conversion is a work of grace and grace alone. Don't be surprised, even, if God does a great thing in your life and others who ought to be rejoicing with you are totally unmoved by it. The Pharisees are not dead, even yet. There are plenty of them still around.

May   *twenty-sixth*

"And one of them, Caiaphas, being High Priest that year, said to them, 'You know nothing at all, nor do you consider that it is expedient that one man should die for the people, and not that the whole nation should perish'" (John 11: 49-50).

*I*t was a diabolical speech. It was one of the most tragic utterances ever put on record. It was not very long but it carried the 71 membered Sanhedrin, the Supreme Court of the Jewish nation. It was devilry packaged in expediency.

The argument put forward by Caiaphas was that if Christ was left alone His popularity would lead to an uprising against the Romans and they would react by putting it down and taking away Jewish privileges and nationhood. Better, argued Caiaphas, that Christ be made the scapegoat and die than a whole nation perish. How wise it sounded but how wicked it was.

In the end even Pilate gave in to Caiaphas' argument. Justice took second place to prudence. One man dead is better than thousands you know, ran the argument, even if that man be a completely innocent person.

In the end the Scribes and Pharisees did lose their power, their temple, their privileges and nationhood as the Romans crushed them. But it was not the lovely life and teaching of the Lord Jesus that made the Romans do it. The lesson from this ugly speech of Caiaphas' is very pertinent. Watch the issues of your heart, today. In its natural state it is deceitful above all things and desperately wicked. Who can know it?

May twenty-seventh

"Now this he did not say on his own authority; but being High Priest that year he prophesied that Jesus would die for the nation, and not for that nation only, but also that He would gather together in one the children of God who were scattered abroad" (John 11: 51-52).

*T*he most dastardly speech when gripped and mastered by God became a statement of sublime hope. That which was dark with sin became radiant with spiritual light and eternal truth. How? John tells us that Caiaphas was actually speaking more than He knew. Caiaphas poured one meaning into His words but God poured another. Caiaphas was responsible for the wicked meaning his words conveyed. The blame lies entirely at his door. Yet God used His words to express perfectly His plan of salvation. Here you have human responsibility on the one hand and divine providence on the other. The deceiving, wicked villain was being a prophet though he didn't know it. Here you have a classic example of how God uses the wrath of man to praise Him. William Cowper called the person happy who "sees God employed in all the good and evil that chequers life". It is comforting to know that that wicked thing that has happened to you can be used by God to bring about incredible blessing.

May twenty-eighth

"Therefore Jesus no longer walked openly among the Jews, but went from there into the country near the wilderness, to a city called Ephraim, and there remained with His disciples .... Then they sought Jesus, and spoke among themselves as they stood in the Temple, 'What do you think - that He will not come to the Feast?'. Now both the chief priests and the Pharisees had given a command, that if anyone knew where He was, He should report it, that they might seize Him'" (John 11: 54, 56-57).

*T*he drama of these days is building. The resurrection of Lazarus has caused great hostility and the Jewish Council has issued an order that if anyone sees Jesus they should report it and He would then be arrested. As hundreds of thousands of Jews went to Jerusalem to prepare for the Passover, the Lord Jesus now occupies a huge place in public thought. His Name is familiar, His destiny is fascinating. Many people were seeking Him and wondering if He would appear. It was to be a Passover as no other before or since; the Lamb was about to be led to the slaughter, silent before his shearers. Meanwhile Christ was quietly awaiting His hour at a city called Ephraim on the edge of the wilderness with His disciples. It was a period of quietness before the storm broke.

We are now far from those momentous days, but all over the world people are asking a similar question to those crowds in Jerusalem. As sin and iniquity increase, as millions are lovers of pleasure more than lovers of God, believers in particular are aware that the coming of the Lord is drawing very near. They are saying, "Will He come today?" That momentous moment cannot be too far away. Don't you feel a thrill in your heart, Christian? This is your great hope for He that shall come, will come and will not tarry. Will He find you working, waiting and watching?

May *twenty-ninth*

"Then, six days before the Passover, Jesus came to Bethany, where Lazarus was who had been dead, whom He had raised from the dead. There they made Him a supper; and Martha served, but Lazarus was one of those who sat at the table with Him" (John 12: 1-2).

No-one can tell me that the Scriptures are merely historical. Underlying these stirring events is a sequence. First, Christ comes to Bethany and raises a believer who had died who then joins believers who are alive and remaining. What did they do then? Both the raised and those who are alive and remaining sit down with the Lord for a supper. Isn't that the sequence of events laid out for the church of Jesus Christ in the future? The church awaits Christ's personal coming. The dead in Christ will then rise first and those alive and remaining will be caught up with them to meet the Lord. They will then sit down together for a supper. It is called the Marriage Supper of the Lamb (see Revelation 19; 7-9).

That supper at Bethany prefigured the supper of all suppers. In our culture there is a wedding ceremony followed by a reception. In Biblical times parents arranged a marriage contract for their children, then when the couple became adults the bride and groom accompanied by his friends would go to the bride's home and escort his bride home. Having brought his bride home, he would invite his friends to the marriage supper. Invitations for the Marriage Supper of the Lamb are out. Have you accepted? You would be a fool to miss it.

May thirtieth

"And Martha served .... " (John 12: 2).

Martha was acting according to character. She served. Mark tells us that this supper was not in her home but in the home of Simon the leper. She was obviously the hostess. Now we have met her earlier preparing a meal for Jesus and as far as we know there were only four people there. How many were here? There were seventeen, at least. There was, presumably, Simon. There was Mary, Martha and Lazarus. That's four. There was Christ and His disciples. That's seventeen. What was the difference between this occasion and the first occasion?

At that time Martha was distracted by her serving. Now, she isn't. She is now serving as wholeheartedly as ever but not to the detriment of ignoring what God wants to say to her. She has now learned the secret of balance in her life. Is she busy? Certainly. Hostess to seventeen is as hard work then as it is now, but, it wasn't, for her, a top priority. It no longer distracted her from the thing that mattered most. Say, what about us? Are we balanced or distracted? Let's put first things first.

May thirty-first

"Then Mary took a pound of very costly oil of spikenard" (John 12: 3).

Love is not content in giving what it must. It is not expressed in merely giving what is expected. That the spikenard was costly did not weigh heavily in Mary's mind. Love cannot be weighed in scales. Cut a channel for it and it will overflow. It cannot be calculated mathematically, it forgets calculation.

One thing is certain, if we have not what the Bible calls "first love" for Christ we will do more harm than good by the defence of the Christian faith. People have risen in the history of the church with a zeal for truth but because there is no first love for Christ behind it, their zeal narrows into hate. All service for Christ that is not the outcome of love to Him is worthless. Activity in the King's service will not make up for neglect of the King.

So, you would follow Christ? Then you must come His way and that way is the way of self-sacrificing, self-giving, self-abandonment. The same way, though it means death to self, also means the gate to life.

It was Epicurus who once said, "Wealth consists not in having great possessions but in having few wants". If you only want what the Lord wants, then selfishness will never dominate your life. You will only want to do His will.

J U N E

June   first

"Then one of His disciples, Judas Iscariot, Simon's son, who would betray Him, said, 'Why was this fragrant oil not sold for 300 denarii and given to the poor?'. This he said not that he cared for the poor, but because he was a thief, and had the money box; and he used to take what was put in it" (John 12: 4-6).

I f you wait until everybody commends and praises you, then you will never do any good in this world. There are always Judas's around who will not tell you outright that you should not have done a certain thing but they will tell you how you might have done something much better. Carpers will always be carping at your motives and actions when you set out to do something for the Lord. Isn't it a blessing that Mary did not take any notice of Judas?

Be sure that if you have done something for the glory of God it will come to no harm. The Lord knows your motivation and will use that act of yours to His glory. Not only was the house filled with the fragrance of Mary's perfume, millions of hearts have been inspired by her act ever since. Indeed her lovely act has become the possession of the whole world. An act done for God's glory is permanently precious. Judas's carping only showed what was inside him, Mary's pouring of the ointment showed where her heart lay. Say, where does your heart lie?

June   second

"Mary .... anointed the feet of Jesus ...." (John 12: 3).

M ary teaches us that it is absolutely vital to spend time in worship. Devotion to Christ overflows in worship. And not just on average days either. The Scripture constantly brings Mary before us as being found at the feet of Jesus. On a pleasant day when He called at Bethany she sat at His feet listening to His Word. On a very unpleasant day in Bethany when Lazarus had just died and her heart was heavy with sorrow, when Christ called for her, she went straight to His feet. Now as the Saviour faces His day of sorrow above all sorrows, where is Mary found? At His feet.

At Christ's feet is the place of power. Saturate your mind and heart there with His fragrance and humility. No pride will mar you, there, ambition fades. Bitterness is neutralised, anger is assuaged, hatred is dissipated, envy is made look ridiculous, lust is seen for the selfish monster it is, restlessness is calmed when you steal away to the feet of the Saviour in prayer and worship. How long is it since you have been there?

June   third

"Then Jesus said, 'Let her alone; she has kept this for the day of My burial. For the poor you have with you always, but Me ye do not have always'" (John 12: 7-8).

*T*he Lord Jesus justified Mary's actions. How? On the grounds of His death. Kindness could be shown to the poor at any time but as He was approaching death, Mary's opportunity to anoint Him for His burial would not come again. If your teenager or your wife or husband asked you for a trip to Florence this coming winter you might immediately assert that you simply couldn't afford it. If, however, the one you loved had but a year to live and asked you if they could see Florence before they died, how would you react? Would you tell them it was too extravagent to help them to get to Florence?

Mary understood what Christ's burial was all about. The custom of using perfume to anoint the body of a loved one was done to overcome the stench of death. When Jesus was laid in the tomb He would not see corruption (Acts 2; 23-28: Psalm 16; 10) so He wouldn't need perfume on His body to mask the stench of death. So Mary poured it on His feet while He was alive.

The lesson? If the Lord requires something from you at this time in your life then give it to Him immediately.

June   fourth

"Then a great many of the Jews knew that He was there; and they came, not for Jesus' sake only, but that they might also see Lazarus, whom He had raised from the dead. But the chief priests took counsel that they might also put Lazarus to death, because on account of him many of the Jews went away and believed in Jesus" (John 12: 9-11).

*I*t is so easy in life to hold on to power for one reason or another. People build their little empires and hold on to them as if that it all there is in this world. What they think is so important is in fact often ultimately useless.

Take a look at the Sadducees in the Jewish leadership. They simply did not believe in life after death. They regarded the situation with Christ as theologically intolerable. To see Lazarus walking about as a result of Christ's clear call into his tomb shook the very foundations of their theological empire of influence and teaching. People were turning away from their teaching, and no wonder; having Lazarus in town rendered it absolutely bogus.

So, what did they do with the evidence? They proposed to destroy it! Not only did they propose to kill Jesus, they proposed to kill Lazarus as well. That's what holding on to power can do to people. Some of them would do anything to preserve it. Don't live, Christian, to hold on to earthly power. Walk loose to it. Your aim is to know Him and the power of His resurrection.

June   fifth

"The next day a great multitude that had come to the Feast, when they heard that Jesus was coming to Jerusalem, took bunches of palm trees and went out to meet Him ..... the Pharisees therefore said among themselves. 'You see that you are accomplishing nothing. Look, the world has gone after Him!'" (John 12: 12-13, 19).

This wonderful story is certainly teaching us very clearly the sequence of events which will take place at the coming of the Lord. First, the dead in Christ will rise first after the Lord's shout. Second, those that are alive and remaining will be caught up with them to meet the Lord. Third, there will be the Marriage Supper of the Lamb at which both groups will sit down with Christ.

What then? Watch what happens in the Lazarus story. The Lord comes to Jerusalem with His own and the crowds in Jerusalem pour out to meet Him, a foreshadow of Zechariah's prophesy which will one day be literally fulfilled when Christ's own shall reign with Him and "His dominion shall be from sea to sea, and from the River to the ends of the earth" (Zechariah 9; 9). Further, "All kings shall fall down before Him; all nations shall serve Him .... His Name shall endure for ever .... all nations shall call Him Blessed" (Psalm 72; 11, 17). It is very clear that the entrance of Christ to Jerusalem foreshadowed the return of Christ to reign with His people. The old Pharisees stood by and watched the proceedings in Jerusalem and scoffed. "Look", they said, "The world has gone after Him". They spoke more truth than they knew.

June   sixth

"Now there were certain Greeks among those who came up to worship
at the Feast. They came to Philip, who was from Bethsaida of Galilee,
and asked him, saying, 'Sir, we wish to see Jesus'. Philip came and told
Andrew, and in turn Andrew and Philip told Jesus. But Jesus answered
them, saying, 'The hour has come that the Son of Man should be
glorified'" (John 12; 20-23).

G reece? It was the cradle of democracy. Philosophers captured
the imagination of its population. The Olympic Games started
there. If you had an enquiring mind, it was the place to be.
From Greece came certain Greeks to the Passover Feast at Jerusalem.
News of Christ had reached them and they were keenly anxious to see
Him. When they eventually met Him they heard Him make an amazing statement. "The hour has come when the Son of Man should be
glorified", He said.

Every committed Jew who had read the Old Testament knew that
Daniel had prophesied that the wicked kingdoms of this world would
be subdued by the one "Like the Son of Man coming with the clouds of
heaven" (Daniel 7; 13). The Saviour, though, meant something entirely
different. By "glorified" they meant the subduing of earthly kingdoms
grovelling at His feet. By "glorified" He meant His crucifixion.

The cross still leaves many people bewildered. Far more important
than the question, "Why did God become a man?" is the question, "Why
did Christ die?" Christians will immediately answer that question by
stating that the cross is the ground of their acceptance with God, the
means of their justification, the subject of their witness and the sole object of their boasting. God forbid that we should glory in anything else.
Before the glory of the cross, the glory of Greece or anywhere else, fades.

June   seventh

"Most assuredly, I say to you, unless a grain of wheat falls
into the ground and dies, it remains alone; but if it dies, it produces
much grain" (John 12: 24).

T he history of a grain of wheat is an absolutely superb illustration of a very profound spiritual truth. Drop a grain of wheat
into the earth and let it die. Wait and carefully watch and in
time the grain becomes the blade, then the ear, and then the full corn in

the ear. The field of golden grain which you eventually see was hidden in those tiny grains of wheat long hidden in the soil.

So it was that men and women did not see in the death of the Saviour the world-wide harvest that would eventually emerge from His death. On and on through the running centuries, that Divine grain of wheat has brought a harvest which is simply incalculable. He died alone but through His death innumerable multitudes have lived. Are you lonely and leading a solitary life? The best cure for loneliness comes through sowing yourself in daily self sacrifice. One thing is then guaranteed; your life will bring an undisputed harvest.

June eighth

"He who loves His life will lose it, and He who hates his life in this world will keep it for eternal life" (John 12: 25).

Here is the great paradox of Christian living. The person who lives merely on "this life" level will lose it and the person who lives for the Kingdom of God, even in this life, will keep it for eternal life. It could not be otherwise. Make yourself the centre of your life and you will become an idolator. Idolatory lies at the heart of all sin. Such a person chooses and causes his or her own perdition. Hate your life? It does not mean hatred in an absolute sense. It does not mean that you are called to hate the trees and the flowers, the joys of human love, the pleasures of a summer's day, the laughter of little children, or the beauty of a snow-blanketed landscape. Such would mean ultimate depression and absolute psychological breakdown.

Yet, we must never overvalue this world. The contrast of love and hate in our text is a Hebrew idiom that really asks us, "What is your preference in life?" Are you the centre of your existence, does self-interest dictate your decisions, does your life have priority over the interests of God and His Kingdom? At the heart of worldliness is Satan's lie which states that this world is all there is. The significance of life in this world cannot be truly lived without reference to the world which exists outside of this one. Don't overvalue this world and its applause. Its attractions are very fleeting things.

June ninth

"If anyone serves Me, let him follow Me, and where I am, there My servant will be also. If anyone serves Me, him My Father will honour"
(John 12: 26).

So, you would follow Christ? Then you must come His way and that way is the way of self-sacrificing, self-giving, self-abandonment. The same way, though it means death to self, also means the gate to life.

It was Epicurus who once said, "Wealth consists not in having great possessions but in having few wants". If you only want what the Lord wants, then selfishness will never dominate your life. You will only want to do His will.

Is such a life worth it? Certainly. All along your life you will experience the Lord honouring you in all sorts of ways. As F.B. Meyer put it, "The soul that dares to live this life will find streams flowing from every smitten rock, honey in the carcass of every slain lion; day out of night; spring out of winter; flowers out of frost; joy out of sorrow; fruitfulness out of pruning; Olivet out of Gethsemane; the Ascension out of Calvary; life out of death".

June tenth

"Now my soul is troubled, and what shall I say? Father, save Me from this hour"? But for this purpose came I to this hour" (John 12: 27).

The Lord Jesus does not ask us to do anything which He would not do Himself. How will He face up to the paradox He has been teaching others about? Will He renounce present interests for future inheritance? Present interests could have diverted Him from lonely resistance to the onset of the powers of darkness. Had not the crowds just lauded Him? It would have been very easy to stay popular and not turn to deal with the weight of the world's sin. It would have meant not having to be made a curse. His resolution, though, was absolutely firm. He had come for this hour.

Notice what He said in His hour of anguish. He said, "Father!" Again and again in His life on earth He murmured that Name. Are you overwhelmed? Cry, "Abba". Are you frightened? Say, "Abba". There is no pain, or hurt, temptation or challenge, trial or perplexity that the thought of your having a Heavenly Father will not console and temper. You are not the sport of circumstance. Your Heavenly Father is guiding your every step. He is your cleft in the rock.

June   eleventh

"Father, glorify Your name. Then a voice came from Heaven, saying, 'I have both glorified it and will glorify it again'" (John 12: 28).

Here is the greatest and highest thing we can ask God to do. The glory of God is the purpose for which all things were created. Did not Paul say, "As always, so now also, Christ will be magnified in my body, whether by life or death"? Christ was willing to suffer whatever was necessary if only the glory of God would be promoted. If people were to think better of His Father through what they saw in Him, that was what really mattered.

The Father simply couldn't keep silence in the light of such a statement. Right out of the April sky came a voice in which was all of the past ("I have glorified it") and all of the future ("and will glorify it again"). The Father had heard Christ's petition and would through His coming death and resurrection glorify His name.

Whatever these days in your life holds for you, make sure that God's name is glorified. It adds true dignity to even the plainest and dullest of daily duties if we can do them to the glory of God. Let your motive for all that you do today be "Blessing, and honour, and glory, and power, be to Him who sits on the throne and to the Lamb for ever and ever". Such a motivation will lift your day.

June   twelfth

"Therefore the people who stood by and heard it said that it thundered. Others said, 'An angel has spoken to Him'. Jesus answered and said, 'This voice did not come because of Me, but for your sake'" (John 12: 29).

Does God still speak? He certainly spoke to Jesus at the great moments of His earthly life. He spoke to Him at His baptism, on the Mount of Transfiguration and now as he turned to face the ordeal of the cross. Does He do the same for us? He certainly does.

He speaks to us through nature, He speaks to us through the Scriptures and he also speaks to us through the Lord Jesus. I believe that He also speaks to us through all sorts of tiny details in our lives, if we had but the eyes to see it. He uses a telephone call, a magazine article, a "bumping into" a friend, a timely conversation with a sympathetic heart; they are secondary causes but they are backed up by the primary cause, namely the serendipity of God. Serendipity? The dictionary calls it "the gift of making fortunate discoveries by accident". Yet what the dictionary and we often call an accident is in fact the voice of God. Listen for His voice, today.

June   thirteenth

"Now is the judgment of this world ....." (John 12: 31).

T he spirit of worldliness says that it wants all the gifts that the Creator gives but it does not want to receive the rule of the Creator. The spirit met the Saviour in full force. When the crowds who had strewn His path with palms discovered the true cost of recognising His lordship and rule, they turned the smiles to frowns, their flatteries to threats.

The spirit of worldliness was unveiled at Calvary. It was a full, head-on collision between the life of Heaven and the life of this world. The world, of course, as personified by Caiaphas and Pilate, thought they were passing judgment on Christ but in reality He was passing judgment on them. They revealed their true character by the way they treated Him. If you as a Christian are being persecuted and hated by worldly people who cannot stand you, then take heart because the Saviour said, "If the world hates you, you know that it hated Me before it hated you". You are in the best of company.

June   fourteenth

"Now the Ruler of this world will be cast out" (John 12: 31).

S atan is not yet cast out of the world, entirely. The text says, though, that he will be. It is a process that began at the cross when, we are told, his head was bruised. At the cross he was dethroned. To every person who offers him or herself to Christ for deliverance, Satan will be cast out. Greater is He who is in you, Christian, than He who is in the world. Satan can no longer possess you. At the cross Christ did battle with Satan and stripped him of a large portion of his authority and cast him out of a large portion of his dominion. Satan is, then, a vanquished enemy. In Christ's power he can be resisted, and will flee. Against prayer he has no defence. At the second Advent he will be, says Revelation 20, finally cast out.

What, then, about death? Christ at Calvary through death destroyed him who had the power of death, that is, the Devil and released those who through fear of death were all their lifetime subject to bondage. Was there ever a more heartening, soul-thrilling word to all of us who have known His power than those quiet, deliberate words of our Saviour, "Now the Prince of this world will be cast out"? Hallelujah!

June fifteenth

"'And I, if I am lifted up from the earth, will draw all peoples to Myself'. This He said, signifying by what death He would die" (John 12: 32-33).

One has often wondered how the Greeks felt who had first asked to see the Saviour. The amazing statements that followed this request have occupied our thinking over these past few days, but how did those Greeks react? They had asked to see Him but are now being told that if the Lord Jesus were "lifted up" then they could approach Him as never before. Indeed, not only could they approach Him but "all peoples" no matter of what race, could do the same. Christ is literally the Saviour of the world. This, of course, does not mean that everyone will yield to Him but it does mean that there will be those who will yield from every clime and nation and tongue. He is the Lamb of God who takes away the sin of the world.

What did He mean by "lifted up"? He primarily meant His cross but the verb has a double meaning and is deliberately chosen; it can signify not only literal elevation but exaltation in rank or honour. So the Saviour was raised on a cross but He was also raised in resurrection, ascension and exaltation. Through it all He has become as a spiritual magnet drawing people to Him without distinction. In Him there are no racial or religious barriers. Those Greeks certainly got an answer if anybody ever got an answer, didn't they?

June   sixteenth

"The people answered Him, 'We have heard from the law that the Christ remains forever; and how can you say, 'The Son of Man must be lifted up'? Who is the Son of Man?'" (John 12: 34).

I went to a school with a chap called Horace and he once sent me a series of photographs which he took of the wreck of Osymandias in the Egyptian desert. Underneath each photograph was an appropriate line from Shelley's great sonnet on Osymandias which he and I had studied under our English teacher, Norrie Watts. Let me quote to you from Shelley's sonnet;

"I met a traveller from an antique land,
Who said, 'Two vast and trunkless legs of stone
Stand in the desert ..... Near them on the sand,
Half sunk, a shattered visage lies, whose frown,
And wrinkled lip, and sneer of cold command,
Tell that the sculpture well those persons read,
Which yet survive, stamped on these lifeless things,
The hand that mocked them, and the heart that said:
And on the pedestal these words appear:
"My name is Osymandias, king of kings,
Look on my works, ye mighty and despair! "
Nothing beside remains. Round the decay
Of that colossal wreck, boundless and bare,
The lone and level sands stretch far away".

In the light of today's text the people in the Saviour's time obviously couldn't understand how a Messiah could die and live forever. We now know how that was possible. The King of Love had founded a Kingdom which grows by the year and all its members love Him because of His death on their behalf. Most empires of the world are founded on force. Those empires soon fade and are forgotten. Which kingdom are you living for?

June   seventeenth

"Then Jesus said to them, 'A little while longer the light is with you. Walk while you have the light, lest darkness overtake you; he who walks in darkness does not know where he is going. While you have the light, believe in the light, that you may become sons of light'" (John 12: 35-36).

*T*here is no more beautiful idiom of Christ than the idiom of light. Light is gentle, pure, penetrating, vivid, all-revealing. Think of the views and vistas that light opens up at dawn; look at the entirely different aspect morning light gives to those things long held in the darkness of night.

The people had asked Jesus a theological question. They wanted to know who the Son of Man was. He ignored the question and told them the thing that they should do was to follow the light that they had and they would soon see that it led to Him. We are back to John's assertion that Christ is the true light which lightens every person who comes into the world.

Christ also asserts that if people believe in Him as the light they will become children of light. In life you become like what you follow. The light of Christ can shine right through you on to the lives you touch today. Imagine bringing joy and gladness and beauty into unhappy, dark, hard, ugly lives. So, be what you are, children of light, wherever you go today.

June   eighteenth

"But although He had done so many signs before them, they did not believe in Him, that the word of Isaiah the prophet might be fulfilled, which He spoke: 'Lord, who has believed our report? And to whom has the arm of the Lord been revealed?'. Therefore they could not believe, because Isaiah said again: 'He has blinded their eyes and hardened their hearts, lest they should see with their eyes and understand with their heart, lest they should turn, so that I should heal them'. These things Isaiah said when he saw His glory and spoke of Him" (John 12: 37-41).

*T*he results of the signs of Christ were not thick on the ground, were they? From turning water to wine to raising Lazarus, His mighty power had resulted in a comparatively small number of people believing in Him. To whom was the arm of the Lord revealed? Many, but few believed. It would take the cross and the resurrection to bring about the complete revelation of Christ and then millions would believe. The signs and teaching of the Saviour on their own were not enough.

Instead of this fact of the Lord's ministry bringing few immediate results leading to John's discouragement, he writes that it actually proved the Lord's authenticity. Isaiah had prophesied it would happen. Their unbelief came because God ratified their decision and attitude. God never hardens a person's heart until that person hardens their own heart. The Lord, for example, hardened Pharaoh's heart but it was not until Pharaoh had hardened his own heart that there came a moment when God sealed Pharaoh's choice.

This is a very important truth. Nobody is ever fated to be incapable of belief in Christ any more than anybody in Israel was incapable of believing Isaiah's message. The people's unbelief, then, and people's unbelief now, is not the result of divine action. It is as a result of their own decision. Selah.

June   nineteenth

"Nevertheless, even among the rulers many believed in Him, but because of the Pharisees they did not confess Him, lest they should be put out of the synagogue; for they loved the praise of men more than the praise of God" (John 12: 42, 43).

*T*his has got to be one of the worst indictments any individual could ever have; it is to love, above everything else, to be well thought of by others. There are people who, like these rulers, believe in Christ, are convinced of the truth He teaches but they will not confess it because it would threaten their position in society where they are well thought of. It is, at heart, a cowardly faith. It puts prestige and position amongst their fellow men and women before pleasing God.

Let me ask you a simple question; do you prefer to stand well with people rather than God? It is obvious that the people in today's text thought far more of what people thought of them than what God thought of them.

Theirs was a secret faith and it will not do. "If you confess with your mouth the Lord Jesus and believe in your heart that God has raised Him from the dead, you will be saved", says Scripture. If you do not confess Christ before others, He will not confess you before His Father. It is worth remembering that the opinion of others may matter during your lifetime but the opinion of God matters for eternity. In the light of this fact, whose opinion matters most? Whose praise counts a million years from now?

June   twentieth

"Then Jesus cried out and said, 'He who believes in Me, believes not in Me but in Him who sent Me. And He who sees Me sees Him who sent Me'" (John 12: 44-45).

We now come to the last phrases in Christ's public teaching and the end of His public ministry. He would soon turn to privately teaching His disciples in the Upper Room and then to stand before Ciaphas and Pilate and then move on to death. Here is a summary of all that He taught. He, note, "cried", i.e. He gave a loud cry, He raised His voice in an emotional appeal calling attention to what He had to say.

The first movement of His final public appeal sums up Christ's relationship with God. It is a remarkable statement insisting on the entire unity between Himself and the Father. They cannot be divided. He is saying that it is no small and insignificant thing to believe on Him. It is the same thing as believing on God the Father. If people have seen Him they have seen the Father.

He holds a supreme place. In Him God meets man and man meets God. No wonder He raised His voice as he came to His very last declaration of this truth. We too need to raise our voices in these days to declare it in our generation when many would relegate Christ to a role on par with other religious leaders. He is on par with no-one. He is God. Don't be afraid to raise your voice on the issue.

June   twenty-first

"I have come as a light into the world, that whoever believes in Me should not abide in darkness" (John 12: 46).

Was ever so much truth packed into so few words? The verse tells us that the world is in spiritual darkness and that Christ is the light. It tells us that He was the light long before He came into the world just like the sun exists before it appears at dawn. It tells us that faith is the way to finding Him. It emphasises that the person who believes in Him no longer abides in darkness but has spiritual light. It teaches that the unbeliever remains in spiritual darkness. It teaches there is only one Saviour in the world. It teaches that He did not come just for one nation but everyone. It proves there is a place for you.

This is a very personal statement of the Saviour. Let no-one ever tell you that the Saviour came to condemn you. He came to deliver you from darkness. He came to transform you. He is describing His mission in terms of having brought into the world what it had lost. When God is recognised, that is the light. So when we recognise Christ we recognise God. That was His mission and nobody, but nobody, could give such a majestic description of His work but He. Bless God for the Lord Jesus!

June   twenty-second

"And if anyone hears My word and does not believe, I do not judge Him; for I did not come to judge the world but to save the world"
(John 12: 47).

All over the country I hear the little expression, "After all, at the end of the day". Football managers use it. Politicians use it to sum up their speeches. Businessmen use it to drive on their sales staff to a greater turnover. It is a phrase that implies that when all is said and done, this is the thing that really matters.

At the end of the day, then, what really matters? The Lord Jesus says that it is His word that matters. He did not come into the world to condemn it, to believe His word is to find life. In fact Christ taught that to hear His word and to obey it is like building your house on a rock. To turn one's back on God's word, though, and to disobey it is like building your house on sand. When the rain and wind comes and the storm blast hits the house, it will fall. It cannot stand on such a foundation. The message that proclaims life to those who believe it is the same message which proclaims judgment to those who disobey it. At the end of the day it is what you do with the Saviour's word that matters. Your word on His word will determine your final judgment.

June   twenty-third

"Now before the Feast of the Passover, when Jesus knew that His hour had come that He should depart from this world to the Father, having loved His own who were in the world, He loved them to the end"
(John 13: 1).

Why didn't the Lord Jesus stay on this earth? I mean would it not have been better for us all if He had? Would all who believe in Him not find it easier to be Christians if we could, at least, go to hear Him speak at some venue, some stadium or on television or spend a day in His company? Would it not make the Christian life more meaningful if we could take a trip to Israel every summer to spend time at some summer school Christ taught? Would it not prove that He loved us if He had stayed with us?

No. It was not because He did not love us that He left us. He loved His own to the end, to the very uttermost. Nor was it that He left this world as a weak victim. He left deliberately. His resurrection and ascension to the Father would liberate the Holy Spirit's power to help us live a holy life. In the place of ugly strife and selfishness, hatred and broken promises would come holy lives.

Holiness, please note, is lovely. It certainly hates sin but its outcome is transformed sinners. Only by departing would the Lord Jesus make room for the Holy Spirit to enter His people, everywhere, and make them holy. That's a lot better than just spending a day or two with Christ or catching an odd glimpse of Him, is it not?

June   twenty-fourth

"Now there was leaning on Jesus' bosom one of His disciples, whom Jesus loved. Simon Peter therefore motioned to Him to ask who it was of whom He spoke" (John 13: 23-24).

There was a Satanic plot afoot. The Devil and Judas were in a conspiracy of evil to bring the Saviour to death. Not only Judas, though, but others around that supper table would soon come under his influence. In a few hours Peter would, with oaths and curses, deny that he knew the Saviour and everyone of the disciples would forsake Him and flee. What's more, the whole lot of them were so selfish they didn't even perform the simple courtesy, customary at the time, of washing each of the guests' feet before the meal. The Saviour was obliged to do it Himself. What hope had Christ in making His disciples holy?

What hope, even, if they had their problems, has He of making us holy? The answer is that because Christ would die at the cross and then return to His Father, the Holy Spirit would enter us and Satan's ultimate intention of blocking Christ's work of making us holy would be defeated.

Recently I had lunch in Vancouver with the great evangelical theologian, Professor J. I. Packer. I cannot remember all that we ate but I can sure remember what was said as we talked together of the things of the Kingdom. In his classic book, "Knowing God", Professor Packer makes four points on Paul's great writing in Romans 8. He says that it teaches that ultimately no opposition can finally crush us, no good thing will finally be withheld from us, no accusation can ever disinherit us, and no separation from God's love can ever befall us. My, doesn't that cheer your day!

June   twenty-fifth

> *"After that, He poured water into a basin and began to wash the disciples' feet, and to wipe them with the towel with which He was girded" (John 13: 5).*

W ords beggar me to describe this incident. It is so majestic in its symbolism. A look, though, at the circumstances out of which it sprang is most revealing. There was something going on in the hearts of the disciples for some time which surfaced even at this momentous hour. Luke, in describing the Upper Room incident, gives us its backdrop; "But there was, also", he says, "rivalry among them as to which of them should be considered the greatest" (Luke 22: 24).

What? Rivalry even after three and a half years teaching from the lips of God Incarnate? What? Even after witnessing the seven great miracles He performed and the kindnesses He showed was there rivalry amongst them? In the face of it all the greatest One in the universe takes the servant's place and washes the disciples' feet while they nurse in their hearts thoughts about who would be the greatest among them. Incredible, isn't it?

If they had it in their hearts then be sure of one thing, we have it too. We forget the rock from which we were hewn. We forget the blessings of God on our lives and the assurance of His promises. We get carried away and rotten pride sweeps in and makes us behave pathetically. Just remember; if you insist on your own glory, God will withdraw His.

June   twenty-sixth

"Then He came to Simon Peter. And Peter said to Him, 'Lord, are you washing my feet?'" (John 13: 6).

*P*eter was embarrassed as well he might be. There was silence from the rest of the disciples but Peter, true to his nature, spoke up and expressed what the others felt. His motivation was well intentioned for the Greek construction of his question emphasises his extreme embarrassment; "Are you going to wash my feet?"

The Saviour, by His answer, though, hinted that there was deeper significance to what He was doing. In fact there was more to what He did than a lesson in humble service. Peter would not grasp what it was all about there and then but there would come a day when he would.

Peter's experience, no doubt, mirrors your situation today. There are things going on in your life which the Lord has brought about. You are completely mystified as to what they are meant to accomplish but one day you will understand it all. The day will come when you will bless the Lord for bringing you into today's circumstance. Be patient. Don't panic. Trust. You'll see.

June   twenty-seventh

"Peter said to Him, 'You shall never wash my feet!' Jesus answered him, 'If I do not wash you, you have no part with me'. Simon Peter said to Him, 'Lord, not my feet only, but also my hands and my head!'" (John 13: 8-9).

*T*here are two loves at work here. There is the love of the Lord Jesus for Peter and there is Peter's love for the Lord Jesus. Christ's is a love that cleanses believers (see Titus 3: 3-7). Peter would fully understand this cleansing in the light of the cross and it is the cleansing that comes at conversion. Praise God that the Saviour cleanses with the washing of regeneration that comes with the experience of the New Birth, puts a whole new nature in us and cleanses our lives from the guilt of sin. We can have no part with Christ if we deny such cleansing.

Peter, though, not understanding what Christ was doing symbolically bursts out, "Lord, not my feet only but my hands and my head".

What an endearing character Peter had! He is basically saying, "I love you, Lord, and if I must be washed then don't stop at my feet". There was, despite his feelings, a deep love for Christ which would soon take him to the service that would be a blessing to untold millions. If Peter erred here, which he certainly did, he erred on the side of love. Do you?

June   twenty-eighth

"Jesus said to him, 'He who is bathed needs only to wash his feet, but is completely clean; and you are clean, but not all of you'. For He knew who would betray Him; therefore He said, 'You are not all clean'"
(John 13; 10-11).

The Lord Jesus made, in this statement, a distinction between the rest of the disciples and Judas. He was talking about a washing which Judas had never had and would never experience.

There are two cleansings mentioned in the New Testament. There is cleansing by blood (see 1 John 1; 7) and cleansing by water (see Ephesians 5: 25-27). The first cleansing by blood is dealt with by Matthew, Mark and Luke and is symbolised in the cup of communion. John, though, concentrates on the Lord's other provision for our cleansing, i.e. cleansing by water.

When you trust Christ as Saviour the blood of Christ shed at Calvary cleanses your conscience from the guilt of sin. But as we go on in the Christian life we will soon discover ugly things which spoil our personalities and character. So the second cleansing is by the power of the Word of God, called by Paul "The washing of water by the Word". When you sin as a Christian, you don't need the washing of regeneration again but you do need the Holy Spirit to renew you. So you will need to read God's Word and let it challenge you and the Lord will show you the attitudes and actions that displease Him. The Holy Spirit will strengthen you to stop doing these things. It is a constant process, a constant cleansing. The first cleansing you have had if you have been born again but all your days you will need the second cleansing, daily. The first cleansing is described as a bathing all over, the second the washing of your feet. Let the Lord wash you feet today. If you don't you will enjoy little practical fellowship with Him.

June   twenty-ninth

"If I then, your Lord indeed, have washed your feet, you also ought to wash one another's feet" (John 13: 14).

*T*his statement is saying that practical holiness is not just a theological doctrine. It is challenging us to remember that holiness involves an attitude of mind which looks for opportunities to serve.

If, as the man said, life is ten per cent what happens to us and ninety per cent how we respond to it, then our choice of attitude is vital. There is nothing, no nothing, that will affect my day like my choice of attitude.

So Christ says our attitude should be as servant's attitude. The Old Testament story of Elisha's servant Gehazi stands as a powerful warning across the century. He started out with a very healthy servant attitude but soon fell foul to a "I'll-take-something-for-myself-thank-you" attitude. It turned him into a cheating, lying individual. God, as a warning to us all, struck him with leprosy. If God treated all who lost their servant attitude with leprosy, we would all be lepers. Selah.

June   thirtieth

"You call Me Teacher and Lord, and you say well, for so I am. If I then, your Lord and Teacher, have washed your feet, you ought also to wash one another's feet" (John 13:13-14).

*W*hy the reversal? It has to do with attitude to Christ. We often come to Christ as a Teacher and hear what He has to say and make up our minds as to whether or not we are going to carry it out. Recently in the United Kingdom a Bishop stated that Paul did not understand humanity in his attitude to homosexuality. Indeed? And what about Christ? They say He never mentioned homosexuality. That is true. He simply said He had come to fulfil the law and the Old Testament law categorically states that homosexuality is an abomination (see Lev. 18: 22). So, if we are going to be truly holy then we should come to Christ as Lord absolutely committed in advance to obeying Him. Then when He teaches us our attitude to Him will be seen very clearly in that we obey what He teaches, unequivocally. So let's get it right, "It's Lord and Teacher, not just Teacher and Lord".

*S*urely if you long to be in the Father's home you long for the Father to make His home with you. To have a guest in your home and not care about what they like or dislike would be extremely discourteous. So, if we would have mutual fellowship with God we must love Him and do the things He likes and abhor the things He dislikes. To do otherwise would be to dishonour the One who makes His home with us. Selah.

JULY

July first

"For I have given you an example, that you should do as I have done to you" (John 13: 15).

The Lord Jesus, by His act of feet-washing has established forever the measure of service for those who claim to be His disciples. If our Lord did not think it beneath His dignity to perform a menial task for those who follow Him, then they should never think it beneath theirs to do the same for each other.

Notice, though, the teaching here in the wider context. We all get our feet soiled on the highway of life, we all have attitudes that are wrong. If, then, you approach someone to wash their feet you will be advised not to use boiling hot water lest you scald them. The Lord Jesus got down below the level of their couches and washed their feet, gently. So if we would seek to correct, say, someone's attitude problem we must not do it in an arrogant and proud manner, else we will do them more harm than good. Humility of attitude and helpfulness goes a long way to guiding those who have been soiled to a place of cleansing. If you would be a true foot-washer, imitate the Lord's method. Christians are often hopeless at this ministry simply because they are not willing to stoop low enough. So, gently does it.

July second

"Most assuredly, I say to you, a servant is not greater than his master; nor is he who is sent greater than He who sent Him" (John 13: 16).

There is nothing more annoying than someone who is too big for their boots. In the history of the Christian church a woeful string of individuals have risen to high office within the church and the higher they rise the more arrogant they have become. Woe betide the church where their place is not recognised! There are even churches where rows have erupted because people did not get the place that they sought. They weren't asked to speak, so they won't speak any more. They weren't asked to sing, so they won't sing any more. They weren't asked to lead something so they refuse ever to lead again.

Arrogance in those who lead and arrogance in those who want to lead often brings chaos in the Christian church. The answer lies in asking a simple question. Who commissioned us to serve? The Lord Jesus.

Who sent us to carry His message? He did. Well, then, let's not play God in our local churches for a servant is not greater than his Lord. As Winston Churchill said; "I know of no case where a man added to his dignity by standing on it".

July   third

"If you know these things, happy are you if you do them" (John 13: 17).

*JH*ere is a beatitude worth learning. It is telling us about the person who is considered truly blessed in the eyes of God. This kind of person will know the smile of God upon them. Surely God's evaluation is the very best evaluation. Here God promises that the practice of humility brings happiness. That's His evaluation and it is worth noting.

The practice of humility, of course, may not bring you immediate ease in your circumstances. Joseph practised humility in the prison, David practised humility in the caves and dens of Israel, Hannah practised humility in a very unhappy Shiloh, Mary practised humility in the poverty of Nazareth, Paul practised humility before the very arrogant Corinthian church and they called him some very nasty names. All of these people knew pressure in their path. Yet, before it was all through, they experienced the peace that passed all understanding and a happiness and contentment which the pride of their day never knew. Practice humility today and although it may not bring you ease of immediate circumstance, it will bring you ultimate happiness. God guarantees it.

July   fourth

"I do not speak concerning all of you. I know whom I have chosen; but that the Scripture may be fulfilled, 'He who eats bread with me has lifted up his heel against me'. Now I tell you before it comes, that when it does come to pass, you may believe that I am He" (John 13: 18-19).

*T*here sat, at the Lord's table, a man who had absolutely no intention of carrying out Christ's commands on humility or on anything else. He intended to disobey Him not by kicking Him openly but by kicking Him when He wasn't looking. He would lift up his heel against Him.

There was no way, of course, that Judas could deceive the Saviour. Jesus identified him as the betrayer before he betrayed so that he could underline for the disciples that He knew all things. The disciples' faith in Christ was strengthened by the fact that they could see that He was indeed the all-seeing, all-knowing God.

Judas had never been a believer. He played a part and he was a hypocrite and took cruel advantage of the Saviour. It is a solemn reminder that even at the Lord's table today people can sit and play a part. They have no intention of being loyal to the Lord Jesus. There can be no greater sin in all the universe than to take a friend's bread and then to betray him. To do that to your Heavenly Benefactor is despicable. Beware of being two-faced.

July   fifth

"Most assuredly, I say to you, he who receives whomever I send receives Me; and he who receives Me receives Him who sent Me" (John 13: 20).

Are you busy in the service of God? You will then know that what your Lord suffered you too, as His ambassador, will often suffer. You will be betrayed and receive rough treatment. You will be misunderstood. You will face disappointment, grief and loss. You will often be unpopular.

Through it all, though, you must seek to remain conscious of the dignity of your calling. An ambassador may get it rough in the country in which he or she is placed but they have the added knowledge that they do represent their king or queen or government and that what people do to them they do to what they represent.

What Judas did to the Saviour, He did to the God of the Universe. What they do to you as the Lord's ambassador they do to the Lord who sent you. Never lower your dignity as an ambassador for Christ. If you then as an ambassador for Christ beseech people to be reconciled to God and they reject you, remember they are rejecting Him.

July   sixth

"When Jesus said these things, He was troubled in spirit, and testified and said, 'Most assuredly, I say to you, one of you will betray Me'. Then the disciples looked at one another, perplexed about whom He spoke.

Now there was leaning on Jesus' bosom one of His disciples whom Jesus loved. Simon Peter therefore motioned to Him to ask who it was of whom He spoke. Then, leaning back on Jesus' breast, He said to Him, 'Lord, who is it?'" (John 13: 21-25).

*I*t is important to understand what was going on in this situation as to the seating arrangements. The table was a low one and U-shaped with the place of honour in the centre of a single side. Jewish people reclined at table and reclined on the left hand side, resting on the left elbow leaving the right hand and arm free to eat food. They reclined on couches and a man's head was literally in the breast of the person on his left. Rabbinical sources tell us that reclining was a posture reserved for special meals, such as parties and wedding feasts.

The news that one of the disciples would betray Christ came like a bolt out of the blue. Peter, obviously at a distance, motioned to John who was at Christ's immediate right to ask Christ who the betrayer was. So, leaning his head back on Jesus' breast he asked him, "Lord, who is it?" Christians to this day talk of John as the "disciple who leaned on Jesus' breast". We need not, by today's texts, think that the Saviour has favourites in His circle. He loved all His disciples, even Judas. What the texts show us is that this teacher is approachable; you too can come close to His very heart with your questions. Selah.

July   seventh

"Jesus answered, 'It is he to whom I shall give a piece of bread when I have dipped it'. And having dipped the bread, He gave it to Judas Iscariot, the son of Simon" (John 13: 26).

*T*he way that the Saviour dealt with the treachery of Judas stands forever as the epitomy of His incredible heart of love. In our culture, say, at a wedding feast, people will drink to the "the bride" or at a banquet to the guest of honour. In the East the giving of the sop was a similar gesture; it was a sign of special friendship. It entailed offering the guest a special morsel from the dish on offer.

Jesus knew that Judas would betray Him but having foreknowledge did not mean that Christ caused Him to do it. Judas was a human being, he had intelligence and emotions and was responsible for his actions. Jesus knew what Judas was about to do but still offered him one last chance. He broke a piece of unleavened bread from one of the flat cakes lying on the table and having dipped it into a vessel filled with bitter herbs, vinegar and salt or into a fruit puree, He took it out and gave it to Judas. He was saying, "Once more I offer you My friendship. Will you accept it?" He could have repented at that moment but he didn't. His was a self-chosen hell.

I recommend a little Bible study for you today. It is suggested by William Hendriksen and shows very clearly that the love of God goes out even to the worst reprobates. Look up these passages; Genesis 4: 6, 7; Isaiah 5: 1-7; Ezekiel 3: 18-21; 18-32; 33: 11; Proverbs 29: 1; Luke 13: 6-9; 13: 34,25; Acts 20: 31.

July eighth

"Now after the piece of bread, Satan entered him. Then Jesus said to him, 'What you do, do quickly'. But no-one at the table knew for what reason He said this to Him" (John 13: 27-28).

Catch the awful drama of this historic moment. Judas made his choice, he took the sop but not the friendship. Mary might pour out her precious ointment and her life for the Master, if necessary, but Judas despised her for it. No love lay in his heart toward Christ. He stole his heart against the Saviour's love and, we are told, Satan entered him.

Obviously, had Judas been willing to refuse Satan, the Saviour's power would have been available to strengthen him. How did Satan get in? Judas let him in. The Prince of Light offered him friendship. The Prince of Darkness offered him money and land (see Acts 1). He yielded to the second and Christ ratified his choice. Judas chose and Christ told him he might as well get on with his treachery and be done with it.

Could it be that someone reading this page is hesitating at the call of Christ? Satan, notice, first "put it into the heart of Judas .... to betray Him" (John 13; 2). Satan is not suggesting now, though, he is completely overpowering. Satan possesses Judas and makes him his minion. Beware, my reader. Do not hesitate to receive Christ for another stands at your door waiting to enter.

July   ninth

"So, when He had gone out, Jesus said, 'Now the Son of Man is glorified, and God is glorified in Him'" (John 13: 31).

Was there ever such a contrast? Was there ever such an antithesis? Judas went out to a spiritual and moral night that would never know a dawn. Christ was to go to Calvary, and, instead of being defeated, His cross would be the greatest display of the glory of God the world or the universe would ever see.

Just as Christ offered friendship to Judas in the Upper Room, so God offers the Saviour to the world as the pledge of His love. Even as they would drive the nails into His hands on the cross He would cry, "Father, forgive them, they know not what they do". Now we say, "God forbid that we should glory save in the cross of our Lord Jesus Christ".

The contrast is still there for all of us. It is heaven or hell. It is good or evil. It is me-ism or God-first. It is God or Mammon. It is not the New Age teaching which says that good and evil are just two sides of one. It is one or the other. Judas insisted that he wanted something for himself without any reference to God. God let him have what he chose. Say, what have you chosen? Remember; it is always night when anyone turns away from the Saviour. Always.

July   tenth

"Little children, I shall be with you a little while longer. You will seek Me; and as I said to the Jews, 'Where I am going, you cannot come,' so now I say to you" (John 13: 33).

When the Jews sent officers on an earlier occasion to arrest the Saviour and when He had pointed out that He was going away of his own accord they thought He was going on a lecture tour of Greece! Truth is, when He had talked of going away the disciples didn't understand it either. Now the Saviour insists that they understand; it was of utmost importance to them, especially in their growth in devotion to Him.

In going away He was referring to His death, burial, resurrection and ascension. Why would His going away benefit them? Because by going away He would in fact get nearer to them! Now He would only presence Himself with them; then He would actually dwell in them. The Holy Spirit would come and be the guarantee of every single Christian's perfect glorification (see Colossians 1; 27-28). Notice how Christ refers to the disciples as "little children". He had never used that expression before. It is the plural of the word used by Mary when she found the Saviour in the Temple when she lost Him. "Child", she said. It was a phrase of exquisite tenderness. He was going on a journey in which they could not join Him. It was a journey which was to prove of immeasurable and eternal benefit for them and us.

July   eleventh

"A new commandment I give to you, that you love one another; as I have loved you, that you also love one another" (John 13: 34).

T he Lord bequeathed special treasures on His own; He bequeathed for example His joy (John 15; 11), and His peace (John 14; 27) and now this new commandment. What was new about it? It was new in its inspiration. It was new in its standard, quality and extent. It was a commandment to love as Christ loves.

C.S. Lewis has pointed out that there are four kinds of love. There is affection which you could have even for an inanimate object. There is friendship which you have for people who have the same tastes and outlook as yourself. There is infatuation which lovers have. These are various kinds of love. But then there is God's love. That is a love which is different to all other loves because it loves that which is unlovable. This love reached out to this group of men, even though one had just left the room to have Christ crucified. The others were about to forsake Him and flee. Yet, He loved the unlovable. That is how we are to behave.

July   twelfth

"By this shall all men know that you are my disciples, if you have love for one another" (John 13: 35).

H ow does the world measure the true value of Christianity? By the creed you recite? By the hymns you sing? By the church order you adhere to? By the size of the church building you worship in? By the number of members you have? By the quality of the preaching and teaching? By the Christian books you produce?

None of these things are the final measure of Christianity. Only one fact will carry weight and that is that Christians love one another. Christ is not asking that they consider this, He is commanding that they do it. The measure in which Christian people fail in love of each other is the measure in which the world does not believe in them.

The story is told that Archbishop Usher once visited, incognito, the home of the godly minister, Samuel Rutherford. The master of the house was leading worship in his home on the Saturday evening and, unaware of who his guest was, asked, "How many commandments are there?" "Eleven", said his guest. The servants were scandalised! Rutherford, though, knew what lay behind it and after a private talk with Archbishop Usher asked him to preach the following Sunday morning in his pulpit. To the amazement of the household the stranger of the previous evening rose and announced the text I have chosen for today's reading, saying, "This may be described as the eleventh commandment". Have you kept it?

July thirteenth

"Simon Peter said to Him, 'Lord, where are you going?' Jesus answered him, 'Where I am going you cannot follow Me now, but you shall follow Me afterward'. Peter said to Him, 'Lord, why can I not follow you now? I will lay down my life for your sake'. Jesus answered him, 'Will you lay down your life for My sake? Most assuredly, I say to you, the rooster shall not crow till you have denied Me three times. Let not your heart be troubled; you believe in God, believe also in Me'" (John 13: 36-38: 14: 1).

There is no question that Peter thought the Lord was calling his courage into question. What? Had he not given up everything for Christ? Why couldn't he follow Christ, now? As far as Peter was concerned, no mountain would have been too high, no valley too deep to follow Christ. He would go anywhere on earth with Christ. Why, he would lay down his very life for Him.

The Saviour, though, was not calling Peter's devotion or courage into question. What He was doing, though, was exposing a weakness. Peter didn't know himself. Before the sun was fully up in the morning Peter would, by oaths and curses, deny His Lord. He thought he was strong enough to overcome temptation but he wasn't. He would learn a lot from his failure but most of all he would learn that despite his failings he would one day follow the Lord into heaven; "You shall follow Me afterward", said Christ. Here is the truth of the eternal security of the believer. We can all rejoice that the Saviour we have trusted is eternally strong. We shall follow Him, by His grace, to heaven soon. It is important to remember that there is no break in the original manuscript between John 13: 38 and 14: 1. Christ was going to prepare a place for Peter and despite his failings he would be there. So will you, Christian.

July   fourteenth

"In My Father's house are many mansions; if it were not so, I would have told you. I go to prepare a place for you. And if I go and prepare a place for you, I will come again and receive you to Myself; that where I am, there you may be also" (John 14: 2-3).

Here we have a verse much discussed, and, no wonder, because the subject matter is mind-bending. The Scriptures show that the dwelling place of God is above in heaven (see Psalm 33; 13-14; Isaiah 63: 15). Earlier Christ had referred to the temple as being His Father's house or dwelling place on earth. There, of course, you would have found many rooms where Priests and Levites were accommodated, each according to the work assigned to them. Every day they worshipped and served God, each in their own capacity.

The simplest explanation of what it all means is best. In the heavenly house the temple not made with hands, eternal in the heavens, has, like the earthly temple, many rooms. The word "mansions" simply means "dwelling places". The Lord implies that if the temple were God's only dwelling place He would have said so.

Think of it, Christian! A multitude which no person can number will inhabit that eternal temple, each with their own distinct contribution to make to the service and worship of God. Young people talk about giving them "space". Here is eternal space. Obviously the language is metaphorical, it is likening God's heaven to a house and our place in it, to rooms. This is earthly language used for a heavenly concept. The actual, though, will be much greater than the description. Here is a promise beyond all promises; here is an eternal and perfect place for you. In a million years from now it will still be your place in His place. It beggars description.

July   fifteenth

"And if I go and prepare a place for you, I will come again and receive you to Myself; that where I am, there you may be also. And where I go you know, and the way you know" (John 14: 3-4).

The temple, God's dwelling place on earth, at the time Christ spoke our text, was a beautiful place. So was the tabernacle in the wilderness before it. Forty chapters in the Bible are given over to the details of its intricate construction. The spiritual lessons inherent in its every detail are a shadow of the substance of the final tabernacle of God, heaven itself. When eventually the tabernacle in the wilderness gave place to the Jewish temple, God still dwelt there.

Beautiful though it is, the temple at Jerusalem was a place of great restriction. A Gentile crossing into its sacred precincts did so on pain of death. A Hebrew was not even allowed to enter certain priestly precincts. Even a priest himself was not allowed into the Holy of Holies. Only the High Priest could go there and that only once a year to offer a sacrifice on behalf of the people. When our Lord comes again we shall enter the eternal temple where there will be none of the restrictions of the ancient one. Every believer is a priest. All the people of God will be where He is. So shall we ever be with the Lord. Think of it; eternal access to the immediate presence of God! "And we shall serve Him day and night in His temple" (Revelation 7: 15) and go out, "no more" (Revelation 3: 12).

July   sixteenth

"Thomas said to Him, 'Lord, we do not know where you are going, and how can we know the way?' Jesus said to him, 'I am the Way, the Truth and the Life. No-one comes to the Father except through Me'"
(John 14: 5-6).

There is something in Thomas that touches us all. There are times when all identify with his bluntness and appreciate his down-to-earth attitude. He was a man in whom there was no pretence. In this instance he simply does not understand what the Saviour is saying and says so. He feels that Peter's question has not been answered. He is basically saying, "How can anyone know the way who does not fully understand the destination?" Thomas had not come to grips with what was meant by an eternal house with many rooms and said so. Don't be too hard on Thomas for asking. He was about to get what is arguably the greatest answer that anyone ever got to a question on the after-life. He asked and it was given to him, so, don't be afraid to ask.

Recently in a newspaper column I asked a lot of people across our community about heaven. Their answers ranged from Rabbi Neuberger saying she didn't believe there was one to the answer of my friend, Professor David Gooding which really got us all thinking. I asked him, "What do you think people will be doing in heaven?" and he replied, "Music is one of the highest expressions of the human spirit; its composers and performers are highly acclaimed. If the redeemed in heaven did nothing but worship God in music, no higher or nobler activity could be imagined. But there is more than one kind of music. All the activities of the redeemed will be under the baton of the Great Conductor. The whole vast co-ordinated activity will together express the verigated wisdom and love of God and its unimpeded, uncompromised goal will be the glory of God. It will fill the universe with rapturous music, a welcome relief from the strident voices of self-seeking party politics, the ugly noises of international discord, the jarring jangling of family break-ups, and the insane cacophonies of genocide and the dirge of death." I'm glad I asked him!

July *seventeenth*

"Jesus said to him, 'I am the Way, the Truth, and the Life. No-one comes to the Father except through Me. If you had known Me, you would have known my Father also; and from now on you know Him and have seen Him'" (John 14: 6-7).

I used to visit a friend's house in Aberdeen. "Come away in", he would say when I arrived. I felt so welcome. His beautiful garden was over one hundred and forty years old and my children used to play in the little stream that flowed through it. He gave me his home for a fortnight once while he and his family were on holiday and my wife loved his garden so much she was found working in it on her holiday! Squirrels ran through the fir trees, wild ducks waddled to the back door for food at breakfast time, deer even came down from the nearby forest.

"Lynwood", where my friend Mr. Stephen Cordiner lived, was, in our family, one of the most beautiful places we have known. Then, one day, I called with Carol, his wife, a few months after his death. She was at the point of selling the house and moving into a smaller one. As I sat in the old familiar kitchen I was suddenly overwhelmed with a sense of indescribable loss. My friend was not there any more. The house was not the same. It was but a shell without him. It broke my heart. I keep a picture in my study of Mr. Cordiner walking with Dr. Billy Graham around the garden at "Lynwood". I grieve, still.

I am glad the text doesn't say, "No-one comes to the Father's house but by Me." Rather it says, "No-one comes to the Father". There is all the difference in the universe between the two. What would the heavenly house be like if the Father wasn't there? A shell.

July *eighteenth*

"Philip said to Him, 'Lord, show us the Father, and it is sufficient for us'"
(John 14: 8).

The Saviour was a teacher who did not mind being interrupted. He showed no irritation whatsoever when either Peter or Thomas or Philip interrupted Him. He was in the process of teaching some of the most sublime and profound truth this world has ever heard, or ever will hear, but the questions of a fisherman like Peter or a doubting Thomas or an enquisitive Philip did not annoy Him. Teachers, take note.

Philip wants an immediate physical display of God. Who of us haven't wanted such a thing? Hadn't Moses asked for it? Who has not longed in the fury of life with all its burdens and responsibilities to see God face to face? We feel it would boost our faith and solve our problems.

The Lord, then, did not rebuke Philip for his request but he was saddened by what it revealed. It revealed that Philip had not realised the source of the Saviour's words and work. He had not passed from the river to its source. He had not realised that in seeing Christ he had seen the otherwise invisible Father. John had already stated in his prologue that "No-one has ever seen God: the only-begotten Son, who is in the bosom of the Father, He has declared Him" (1: 18). Are you looking for God? You shall never learn something about the Father that Christ has not or could not tell you.

July   nineteenth

"Do you not believe that I am in the Father, and the Father in Me? The words that I speak to you I do not speak on my own authority; but the Father who dwells in Me does the work. Believe Me that I am in the Father and the Father in Me, or else believe Me for the sake of the works themselves" (John 14: 10-11).

Put these words on the lips of anyone else and they are unthinkable. Beautiful words, wonderful words, wonderful words of life! But for some they are not enough. They need more than words, they say, before they can believe. And God by His grace gives them what they need. It was true that as those men lay by the table they were watching the light of the knowledge and glory of God in the face of Jesus Christ. It is true that in every move He made He was revealing the Father. The wonderful thing is, though, the Saviour did not just reveal the Father in words, He revealed Him in works. If people still find it difficult to penetrate the meaning of His words and so believe in Him, then let them believe on Him for his very works sake. Every miracle was a sign that God did not just reveal Himself in words but works. In the seven great recorded miracles are enough signs to point us to Christ as God. Think them through and they will point you to the fact that if you follow Christ you will have direction anywhere in God's universe. So, if you can't believe Him for His words, believe Him for His works.

July   twentieth

"Most assuredly, I say to you, he who believes in Me, the works that I do he will do also; and greater works than these he will do, because I go to my Father" (John 14: 12).

Greater works than these? Than walking on water? Than feeding five thousand? Than healing a paralytic man? Than healing a nobleman's son at a distance? Than healing a blind man? Than raising Lazarus? Certainly. Is not the conversion of a soul a greater miracle than feeding five thousand? More people were converted on the day of Penetcost than during Christ's entire ministry. The Holy Spirit came and all believers ever since have received Him as a gift and as they witness and spread the Gospel, people believe it and millions have been transformed from darkness to light. To introduce a child, a young person or a grown up to Jesus Christ through the help of the Holy Spirit is to bring them to know God. To see them converted is, the Scriptures say, to hide a multitude of sins and to save a soul from death. That is the greatest work of all. So, Christian, get on with it and remember that those who turn many to righteousness shall shine as the stars forever.

July   twenty-first

"And whatever you ask in My Name, that I will do, that the Father may be glorified in the Son. If you ask anything in My Name, I will do it"
(John 14:13-14).

*I*f we had access to the presence of God once a year to bring our requests to Him, we would think well before we entered that presence about the requests we would make. We wouldn't fritter away our time, we wouldn't let our minds wander, we would concentrate on every word we spoke.

Why then, when access to God's presence is available day and night, do we often treat prayer so carelessly? If a mother stirs to the slightest whimper of her child, does not God move to even the slightest prayer given in Jesus Name? Today's text obviously doesn't mean we will receive whatever we ask, full stop. That could often lead to disaster. It implies, though, that if our request is asked in Jesus Name then it is monitored by what are His interests and purposes. Those interests and purposes are those things which glorify the Father. If what I am asking for augments the Father's glory, then it will be granted. We need to write over our prayer requests just as much as we do over our church buildings, "For the greater glory of God".

July   twenty-second

"If you love Me, keep my commandments" (John 14: 15).

*T*here is a love which precedes obedience. It is love for Christ which precedes obedience to all He commands. If you do not love Him you will have no desire to do what He says. Churches can hold, for example, all the seminars they like on evangelism but there will be no evangelism if Christians do not love Christ. When you love Him then you obey His command to go to those who are spiritually lost. The one naturally flows from the other.

A friend of mine would put it this way. Let's say you come across someone who says they love Switzerland. You ask them if they like lakes but they say they can't stand them. You ask them if they like high mountains and they say they don't like heights. You suggest that they might perhaps have an appreciation of chocolates but, no, they don't like chocolates. In exasperation you mention Alpine slopes where cows who wear little bells roam; do they like such a pastoral idyll? No, they think it ridiculous. And they said they loved Switzerland!

July   twenty-third

"And I will pray the Father, and He will give you another helper, that He may abide with you forever" (John 14: 16).

When the Saviour offered His disciples "Another helper" He obviously implied that they already had one. He was that helper but He was going away. Now He will send another to come alongside them to be their helper; He spoke, of course, of the Holy Spirit. The Holy Spirit, Christian, is your "champion". In Greek the word helper means your advocate (see 1 John 2: 1). He has been called in to guide you, to give you the strength to face your difficulties. He will give you power to overcome.

Our text implies that the Holy Spirit is like Christ. He is as distinct and helpful as Christ is. The word "another" indicates that Christ meant "one like Myself". He is a Person, a divine Person. Just as Christ does things for us, so does the Holy Spirit. He compensates for the visible loss of Jesus' presence. He will abide with us forever. With such a helper you need not be afraid of any task the Lord sends you on today. He will help you to cope. Aren't you glad that when Christ sent you a helper, in His absence, it wasn't in the form of words but that it was the form of such a wonderful person?

July   twenty-fourth

"Even the Spirit of truth, whom the world cannot receive, because it neither sees Him nor knows Him; but you know Him, for He dwells with you and will be in you" (John 14: 17).

I t is not easy as a Christian to understand how the world remains so blind and so indifferent to the Holy Spirit. The word for "world" in Greek is "kosmos", meaning the world of human beings and their affairs in rebellion against God, determined not to allow God to have His place. He is, to them, an irrelevancy.

How could it, though, be otherwise? If they did accept and know the Holy Spirit, they would no longer be "the world", would they? You either bow to the Lordship of Jesus Christ and the Holy Spirit enters your life to stay or you belong to that system and lifestyle that remains blind to Him . Receive Christ and you will become very aware of the presence and power of the Holy Spirit for He will live with you and dwell in you. He will reveal God to you and shed His love abroad in your heart. Remember, the knowledge of the Spirit of God is to be experienced. He is more than a doctrine.

July   twenty-fifth

"I will not leave you orphans; I will come to you" (John 14: 18).

Y ou did not have to lose both parents in the ancient world to be called an orphan: you only had to lose one. The word is also used of students and disciples bereft of a beloved teacher or master. Just the other day I delivered a eulogy at the funeral service of my English teacher, the man who first introduced me to the beauty of words and literature. A hero of the second World War and a veteran of "The Great Escape" in which he was an tunneler we, as boys, thought the world of him. As an adult, bidding him goodbye was sore. I felt, in the Greek sense, orphaned.

There will be no such goodbye between the disciples of Jesus Christ and their Master. Students of His word will never be orphaned from the living word. He will "come to us". Throughout life's journey His manifestations are real. He will be there in a special way, just when you need

Him most, revealing Himself through all sorts of circumstances. Remember that for the Christian, "something lives in every hue that Christless eyes have never seen". You will never be orphaned from Christ.

July   twenty-sixth

"A little while longer and the world will see Me no more, but you will see Me. Because I live, you will live also" (John 14: 19).

I t is now Thursday night and on Friday the Lord Jesus will die. The world, in a few hours, will no longer see Him. Even in resurrection He would be revealed only to His own. But because of His resurrection life, those who follow Him will know the same resurrection life. "You will live", says Christ.

How long will they live? The reference is to the cause of their spiritual life. Christ is its cause and because He lives in the power of an endless life, so will they. We are talking about an unchangeable situation here. Their bodies might die but their souls will live forever. Here is a promise and the Lord Jesus stands behind all His promises, and demands, and statements of purpose. The Scripture cannot be broken. "Because I live you will live also". Even Satan himself cannot quench this life.

Hard times of deep sorrow and great stress cannot break this supply of life to the believer. On and on through wind and storm, hassle and opposition, enemies galore including principalities and powers trying to ditch you, this gift of spiritual life is yours and nothing can cut off its supply. As long as He lives, so will your soul!

July   twenty-seventh

"Jesus answered and said to Him, 'If anyone loves Me, he will keep My word; and My Father will love Him, and we will come to Him and make our home with Him'" (John 14: 23).

A ll the wonderful truth in Scripture about the Lord preparing a place for us in heaven is extremely comforting. It lifts your day to know that place is being prepared for you. But what

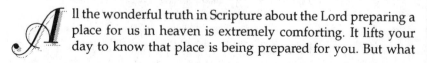

about the meantime? Christ does not propose to wait until we get to heaven before He introduces us to the Father. He proposes to bring us to the Father now, already, in this life. How? By the Father and Son making their home in our hearts through the Spirit here on earth. Mark well the sentence, "We will make our home with Him".

Surely if you long to be in the Father's home you long for the Father to make His home with you. To have a guest in your home and not care about what they like or dislike would be extremely discourteous. So, if we would have mutual fellowship with God we must love Him and do the things He likes and abhor the things He dislikes (See John 14: 21). To do otherwise would be to dishonour the One who makes His home with us. Selah.

July *twenty-eighth*

"These things I have spoken to you while being present with you. But the Helper, the Holy Spirit, whom the Father will send in My Name, He will teach you all things, and bring to your remembrance all things that I said to you" (John 14: 25-26).

The Holy Spirit is a remembrancer and an interpreter. In the context this had particular application to the disciples because between the time He said these words and Pentecost, the Crucifixion, Resurrection, Ascension and Coronation of Christ happened. Yet, the words do apply to us. How often when we are faced with some difficult question, some circumstance that overwhelms us and perplexes us, some decision that needs to be made quickly, does a word of Christ's surface in our minds? As that word has come fresh to our minds, it has answered our questions, kept us sane in overwhelming circumstances and given us a sense of direction as to the decision we have to make. I have found in the hour of temptation, in the moment of rash action, in the time of testing, something the Saviour said has pulled me back from the brink. This is the work of the Holy Spirit.

And interpreting? This means He will help you to understand what Christ is saying and to grasp its significance. In John's Gospel itself John draws attention to some things the disciples only remembered and understood after Christ had risen (see 2: 19-22; 12: 16; 20:9). So it is that the Holy Spirit will lead us deeper into the truth of God. It will not be to help us continually to seek the truth, for in Christ we have already found it, but it will be to help us understand the truth as it is in Jesus. He is the revealer and He lives in you, today. What a comfort!

July twenty-ninth

"Peace, I leave with you, My peace I give to you; not as the world gives do I give to you. Let not your heart be troubled, neither let it be afraid"
(John 14: 27).

*H*ere is a gift for you. You will not be able to see it for sale at Tiffany's or in Knightsbridge. All the gold in Fort Knox or the Bank of England combined could not buy it. It is the bequest of Christ. He gives it to all who trust Him as Saviour. It is the gift of His peace. Having His peace, though, does not imply the absence of trouble. Note carefully that the Saviour had earlier admitted to being "troubled in spirit" (13: 21) and would soon state in the Garden of Gethsamane that He was "overwhelmed with sorrow to the point of death". All Christians will experience storms of sorrow, frustration, disappointment, anxiety and fear. Yet, having Christ in our lives means that we have a security that no storm can sweep away, no fear can overwhelm, no disappointment or grief can crush. He is our peace.

The world simply does not have that security. It does not trust in the Lord. It trusts in its own maxims and principles which are built on sand. When the storm comes it is all easily swept away and death and destruction lie ahead. There is nothing more insecure and transient as that which does not trust in God. The peace which Christ gives, though, is rock solid no matter what hits it. It passes all understanding. Enjoy it. It is a peace to be entered into.

July thirtieth

"Let not your heart be troubled, neither let it be afraid."
(John 14: 27).

*I*s there greater evidence of the peace Christ gives than a heart at leisure? The Christian heart often feels troubled, often feels anxiety and fear but the peace Christ gives can assuage these things. "In everything by prayer and supplication let your requests be made known to God," wrote Paul, "and the peace of God, which surpasses all understanding, will guard your hearts and minds through Jesus Christ."

Peace with God you have through Christ, the peace of God comes when with a grateful heart you pray. It stands like a sentry over year heart and mind. Worry in particular seeks to strangle and choke you. It throttles your thinking and harasses you and cuts off your motivation and joy. If you turn from worry to prayer, you will get this peace from God, a calm serenity that characterises God's very nature which thankful Christians are welcomed by God to share.

This peace will get better results than human planning, it will be far superior to any person's schemes for security, it will be more effective for removing anxiety than any intellectual effort or power of reasoning. Prayer will calm your troubled heart. Prayer will ease fear and replace it with the peace that God has. Look at that peace at work in the next few hours in Christ's life; it healed Malcus's ear, stayed the impetuous Peter, told the women of Jerusalem to stop weeping, opened Paradise to the dying thief and gave His mother an earthly home. And all surrounded by unspeakable horror. That peace can be yours.

July   thirty-first

"I will no longer talk much with you, for the ruler of this world is coming, and He has nothing in Me" (John 14: 30).

*A*t the very moment the Saviour was speaking Satan was coming to attack Him. Judas was mobilising temple police, members of the Sanhedrin, and "a great multitude with swords and clubs" all inspired by Satan. They were hunting for Him as for a criminal but He stated that Satan, when He came, would find no guilt in Him. Satan had no claim on Him whatsoever. If He had, then this coming death would have had no meaning whatsoever for us.

Matthew adds for us the details that "When they had sung a hymn, they went out to the Mount of Olives". So it was that just before the Lord Jesus asked His disciples to accompany Him on his way out to face Satan and before He went to battle against all that Satan would launch against Him, He sang a hymn. Think of it. He went to Calvary, singing. Calvary was not approached in a lightness of spirit, it was not a carefree exercise, it was the most solemn moment in earth's history. Yet, if you had been passing by on the street you might have caught on the night air the strains of a perfect voice singing on the verge of entering indescribable darkness. It was the voice of God's Son singing in confidence before facing a battle that leaves all the battles of earth far behind. Here was assurance of victory if ever there was assurance. He went to Calvary singing! How long is it since God heard a song of worship from us at an unusual hour? Selah.

A bide in me", says the sun to planet earth, "Remain in the solar sphere". So earth is baptised in the sunlight every day. "Abide in me", says the ocean to the alcove and fills it, to fullness, twice every twenty-four hours. "Abide in me", says the air to the lung and oxygen saturates it cells. "Abide in me", says the mother to the child and prepares it for life. "Abide in Me", says Christ to the believer and He is absolutely sufficient to all the needs of the spiritual life.

AUGUST

August first

"I am the true vine, and My Father is the Vinedresser" (John 15: 1).

As the Saviour led His troubled disciples towards the Garden of Gethsamane with the moon shining upon them, they could see growing all around them, almost everywhere, the narrowed little vines of Israel. Even the great outer gates of the temple had a golden vine adorning them because the vine was the symbol of national life.

Prophets like Hosea, Isaiah, Jeremiah and Ezekiel all used the symbol of the vine to teach powerful spiritual lessons to Israel. The Old Testament was entwined with this symbol. And the point of having a vine is, of course, to have grapes, luxurious and refreshing. But Israel as a vine had failed. Lying, cheating, selfishness, bitterness, malice, oppression and exploitation had marked them. And the Saviour was about to replace them with the true vine, the Church? No. The truth is that the Church has often failed every bit as much as Israel has failed. Rather He said, "I am the True Vine". He is the ideal, the perfect and the true. He never fails.

"What", asked the agnostic Professor of Comparative Religion in a Hindu college, "Have you found in Christianity which you have not found in your old religion?" "I have Christ", replied the converted Sundar Singh. "Yes, I know", said the impatient Professor, "What particular principle or doctrine have you found that you did not have before?" "The particular thing I have found", he replied, "Is Christ". Have you?

August second

"My Father is the Vinedresser" (John 15: 1).

The vine is certainly a fruit-tree. Yet, it cannot stand upright like other fruit-trees. Its branches are very pliant and it requires a skilful hand to guide the branches along the trellises. Christ is about to teach that He is the vine and we are the branches. He achieves His purposes through His people and if there is to be a good branch-life producing fruit, then we must yield ourselves to the loving hands of the Vinedresser. We may deeply desire to grow a certain way but our purposes and sense of direction can be far different from what the

Vinedresser wants. He may twist us, fasten and nail us in a certain place much against our will but what is the result? The result is luscious grapes.

Just as Christ, the True Vine, showed subordination to His Father yielding to His will in even being nailed to a cross for the blessing of the world, so if we yield to the Vinedresser we too will be a blessing beyond our expectations.

August third

"Fruit ... more fruit ... much fruit" (John 15: 2-3).

We have always seen that the purpose in the vine is to bear fruit. Notice, though, how the Lord Jesus emphasises that He will not be content to find a few mildewed bunches of inedible grapes. Even a few grapes here and there will not be sufficient. We were not grafted into the new vine by regeneration to become a bunch of sour, unripened grapes. It is quite obvious that He nowhere states that He is looking for a few grapes; He is looking for many.

Let me look well to the question, "Am I bearing fruit for Christ?" Where are the signs of the fruits of love, joy, peace, gentleness, goodness, faith, meekness and temperance? Where are the signs of turning many to righteousness? How can I possibly really abide in Christ and not produce some of His loveliness? If I am spiritually barren and unfruitful there is something wrong. Again, let me not hesitate to yield to the hands of the Vinedresser. It will only result in abundant fruit to His glory.

August fourth

"Every branch in Me that does not bear fruit He takes away; and every branch that bears fruit He prunes, that it may bear more fruit"
(John 15: 2).

Walk into a greenhouse where the Vinedresser has been at work. Walk through a vineyard where the pruning knife has been in use. What do you see? The ground is covered with fronds and shoots and leaves. For a vine to grow luxuriantly, drastic pruning is necessary. Slips are set in the ground at least twelve feet apart because the vine creeps over the ground so fast. A young vine is not allowed to fruit for the first three years.

The emphasis the Lord Jesus gives in this part of His teaching is on the hands that take up the pruning. They are His Father's hands. It is not a work for prophets nor is it a work for angels. It is the Father's work and He often does it through the Scriptures. Christ said that His disciples had been pruned through His word. This word of course He received from His Father. So it is that the Father prunes away false ideas in our lives through the Scriptures and corrects emotional thinking with Biblical thinking. This, of course, is not punishment. It is cleansing. It may seem a loss. It is, in fact, a gain. If you yield to the Word now, you will escape chastisement later. So, yield, Christian, yield.

August fifth

"Every branch in Me that does not bear fruit, He takes away ..... If anyone does not abide in Me, he is cast out as a branch and is withered: and they gather them and throw them into the fire, and they are burned" (John 15: 2, 5-6).

I have no doubt that these verses refer to people who profess to be believers but aren't. Study John 8: 30-44 carefully and you will see that some Jews professed to be believers and Scripture took them at face value and referred to them as believers. When the test was applied to them as to whether their profession was genuine, they were discovered to be unwilling to abide in His word (see John 8; 31). Judas, even, was named an apostle (see Luke 6: 13) and failed the same test.

Faith without works is dead. Genuine faith will express itself in showing spiritual life in the believer, somewhere. You can't have one without the other. The wood of the vine is good for nothing except producing grapes. It cannot even be used to make furniture or a utensil of any kind. It is too soft. A vine branch that does not produce grapes is good only as fuel (See Ezekiel 15: 1-8). Selah.

August sixth

"Abide in Me and I in you. As the branch cannot bear fruit of itself,
unless it abides in Me, neither can you, unless you abide in Me"
(John 15: 4).

Of what use is a vine-branch unless it remains attached to the vine? None at all. The branch's continuous dependence on the vine, its constant reliance upon the living sap flowing into it to produce grapes is absolute. So Christ renews His people with His life and we can say, "I can do all things through Christ who strengthens me". Abiding "in Christ" is indispensible to our Christian identity. It is central to the Gospel: 164 times the expression "in Christ", "in the Lord", "in Him", occurs in the New Testament. It is no mere formal attachment or some nodding acquaintance or merely a personal friendship. It is nothing less than a vital, organic, ultimate union with Christ involving a shared life and a shared love.

"Abide in me", says the sun to planet earth, "Remain in the solar sphere". So earth is baptised in the sunlight every day. "Abide in me", says the ocean to the alcove and fills it, to fullness, twice every twenty-four hours. "Abide in me", says the air to the lung and oxygen saturates it cells. "Abide in me", says the mother to the child and prepares it for life. "Abide in Me", says Christ to the believer and He is absolutely sufficient to all the needs of the spiritual life. As Godet put it, "Abiding is the continuous act by which the Christian lays aside all he or she might draw from his or her own wisdom, strength and merit to desire all from Christ by the inward aspiration of faith".

August seventh

"If you abide in Me, and My words abide in you, you will ask what you
desire and it shall be done for you" (John 15: 7).

There are five tests which a prayer must pass before it is answered. (1) The Father must be glorified by our request (John 14: 13). (2) It must be prayed in the name of Christ (John 14: 13). (3) We must be abiding in Christ (John 15: 7). (4) We must submit our prayer to the correction of God's Word (John 15: 7) (5) Our prayers must be prompted by a desire for a ministry to others for that is what fruit-bearing is all about (John 15: 16).

But remember, though, that while the granting of prayer may be immediate, the giving may be delayed. "Your prayer is heard", said the angel to Zacharias. The giving, though, of the son he asked for came to Zacharias and Elizabeth much later in their lives. "From the first day that you set your heart to understand and to humble yourself before your God, your words were heard and I have come because of your words", said the angel to Daniel. But from the granting to the coming was twenty-one days (see Daniel 10: 12-13).

I know of a castle in Austria which was used for Christian work by some friends of mine. On the fly-leaf of his Bible the owner of the castle asked God to use the castle for His glory. The owner died a very persecuted man. But the prayer was answered seven hundred years later when my friends walked in. Remember, God takes the root that brings the most glory and "on its way to better it may drop by worse".

August eighth

"As the Father has loved Me, even so have I loved you" (John 15: 9).

What kind of love is this? Oceans could not contain it. The Heavens are too limited to circumscribe it. There is no shore to this love and there is no horizon to it, either. It stretches back into eternity, forever, and it stretches on into eternity, forever. It is a perfect, flawless love that has never known interruption or disagreement. It is constant, absolutely committed, undiminished neither by time nor circumstance.

Earthly love has its moments, and frustrations, its tiffs, its making up, its highs and lows: it can sour, it can sweeten. This love, the Father's love for the Son has no strong points because it hasn't got any weak ones. And just as the Father loved Christ, so He has loved you. He knows when you get up and when you sit down. He has the very hairs of your head numbered. His thoughts about you are more than the sand on the seashore. Just count the grains at your local beach: 50 billion? 1,000 billion? Then go count them under the sea at your local bay? Then start on the Atlantic and the Pacific! As the Father loved Christ even so has He loved you. So what are you discouraged for?

August ninth

"If you keep My commandments you will abide in My love, just as I have kept My Father's commandments and abide in His love"
(John 15: 10).

Children do not always like their parents commands. They think them too restricting, too harsh. They think they are being fenced in. They often think their parent's commands are specifically designed to kill their joy. What they don't realise is that those commands are designed to protect them, to enhance their lives and prepare them for even better things in the future. Spoilt children are a pain but they are headed for even more pain in the future if they are not restrained and disciplined.

Let's say my heart rises up with selfish greed and hankers after merely earthbound things. Then comes Christ's command to "seek first the Kingdom of God and His righteousness" and it checks me and brings me back. Is that command designed to ruin my life? Certainly not. It is designed to enhance it. It is designed to give me not what I think is good for me but all that God thinks is good for me. That, of course, in the end, is exceeding abundantly above all that I could ever ask or think.

I am tempted, perhaps, to hug-the-coastline, to play safe, to escape vulnerability. Then I hear the Saviour say, "For whoever desires to save his life will lose it, and whoever loses his life for my sake will find it". Is Christ being vindictive? Never. He is showing me a spiritual law that if yielded to reaps eternal benefit.

To obey Christ's commands is to abide in His love. It is a very necessary practical condition for the continuing deep enjoyment of a love that knows no measure. What's harsh about that?

August tenth

"These things I have spoken to you, that my joy might remain in you, and that your joy may be full" (John 15:11).

The trees once went forth to anoint a king over them", said Jotham (see Judges 9). They approached the olive, but, no, he gave oil and was happy with the blessings that his oil brought to the community. The fig also refused to be king because he was perfectly happy to bring his sweet fruit to hungry people.

The vine, surely, would want to be king? But no, he refused. He brought cheer, to both God and men, so why would he want to go and sway over trees? Strangely the little snitch of a bramble accepted the invitation to be king and declared "If in truth you anoint me as king over you, then come and take shelter in my shade: but if not, let fire come out of the bramble and devour the cedars of Lebanon!"

So what do you want in life? Do you want to be "big boss", no matter what? Would you devour that which has stood for decades just to lord over others? Small joy you'll know. But be glad and satisfied that your life brings joy to others, or some soul to Christ, or some weary spirit to be lifted, some lonely life to be blessed, some child to be inspired; that's the thing. To be a branch in Christ's vine bringing forth joyous grapes in the fulness of the grape harvest, that's the aim. May God make it so in your life.

August   eleventh

"These things I have spoken to you, that my joy may remain in you, and that your joy may be full" (John 15: 11).

I want us to stay with this text for a second day in our readings in order to point out one very important truth. This teaching of the Saviour about His joy remaining in us and our joy being full is independent of our circumstances. We know it even when the pressures are on. You doubt me? Then read this; "Five times I received from the Jews thirty-nine lashes. Three times I was beaten with rods, once I was stoned, three times I was shipwrecked, a night and a day I have spent in the deep. I have been on frequent journeys, dangers from rivers, dangers from robbers, dangers from my own countrymen, dangers from the Gentiles, dangers in the city, dangers in the wilderness, dangers on the sea, dangers among false brethren; I have been in labour and hardship, through many sleepless nights, in hunger and thirst, often without food, in cold and exposure. Apart from such external things, there is the daily pressure on me of concern for all the churches".

These amazing words were written by the Apostle Paul and when eventually he suffered imprisonment in Rome, he wrote a letter to some friends of his in Phillipi. What do you think was the theme of his letter? Joy! Obviously his circumstances had not fettered him or choked him. Arresting him didn't do any good - he brought his joy with him wherever he went! Do you?

August twelfth

"This is My commandment, that you love one another as I have loved you. Greater love has no-one than this than to lay down one's life for his friends" (John 15: 12-13).

Here is a new standard tenderly and beautifully explained. The new standard is that not only are we to love one another but we are to love one another as Christ loved us. Mark Twain once said, "To do good is noble, to teach others to do good is nobler, and no trouble". How many people have exorted others to love each other and then shown by their whole lives that is the last thing they do themselves? They are, as we say, bluffers.

Here is no bluff. When the multitudes came to the Garden of Gethsamane seeking to take the Saviour, He told them, "If you seek Me, let these go their way". Here was no heirling shepherd running when the wolf came. How many people say they are behind you? You look but they are so far behind you cannot see them! Here was a Saviour who loved His own to the end. He laid down His life for them. So are we to love one another.

Who could measure the words, "As I have loved you?" They are immeasurable. Let them be a motto to you, for example, in your marriage. "Husbands", wrote Paul, "Love your wives as Christ also loved the church". And how did He love the Church? He laid down His life for her. If I thought for one moment that Christ would divorce His church or desert her, my whole peace would be devastated, for I am part of that body. His undiminished love is my greatest security. As He has loved, then, so must we. And this love begins at home if it begins anywhere.

August thirteenth

"You are My friends if you do whatever I command you" (John 15: 14).

Is Christ's love conditional? Is it that as long as I do what He asks, I am a Christian and if I fail to do what He asks, I am not? If that were so then Peter who was about to deny Christ wouldn't have stood a chance of remaining a Christian and millions of others like him. In fact the greatest surprise in the life of Peter was that Christ continued to be his friend despite his own failures.

David Gooding has succinctly commented, "Christ does not say 'I am your Friend if, and only if, you do the thing which I command you'". What He says is; "You are my friends if you do the thing which I command you". True friendship, even between the Lord and ourselves, let us never forget it, is a two-way process. It would be a shocking thing if we relied on our Lord always to act as a friend to us, but ourselves made little deliberate attempt to act as friends to Him by doing what He commands us to do.

August fourteenth

"No longer do I call you servants, for a servant does not know what his master is doing; but I have called you friends, for all things that I heard from My Father I have made known to you" (John 15: 15).

The Roman Empire was built on slavery. Slaves simply did what they were told. Roman masters did not inform their slaves of their thinking. They did not sit down with their slaves and explain the whys and the wherefores of their commands. Blind and unconditional obedience was the order of the day.

Christ, though, does not call us His slaves. He calls us His friends. He explains to us His plans, purposes and motives. We are His confidantes. He has passed on to us everything He heard from the Father. Just as a vine passes on nutrients to the branches, so Christ has passed on what His Father told Him for our good. He told, for example, why He was sent to earth, why He was going to lay down His life, why He had come to leave this world, and what He would do when He came back. He told us how we might approach the Father and come to know Him. He did not leave us to wither and die eternally. He passes on His life and reveals the heart of God. As His friends we do not do what He tells us because we have to, we do what He tells us because we love to. A slave's yoke is heavy but Christ's yoke is easy and His burden is light.

August fifteenth

"You did not choose Me, but I chose you and appointed you that you should go and bear fruit, and that your fruit should remain, that whatever you ask the Father in My Name He may give you"
(John 15: 16).

Long years ago my mother, who was a great supporter of missionaries abroad, got discouraged in her ministry. She told me that someone approached her and imagined her in heaven. "There you are, Ruth," said her friend, "walking along through Heaven and you meet someone who says 'thank you'". "I don't know you", you will say. "No", the stranger will answer, "but you sent support for a missionary from your church and her witness resulted in my conversion". You will go along further and someone from another country will say, 'thank you'. Again you will plead ignorance and the stranger will speak of the support you gave to another Christian worker who led that person to Christ. On and on you will go finding out that your work has not been in vain". My mother was encouraged and kept at her work. The story was not as far fetched as you might imagine for today's text says that the fruit borne is your fruit. Christ gives you all you need to produce it but He does ultimately call it yours and it will remain. Remain, that is, forever. My mother, if I may mix metaphors, has gone to see her investments; the fruit is hers, eternally. Say, how are your eternal investments doing?

August sixteenth

"If the world hates you, you know that it hated Me before it hated you. If you were of the world, the world would love its own. Yet, because you are not of the world, that I chose you out of the world, therefore the world hates you" *(John 15: 18-19).*

The greatness of Rome stretched for more than two thousand miles in breadth; it extended from the Western Ocean to the Euphrates for more than three thousand miles in length. It contained more than sixteen hundred thousand square miles of, for the most part, fertile and well cultivated land.

Across this vast territory, situated in the finest part of the Temperate Zone, between the twenty-fourth and fifty-first degrees of northern latitude, a uniting idea force wedded the varied masses into one. This force and idea was, of course, Ceasar worship. At the time of the rise of Christianity once every year every inhabitant of the Empire had to take his or her pinch of incense to the Godhead of Ceasar. A certificate was then given and after the "Ceasar is Lord" act was accomplished, Roman citizens could worship any god they pleased, so long as it did not disturb public decency and order. But the Christians would call no man "Lord" but the Christ and so persecution arose.

When Christians own the Lordship of Jesus Christ it does not mean that every non-Christian will hate every Christian. Yet the truth is that Christians will still face opposition from "the world" shown in John's Gospel as that which Judas epitomised; taking all God's gifts but not recognising God. Christians in the Roman Empire were therefore treated as aliens. Tell me, though, where is Roman glory now? It is mere Mediterranean rubble. And Christ? Of His Kingdom there will be no end. I would rather Christ was for me and the world against me than Christ against me and the whole world for me, wouldn't you?

August   seventeenth

"Remember the word which I said to you, 'A servant is not greater than his master'. If they persecute Me, they will also persecute you. If they kept My word, they will keep yours also. But all these things they will do to you for My Name's sake, because they do not know Him who sent Me"
(John 15: 20-21).

I well remember sitting in a friend's house bemoaning the problems I faced in Christian work. "Did you think you would escape?", said my friend, "If they crucified your Lord, did you think that in serving Him you would escape problems?" His statement brought me up with a jolt. The answer is, of course, that if they persecuted Him they will persecute us. Yet notice the hope here. Christ is saying that just as there were those who persecuted Him, there were also those who deeply appreciated Him and His teaching and followed Him.

That is how it will be with you if you are an active Christian, they will divide around you just as they divided around Christ. Responses, in the end, will not be regarding who you are but regarding who Jesus is. "For My Name's sake", means "Because of Me". What greater privilege could a person have? What more encouraging promise than to know that some will respond and believe when you live for Him? Keep going; some may believe, today.

August   eighteenth

"If I had not come and spoken to them, they would have no sin, but now they have no excuse for their sin ..... but when the Helper comes, whom I shall send to you from the Father, the Spirit of Truth who proceeds from the Father, He will testify of Me. And you also will bear witness, because you have been with Me from the beginning" (John 15: 22-27).

Christ's contemporaries had every opportunity to test, prove and believe that He was God Incarnate. With all those advantages many refused every single piece of evidence. So God wiped them off the face of the earth? He did no such thing. He promised to send the Holy Spirit who would powerfully witness of Him and seek to draw even His enemies to Himself. God does not will that any should perish.

Notice, though, the words, "And you also will bear witness". We don't just suffer in fellowship with Christ, we witness in fellowship with the Holy Spirit. The international witness of the Holy Spirit has been, through centuries of time, against tides of opposition that have risen against Christ and His Church. The Gospel, though, is still the power of God unto salvation to everyone who believes, even as we come to the twenty-first century. When you witness to it, the Holy Spirit will aid you. Try to remember that "five words, in the Spirit are better than ten thousand in an unknown tongue". Those five words may be spoken by you today and a life will be turned around. The words "you also" obviously principally refer to the Apostles but they are certainly not limited to the witness bearing of the Apostles. They include Christians in every century, and you, also.

August   nineteenth

"These things I have spoken to you, that you should not be made to stumble. They will put you out of the synagogue; yes, the time is coming that whoever kills you will think that he offers God's service. And these things they will do to you because they have not known the Father nor Me. But these things I have told you, that when the times comes, you may remember that I told you of them. And these things I did not say to you at the beginning, because I was with you" (John 16: 1-4).

I sat one day with Gerald Grosvenor, the Duke of Westminster, in his office at Eaton Hall near Chester interviewing him about his life and times. It was an absolutely fascinating conversation. It turned to spiritual things and, as a soldier, he pointed out something I had never known before. "Every German soldier in the Second World War", he said, "carried a slogan on his belt which stated, 'God is with us'. He then went on to point out that more atrocities have been carried out in the name of God than anything else.

He is right. Jesus pointed out that people would be so twisted they they would kill some of His followers and think they did God a service. They mistakenly think they have a monopoly of truth and would kill to preserve it. The curse of such thinking is still with us. "It is", said Abraham Lincoln, "not so important that God is on our side as it is that we are on His".

August   twentieth

"Nevertheless I tell you the truth. It is to your advantage that I go away; for if I do not go away, the Helper will not come to you; but if I depart, I will send Him to you. And when He is come, He will convict the world of sin, and of righteousness, and of judgment: of sin, because they do not believe in Me; of righteousness, because I go to My Father and you see Me no more; of judgment, because the Ruler of this world is judged" (John 16: 7-11).

As the little party of men walked through the dark streets of Jerusalem towards the Garden of Gethsamane the Lord Jesus now turned to comfort His grieving disciples. Yes, He was going to leave them but it would be to their advantage, it would be to their gain. His going out meant the Holy Spirit coming in. Here was, according to Christ, progress. The Holy Spirit's work would be to first convince the world that rejection of Christ would be a sin. Reception of Him would mean having sin dealt with. The Holy Spirit would also witness concerning righteousness because via the cross Christ was going to His Father and righteousness was now possible to all who would trust Him as Saviour. He would, thirdly, convince people of judgment, i.e. that Satan had been judged at Calvary and defeated (see John 12: 31). The fact that the Holy Spirit is present proves that Satan has been defeated. You meet a foe who is not invincible. The Prince of this world has been judged and found wanting. He is condemned for evermore. In Christ you can have victory over Him again and again. The Spirit's coming was progress indeed.

August   twenty-first

"I still have many things to say to you, but you cannot bear them now" (John 16: 12).

This is a very tender point which the Saviour makes. The disciples are weary, they have had enough, they have reached saturation point. The teaching has been immensely deep, they have gazed into the very heart and purposes of God but they were, like us, human. There comes a time when enough is enough. So, the Lord calls it a day.

Do I write for some weary one, today? We all want to know many things. We want to know answers to profound questions, to know what God's plan for tomorrow is, or next year, or why that tragedy was permitted, or "what shall I do next?" The Lord says two words to you, "Trust Me". He will explain it when you are strong enough to bear it. All will be revealed to you one day. That's a promise. The Epistle to the Romans or Corinthians or Galatians was to come. The soaring heights of the Letter to the Hebrews was in the future for followers of Christ. But not tonight. So step out of the circle of all those questions you have for tonight and rest and sleep. The future is safe; you can do all things through Christ who strengthens you.

August twenty-second

"However, when He, the Spirit of Truth, has come, He will guide you into all truth; for He will not speak on His own authority, but whatever He hears He will speak; and He will tell you things to come" (John 16: 13).

Quietly slipping into a beautiful church building on Piccadilly one hot summer's day, I sat down on a pew to rest and pray. In a little while I decided I would have a look at the notice board to see what the weekly programme was in order to learn what the congregation was feeding on. I was incensed to learn that a whole array of lectures from the New Age Movement was available with its mixture of art, the environment, holistic medicine, yoga, spirit guides, Buddhism, with bits of Christianity thrown in. The rector of the church had added a statement saying that the church did not necessarily agree with all that these lectures contained but felt that they should be given a platform. It appeared to me that was like letting thieves in to the Crown Jewels.

Let today's text teach us that we shall never know more about God than what the Lord Jesus reveals to us through the Spirit. The Holy Spirit is not Himself an independent source of truth; "He shall not speak 'from' Himself", though He often speaks in the New Testament "of Himself". He speaks what He hears from the Lord Jesus who speaks what He hears from His Father (see John 14:10). What fuller, more perfect, more exquisite revelation of God is possible? None. Exclusive it is but there is enough in it to satisfy the heart of every man, woman and child in the whole wide world.

August twenty-third

"He will glorify Me, for He will take what is Mine and declare it to you" (John 16: 14).

When you see Christ glorified you can be sure the Holy Spirit is at work. When you have a precious insight into the person of Christ, the Holy Spirit is witnessing and working within you. That is the Spirit's work; to show that Christ is all and in all.

Christianity is Christ. He is the One by which every Christian affirmation has to be judged. "Christ is lovely," said Thomas Brooks, "Christ is very lovely, Christ is always lovely, Christ is altogether lovely." The more you think of Christ the more you think of Him.

The Holy Spirit, then constantly seeks to draw us after Christ. He seeks to take us away from plain self-interest and selfish ambition and to have the highest of all motives, which is to live and work for Christ. It is devastatingly sad whenever people in Christian work start to glorify themselves. How easy it is when engaged in the very highest work of all to let self spoil it. Even the Holy Spirit does not glorify Himself, He glorifies Christ. So watch like a hawk the words, "Me", "My," "What I said," and "What I did."

$\mathcal{A}$ugust   twenty-fourth

"Most assuredly, I say to you that you will weep and lament, but the world will rejoice; and you will be sorrowful but your sorrow will be turned into joy" (John 16:20).

Soon the disciples would weep at the sight of the cross. The Christ they now saw they would see no more. But He would return and by Galilee's shore they would see Him again, and in a way they never saw Him before. They didn't understand it but their sorrow and the coming events would be transmitted into joy.

Christ explained it all by describing their experience as being like a woman giving birth. The pangs of childbirth are very real but the joy of giving birth to a new human being is unsurpassed. The pains of Christ were very real to Christ and heartbreakingly sad were the disciples to watch but it was to bring indescribably joy. Indeed for the Lord Himself the joy set before Him helped Him to endure the cross, despising the shame.

Don't you find, as you go through life, that the things that cause you pain, that cause you sorrow, are often turned into joy? "Time," wrote F. W. Boreham, "by an alchemy of its own can sometimes transmute pain as an object of pleasurable contemplation." Ultimately, though, the sufferings and limitations of this present time are not to be compared with the eternal weight of glory which will follow.

August twenty-fifth

"In that day you will ask Me nothing" (John 17: 23).

I t is like Job, isn't it? All those questions he had when he was suffering, dozens and dozens of them. "Why did I not die at birth?", he asked. "What have I done to you, oh watcher of men?""Why have you set me as your target so that I am a burden to myself?" "Will you turn me into dust again?". "Why do you hide your face?". "If a man dies will he live again?" On and on go the questions.

When the Lord, though, eventually took Job on a tour of creation he suddenly found he had no questions left. "I have heard of You by the hearing of the ear, but now my eye sees You. Therefore I abhor myself and repent in dust and ashes", said Job. After the resurrection the disciples' questions were answered. They saw, in seeing the resurrected Lord, what it was all about. So, we too find that when Christ is accepted in our lives we know, without question, that He does live within our hearts. We can no more explain it than explain why we fell in love and know we are in love. We just know. It's bigger than our questions.

August twenty-sixth

"These things I have spoken to you in figurative language; but the time is coming when I will no longer speak to you in figurative language, but I will tell you plainly about the Father" (John 16: 25).

Y es, the Saviour could have revealed Himself in all His incomparable glory right at the beginning. He could have been transfigured and stayed transfigured when He first appeared to John or Matthew or Mary Magdalene. The vast crowds could have fallen at His feet and acknowledged their Creator and that they were His creatures. His purpose, though, was much greater than that. He wanted, through the New Birth, to make them His children and grown-up children at that. He wanted a relationship with them.

God's purpose is not to make you scared of Him, it is to bring you into a relationship with Him. He doesn't want to be your Heavenly policeman, He wants to be your Heavenly Father. So, step by step, He revealed to them what He was in parables and metaphors. He spoke of the temple of His body, of the wind of the Spirit, of the good samaritan and the good shepherd, of the angels and the ladder, of the living water, of the true vine, of the washing of feet, of the marriage feast, of the dragnet, of the darnel and of hidden treasure. He spoke of light and rivers, of the bread of life, of the house of many rooms. It was enigmatic but it was, irresistible. It was gradual but it was unforgettable. It was the mystery of godliness - God manifest in flesh. There has never been anything like it before and there never will be again.

August   twenty-seventh

"For the Father Himself loves you, because you have loved Me, and have believed that I came forth from God" (John 16: 27).

very Christian loves the story of King David's kindness to the disabled Mephibosheth. He gave him a place at his table for his father Jonathan's sake. That David loved Jonathan is certain; that he loved Mephibosheth for Mephibosheth's sake is, in the subsequent story, not so certain.

Now learn this and learn it well. God the Father does not love you just for Jesus' sake. He loves you, full stop. Isn't that what today's text says? Too long have we lived with the idea that God hates us, loathes us, despises us but for the intervention of the Lord Jesus. That is inconsistent with Scripture. What is God? God is love. The fact is that the intervention of the Lord Jesus in history only proves the Father loves us for "The Father", says the Scripture, "sent the Son to be the Saviour of the world". Let's not get it the wrong way around. Yet, let us remember, if we were to despise that love that sent the Saviour, then we must face the eternal indignation of God (See Hebrews 10: 28-29). Selah.

August   twenty-eighth

"I came from the Father and have come into the world. Again, I leave the world and go to the Father. His disciples said to Him, 'See, now you are speaking plainly, and using no figure of speech! Now we are sure that

you know all things, and have no need that anyone question you. By this we believe that you came from God'. Jesus answered them, 'Do you now believe? Indeed the hour is coming, yes, has now come, that you will be scattered, each to his own, and will leave Me alone. And yet I am not alone because the Father is with Me'" (John 16: 28-32).

Words are easy, aren't they? The disciples declared their firm belief in who the Lord was. Their affirmation masked, though, a subtle self-confidence which was soon to be exposed. They would, in a few hours, all turn from their Saviour and run. When He refused to use violence against those who came to arrest Him the disciples left Him to it. They had other ideas about how the Kingdom of Christ should be established. They who had taught with so much self-assurance of their belief in Him baulked under testing. They didn't run because they were afraid. Peter certainly wasn't afraid; he demonstrated that with his sword. The disciples ran because although they believed in who Christ was, they found the cost of obeying Him very high indeed and decided to run, each to his own pursuits and his own affairs.

Be careful when you affirm your faith in Christ: words are easy, actions speak much louder. God will see to it that we are tested. May we be found standing firm and not running.

August   twenty-ninth

"Indeed the hour is coming, yes, has now come, that you will be scattered, each to his own, and will leave Me alone. And yet I am not alone, because the Father is with Me" (John 16: 32).

Catch the anguish of the words, "And will leave Me alone". Here is One who knows the experience of the worship of multitudes of angels, who can send them on an errand at a word. Now He is to be left alone. Here is One who is able to create the stars, amongst whom are the Crab Nebula which is forty-five thousand million million kilometres away and is expanding at one thousand one hundred kilometres a second and twelve of His dearest friends could not stand with Him in His hour of trial. The crowds would leave Him. The nation's religious leaders would leave Him. The Emperor's representative would abandon Him. No-one but no-one would so identify Himself with Jesus as to be arrested and share His suffering. It's mind-boggling.

He may have been left alone by men and women but He was not ultimately abandoned by His Father. One with God is a majority. Even if you stand alone for the right, you stand with God.

August   thirtieth

"These things I have spoken to you, that in Me you may have peace. In the world you will have tribulation; but be of good cheer, I have overcome the world" (John 16: 33).

I stood in a heathen temple and a man showing me around held up a piece of paper upon which, he told me, the blood of priests in the temple had been sprinkled that afternoon. "Take it", he said, "home to Ireland and put in on your door and you will have peace".

"With due respects to you", I said, "I don't need it. I don't need it because nearly two thousand years ago someone died for me who made peace through the blood of His cross". "You are lucky", he said, "all you have to do is to believe. I have to come to the temple and try to get my ancestors out of Hell". He produced a note with "Hell bank note" written on it, obviously the "currency" of the temple. "My children will then hopefully come here regularly to get me out of Hell in their time", he added. Think long on the words of the Saviour. "These words I have spoken to you that in Me you may have peace". There is no peace to compare with the peace available in Christ. It is available without money and without price. I wonder if that man goes to his temple, yet? One thing is certain, he will never get true peace that way. Say, where do you go for peace?

August   thirty-first

"In the world you will have tribulation; but be of good cheer, I have overcome the world" (John 16: 33).

The Christian knows who triumphs in the end. The world did its worst to the Saviour but He was victorious over it. He conquered it. His victory, just like peace, can be shared by all who have faith in Him. For the "Victory that overcomes the world", is, says John, "our faith" (1 John 5: 4).

We are promised tribulation in this world; it goes with standing up for Christ. But then so does victory. As you take your stand for Him and His truth in a world where moral and spiritual values are crumbling, take courage. As you stand for that which is virtuous, and good, righteous and moral, wholesome and godly, do not despair. Who would have imagined that the abandoned and lonely penniless preacher of Galilee would, through His cross, take on the principalities and powers and make an open show of them? Who would have imagined He would have defeated Him who had power over death, that is the Devil, and free those who were all their lifetime subject to bondage? Who would have imagined that two thousand years later His Church would stride on across the world despite unbelievable opposition? Take heart, Christian, you can be more than a conquerer through Him who loves you. So, don't quit.

*W*hat in life can bring more joy, delight and contentment than the knowledge of God? You and I are not big enough to be the goal of our own existence. We need an objective that catches our imagination, that grips our hearts and affections and fires our very lives with purpose. Eternal life will give us those very things and bring us to that very goal, namely, to know God. It is an experience which will thrill your heart in a relationship which will never end.

SEPTEMBER

September first

"Jesus spoke these words, lifted up His eyes to Heaven, and said: 'Father, the hour has come. Glorify Your Son, that Your Son also may glorify You'" (John 17: 1).

*T*he hour had arrived. Jesus had spoken of it before but now it had come. The hour would fulfil those ancient and detailed prophesies and symbols, the hour that even the Father in the council chambers of eternity had planned, the hour in which Satan would meet His defeat, the greatest hour in the history of the world had come. It was the hour which was the consummation of the Saviour's entire ministry. It was the moment of crisis and the moment by which untold millions would be drawn to the heart of God and by which the heart of God would be revealed.

The lotus flower is the symbol of Buddhism. The hammer and sickle is the symbol of Marxism. The swastika was the sinister symbol of Nazi racial bigotry. The Crescent is the sign of Islam. The hexagonal Star of David is the sign of modern Judaism. At first the symbol of Christians was the fish. The Greek word was "icthus" which was an acronym for Jesus Christ, Son of God, Saviour. The cross was not at first the universal sign of Christianity because of its shameful association with the execution of common criminals, but soon it came to be. Not a crib, not a carpenter's bench, not a fishing boat, not a tombstone, not a throne, but a cross. We speak now of the glory of His cross. It was the most revolutionary thing ever to appear among mankind. Nobody who has truly seen the cross of Christ by faith can ever again speak of any situation or any individual being hopeless.

September second

"As you have given Him authority over all flesh, that He should give eternal life to as many as you have given Him. And this is eternal life, that they may know you, the only true God and Jesus Christ whom you have sent" (John 17: 2-3).

*E*ternal life? So many think of it as a kind of life after death but notice what our Lord says. He says it is, in fact, the capacity of knowing God through Himself. That comes through conversion and can be the experience of men and women, boys and girls, now.

Here is an experience available to all who trust the Saviour. We were made not only to have a knowledge about God but the actual knowledge of God. This knowledge does not end in passivity. Those who know God do "exploits" (see Daniel 11:32) i.e. they stand firm and take action. Those who know God find great contentment in God for they know that although everything that happens to them is not good, it works together for good.

What in life can bring more joy, delight and contentment than the knowledge of God? You and I are not big enough to be the goal of our own existence. We need an objective that catches our imagination, that grips our hearts and affections and fires our very lives with purpose. Eternal life will give us those very things and bring us to that very goal, namely, to know God. It is an experience which will thrill your heart in a relationship which will never end. Have you got eternal life? Then take it as a gift, for, "the gift of God is eternal life through Jesus Christ our Lord".

September   third

"I have glorified You on the earth. I have finished the work which you have given Me to do" (John 17: 4).

Think of the lies that Satan spreads about God. So many in the world are silent towards God because they are convinced that to know Him would be boring. They see Him as a kill-joy, as a spoiler, "Who is the Lord that I should obey His voice?", they say with Pharoah. The God of this world blinds their minds and locks them in a prison cell of silence towards God.

It was a great moment when God sent the Lord Jesus into the world. Those lies about God were dispelled as people began to watch Christ. They began to confess that they had never, ever heard anyone speak like Him. The prodigals and sinners began to crowd the tables where He ate and the public places He frequented. They discovered that God certainly hated their sin but that He loved them. They saw the loveliness of God revealed in Jesus Christ. They had never thought of God as lovely. Their prison cells of silence were opened by Christ and they got a new song in their hearts, even praise to His Name. He had come to change people's minds about God and to die for them at Calvary. He already looked on the cross work in the past tense! He was speaking of His place at that moment in the flow of redemptive history. He reported to His Father that He had finished the work He had been given to do. Christ's work is a perfect work for He revealed God perfectly and perfected the work of salvation for us. I know of no greater doctrine than the finished work of Christ. Do you?

September fourth

"And now, O Father, glorify Me together with Yourself, with the glory which I had with you before the world was" (John 17: 5).

What use would the Saviour's finished work be if there was no resurrection? What help or succour would His revelation of God be or His way of salvation if He were dead? If His Father had not raised Him from the dead, back to the position He had before the world was, how the critics would have mocked! What a field day the enemies of the cross would have had through the centuries!

The glory which Christ had before the creation was now about to be restored to Him. What was that glory? It certainly entailed uninterrupted enjoyment of His Father's presence in a sinless place. He yearned to go back to that place. Even at the grave of Lazarus He groaned in the presence of death. Now He calls on His Father to honour His work by restoring Him to his former place. No wonder we say that the greatest news in the world came out of a graveyard.

September fifth

"I have manifested Your Name to the men whom you have given Me out of the world. They were Yours, You gave them to Me, and they have kept Your Word" (John 17: 6).

What's in a name? Well, for a start the Devil never signs His Name to anything, does He? Why? Because of what it stands for? A name has to do with character. Mention someone's name and immediately you get reaction from people. "Oh, her?", or "I know him", "Nice person", or "Nasty character".

But God's Name? Think of His character as revealed in His Name. He is, "Jehovah", the Living One. He is "El-Shaddai", the Almighty One. He is "Adonai", the Lord and Master. He is "Jehovah- Jireh", the One who provides. He is "Jehovah-Rophe", the One who heals. He is "Jehovah-Nissi", the One who brings victory. He is "Jehovah-M'Kaddish", the One who sanctifies. He is "Jehovah-Shalom", the One who is our Peace. He is "Jehovah- Tsidkenu", the One who is our Righteousness. He is "Jehovah-Rohi", the One who is our Shepherd. He is "Jehova-Shammah", the One who is there. All of these attributes of His Father, revealed in His Name, the Lord Jesus revealed in the nitty-gritty of human experience. He has brought God so close that we now breathe His Name in our moments of ecstasy and in our moments of pain and suffering. "Abba", we say, meaning, "Dear Father" and all because in seeing and knowing the Lord Jesus we see and know God.

September sixth

"I pray for them. I do not pray for the world but for those whom You have given Me, for they are Yours" (John 17:9).

There was, of course, no point in the Lord Jesus praying for the world. The Bible defines the world particularly as being composed of those who do not acknowledge the Lordship of Christ and so there was no point in Christ praying for the preservation of the faith of those who didn't have any. He was pryaing for the preservation of those who do.

Was His prayer heard? It certainly was. Despite the failures of His disciples, their preservation was secured and so, Christian, is yours. One of the most comforting verses in all of the Bible is Hebrews 7:25. Learn it well. "Therefore He is able to save to the uttermost all who come to God through Him." Who could define the extent of that word "uttermost"? We joy in it. Yet, do we ever really meditate on why we are saved to the uttermost? "It is," continues the verse, "because He ever lives to make intercession for us." The blood of Christ, freely shed for us, leads to our atonement. The prayers of Christ leads to our preservation. You know how when you are ill or in some kind of trouble, the prayers of people mean a lot to you. Meditate on the fact that Christ is praying for you. He ever lives to do so.

September seventh

"I am glorified in them" (John 17: 10).

Really? Glorified in a doubting Thomas, in a denying Peter, a bad tempered James and John? Yes. Glorified in me? Glorified in you? Yes. That which is displayed as the grace of God in our lives reflects His redeeming power and love. As the musician gives honour to his or her teacher, as the athlete brings glory to his or her trainer, as the patient brings glory to his or her surgeon, so the Christian gives glory to the One who brought about his or her salvation.

Wouldn't it be lovely if today you showed God's grace in your life, perhaps in some tiny action of kindness to another which would, in turn, glorify Christ? What better thing in all the world could you do? What better motivation could you have? You couldn't pray a better prayer than "Be glorified in Me, today, Lord". Who of us would not be proud to bring honour to our school, our college, our nation? But to bring honour and glory to the Lord? Now that's really something!

September eighth

"Now I am no longer in the world, but these are in the world, and I come to you. Holy Father, keep through Your Name those you have given Me, that they may be one as we are" (John 17: 11).

So the idea is to have everybody worship in the same posture, have the same tastes, go through the same formulations, follow the same systematic theology? Is that it? What use would all that be if those in it did not know common spiritual life? It would mean a vast monolithic denomination of univeral uniformity that would sleep the sleep of spiritual death.

Notice the Saviour speaks of a unity that is similar to the one that exists between Himself and His Father. That is a bond of common spiritual life which nothing can break. F. B. Meyer put it this way: "The model for Christian unity is evidently the unity between the Father and the Son by the Holy Spirit; and since that unity, the unity of the blessed God, is not corporeal nor physical, nor substantial to the eye of the flesh, may we not infer - nay, are we not compelled to infer - that the oneness of believers is to be after the same fashion; and to consist in so close an identity of nature, so absolute an interfusion of spirit, as that they shall be one in aim, and thought, and life, and spirit - spiritually one with each other - because spiritually one with Him?" Nowhere does it ever imply that this unity of believers is absolute uniformity. The variety of the human body, from the eyelash to the foot, is great but there is one conscious indivisible unity. So it is in the body of Christ.

September ninth

"I have given them Your Word; and the world has hated them because they are not of the world, as I am not of the world" (John 17: 14).

Those who absolutely refuse the Lordship of Christ will not want you as their friend. You may be amongst them in your everyday work, you may be taught by them at school or university, you may go amongst them in your own community as you seek to be a useful citizen. "In it" but not "of it" is the Bible's definition of your position.

Why the hostility? Because when you bring God's Word before those who refuse the Lordship of Christ, it stirs their conscience, exposes their sins and calls them to repent towards God and to put faith in our Lord Jesus Christ. For a study of how people reacted to the Saviour's teaching on this see Luke 5: 17-21, 7: 49 and John 5: 18-24. You and I will receive the very same hostility. So, isn't it good to know that Christ's prayers will keep you and that Christ's joy will fill you?

Are you tempted to succumb to live for the world? Do you long for friendship with it? Think of the loneliness that will entail. Loneliness? Certainly. Friendship with the world means enmity with God. I'd rather have the whole world against me and Christ for me than the whole world for me and Christ against me, wouldn't you?

September tenth

"I do not pray that You should take them out of the world, but that You should keep them from the evil one" (John 17:15).

If you don't believe in the Devil's existence, just try resisting Him for a while", said Charles Finney. "I believe Satan to exist for two reasons: first, the Bible says so, and second, I have done business with Him", said D.L. Moody.

Anyone who has ever stood up for God is aware of how very subtle and totally self-effacing Satan is. He will use anything or anyone to accomplish His purposes and you'd never know, on the face of it, that it was Him. Yet, the Scriptures teach that He is a murderer, a liar, a tempter, an accuser and an imitator of God, and the god of this world. The Devil may be a secular figure of fun in this world but every Christian knows very well that He is no joke.

The Lord did not pray that His followers be taken out of this world but He did pray that they be kept from the evil one. While the Devil may oppress you, Christian, He cannot possess you. Christ is your Shepherd and the wolf that is Satan may attack the flock, scatter it, harrass it, but Jesus promises that "neither shall anyone snatch them out of My hand". That "anyone" includes Satan. Selah.

September eleventh

"Sanctify them by Your truth. Your Word is truth" (John 17: 17).

To be sanctified is to be set apart, to be "other". In the Bible's original language the adjective "holy" and the verb "to sanctify" are derived from the same root. So to be holy in practical terms means we must be sanctified in our living. That means being devoted to God, consecrated to doing His will, hating what He hates, and, loving what He loves.

How is such a life governed? It is governed by the truth, i.e. God's revelation in Christ is the ultimate standard. Christ is the truth and the Word He gave us is infallible. So we must love His Word and direct our lives by it. We neglect God's Word at our peril; by it we can learn how to be set apart. Christ's heart was a burning heart, consumed with a passion to do His Father's will. Is this my life? Is this yours? Consecration is not an option, it is an obligation.

September twelfth

"As you sent Me into the world, I also have sent them into the world" (John 17: 18).

Have a look at your trail-blazer! See how He set Himself apart to do His Father's will! He delighted to do it. He did it so that we might do it. Was He not tempted in all points, as we are?

Was He not faced with the possibility of a life of ease, of comfort, of popularity, of money-making, of personal ambition? Were not the kingdoms of this world offered to Him if He would but bow down and worship Satan? He refused them all for a carpenter's bench, a Galilean preacher's itinerary, and an unspeakably cruel cross. He never, ever turned aside for a moment.

And what did He accomplish? He touched a dark world in a way no-one has ever done before or since. He brought a light and a love that has transformed millions. Do not think, Christian, that by consecrating yourself to God you are opting out of a position of influence and power to change things in this world. You are, in fact, putting yourself at the centre of a true influence and power.

September thirteenth

"I in them, and You in Me; that they may be perfect in one and that the world may know that You have sent Me, and have loved them as You have loved Me" (John 17: 23).

*A*cross China, at this time of writing, a vast communist monolithic structure ruthlessly holds down millions from any deviation from its line. If you doubt its organisational unity, just try and defy it and see what happens to you. Yet, as David Gooding has pointed out, such unity does not prove that Karl Marx was sent by God, does it? It doesn't prove that Mao Tse Tung was God either. Does it?

The unity Christ speaks of is, of course, the fact that every single Christian is "in Christ": that is indestructible. It is not church membership, nor creed, nor conduct that gives Christians this unique identity. To be a Christian is to permanently live in union with Jesus Christ Himself. As Henry Scougal in his little book, "The Life of God in the Soul of Man" wrote: "True religion is a union of the soul with God, a real participation of the divine nature, the very image of God drawn upon the soul, or in the appropriate phrase, it is Christ formed within us". When people see this most unworldy phenomenon, they will be convinced that the character and mission of Jesus Christ are true.

September fourteenth

"Father, I desire that they also whom You gave Me may be with Me where I am, that they may behold My glory which You have given Me; for You loved Me before the foundation of the world" (John 17: 24).

Without question, one of Christ's deepest longings is that we be with Him in glory. All across the world the words "with Christ which is far better" is one of the most popular gravestone inscriptions. We must remember, though, that to be "with Christ" means more than just being with Him after death.

"We have died with Christ", says the Bible. (See Galatians 2: 20; 6: 14; Romans 6: 13). Our former life of bondage to sin is over. "We have been raised with Christ". (See Philemon 3: 10). Just as He was raised from the dead, so we have been raised from the death of trespasses in sins. Our lives are now "hidden with Christ in God". (Ephesians 6; Colossians 3: 3). If people don't understand where our authority lies, it is Christ who is our secret.

One day, of course, our Saviour will come again. We shall "appear with Him". Our secret will be out. We shall behold and share His glory. The death, resurrection, exaltation and return of the Lord Jesus are more than mere historical events. They are personal. When a Christian speaks of being "with Christ" it says a lot!

September fifteenth

"When Jesus had spoken these words, He went out with His disciples over the Brook Kidron, where there was a garden, which He and His disciples entered" (John 18: 1).

Catch the climactic movement of these moving lines of John. He is now showing the majesty of his Saviour as He deliberately moves to the place where He knew Judas could find Him. Luke tells us that Jesus went there night by night during Holy Week, and John tells us that He "often" went there. It was not a public garden but a private one for He (John) points out "entered" it. Wealthy people had their private gardens outside of the city on the slopes of the Mount of Olives for there were ceremonial strictures on the use of manure on soil in the sacred city. Some wealthy citizen, it would seem, had given Jesus a key. Crossing, first, the Kidron, where the blood sacrifices up at the

Temple would mix with the water in the rainy season, the Saviour of the world walked on His way to shed His blood for our sins.

It was a garden, a place where God Incarnate talked with His disciples. Long distanced from that garden of all gardens, the Garden of Eden, where God once walked with man, Christ now faced, in Judas, Satan who wrecked that first idyll. The flaming sword of the angel banned entrance to Eden but in the Garden of Gethsamane the Saviour faced up to Satan and was to soon remove forever the sword that barred us from heaven and home. What courage! What a victory! Never take all that it accomplished for granted.

September   sixteenth

"Then Judas, having received a detachment of troops, and officers from the Chief Priests and Pharisees, came there with lanterns, torches, and weapons" (John 18: 3).

John makes a very clear distinction that Roman soldiers were involved in the arrest of the Saviour in the Garden of Gethsamane. There were temple police, of course, called here "officers from the Chief Priests and Pharisees". There was, however, a detachment of Roman soldiers. This word, I am told, could mean a detachment of anywhere between 200 and 1000 men. It was, note, a sufficiently large detachment to warrant the presence of the Officer commanding the whole garrison (See John 18: 12). The Jewish authorities obviously expected armed resistance.

Just think of it; torches and lanterns to search for the Light of the World and swords and spears to subdue the Prince of Peace. It showed the dark ignorance they had of His mission but it also showed His singular power in the community in that they felt they needed the help of the army to bring about His submission. He was, after all, in their eyes, a mere carpenter from Nazareth.

In history this phenomenon has long continued. The might of empires and armies, dictators and regimes have been thrown against Christians who are often a very small minority. It proves that you don't need a crowd to make an impact. "You are the salt of the earth", said Jesus. Salt, at times, can be invisible (for example, in bread) but nevertheless a very potent agent. So Christians may not always be seen but individually and collectively they permeate society and constitute a restraining force in a perverse and depraved world.

September seventeenth

"Jesus therefore, knowing all things that would come upon Him, went forward and said to them, 'Who are you seeking?'" (John 18: 4).

J H ere you have the deliberate choice of the Saviour to give Himself as a ransom in exchange for many. He could have walked through the crowd and gone His way, but He refused. He had clear foreknowledge of all that was about to happen to Him and the indescribable suffering He was putting Himself into but He did not flinch. What courage! What love! What incalculable obedience!

We, of course, do not have such foreknowledge but we do have a sense of the implications involved in our actions. We know very well that if we do "this" then "that" will ensue. Are you faced with such a situation, today? You know the will of God points in a certain direction and you also know the implications if you follow it: criticism, loneliness, misunderstanding, ostracisation, financial loss, even. You hesitate? You baulk? Just remember, the fear of man brings a snare. Your doing God's will today will have implications in eternity. Not doing it will have the same. "What will my decision look like in eternity?" is what you must ask.

September eighteenth

"They answered Him, 'Jesus of Nazareth'. Jesus said to them, 'I am He'. And Judas, who betrayed Him, also stood with them. Then - when He said to them, 'I am He', - they drew back and fell to the ground" (John 18: 5-6).

W hat was it that had that detachment of Roman soldiers lying on their backs on the ground? What pinioned them, they who had been trained by the most sophisticated military leadership on the face of the earth? What were these temple police, backed by the priestly aristocracy of Israel, doing sprawled on the ground? What brought about their discomfort?

What did Jesus do? Did He call in a myriad of angels? Did His contained, awesome glory slip out for a moment and push them over? Was it a miracle? We don't know. All we can surmise is that the power lay in the words, "I am He". Earlier the Saviour had said, "If you do not believe that I am He, you will die in your sins". (John 18; 24). Is there not a hint here of God's Old Testament affirmation to Moses of His Name being, "I am that I am"?

On one level the Saviour is saying He is Jesus of Nazareth but on another level He is saying more. There is power in the Name of Jesus; even to lay low his enemies. Yes, Jesus returned in a moment to His attitude of self-surrender for our sakes but in this incident He shows the power of His Name. Don't be afraid to use it.

September   nineteenth

"Then He asked them again, 'Whom are you seeking?' and they said, 'Jesus of Nazareth'. Jesus answered, 'I have told you that I am He. Therefore, if you seek Me, let these go their way'" (John 18: 7-8).

*T*here are many things about Webber and Rice's "Jesus Christ Superstar" that annoy me but the particular thing that hurts me is the impression given that the cross was a good mission gone wrong, that here was a good man overwhelmed by events. This is totally false and no text in Scripture proves it to be totally false better than this one.

There is no doubt that Christ's enemies were intent on arresting Christ's disciples as well as arresting Christ Himself. Mark tells us, for example, of how they tried to arrest a young follower of Christ who had great difficulty in escaping. Yet, the Saviour ensured the release of His disciples. If He could to that He was perfectly capable of ensuring His own release. So, here was no Christ overwhelmed by circumstances. The cross was no good mission gone wrong, it was a good mission gone right. We again emphasise that Christ's death was His own, deliberate, voluntary, act. He was in charge. No-one could lay hands on Him until His hour was come. The merging of majesty and mercy which He showed in this hour is part of our song forever.

September   twentieth

"Then Simon Peter, having a sword, drew it and struck the High Priest's servant, and cut off his right ear. The servant's name was Malchus"
(John 18: 10).

*F*ollowing Peter's pointless hacking at the ear of Malchus, Matthew concentrates on the fact that Jesus taught that those who live by the sword shall die by the sword. John, though, concentrates on the fact of Peter's bravery being based on ignorance of the work to which the Lord has devoted Himself. Along with the rest of the disciples he simply did not understand what Christ's choosing of death was all about (See Mark 8: 31-33 and John 13: 6-10). Jesus was committed to drinking the cup His Father gave to Him and Peter's zeal was zeal without knowledge.

The Lord, with His own finger, touched Malchus' ear, staunched the flowing blood and healed it. Interesting, isn't it, that the last act of supernatural healing performed by the Saviour during his earthly ministry was necessary because of the blundering zeal of one of His followers? Don't you think that the Lord is still constantly healing the wounds made on people's lives and souls by those who ought to know better? There is still plenty of zeal-without-knowledge in the Christian church and it does more harm than good. Of course we admire Peter's honest zeal but Malchus didn't, did he? Be careful you don't wound someone today by enthusiasm for the Lord that does not come from knowledge of Him.

September   twenty-first

"And they led Him away ..... " (John 18: 13).

*I*t is only the early hours of the morning and these people are in a great rush to have the Saviour tried. Why this great haste? It was because the Passover Sabbath, and the week of unleavened bread was following: it would not be possible to crucify an offender during that entire period as it would infringe the holiness of these days. If they were going to have Him executed they had to have Him tried and formally condemned by the Sanhedrin early on the Friday, then they had to get Pilate's confirmation by mid to late morning so that Christ could be on the cross by midday and dead and off the cross again before sundown at the inauguration of the Sabbath. It could be done but it would be very tight.

Amazing, isn't it, these religious leaders went out from studying their Bibles and in deadly haste had the Saviour their Bibles told them about, crucified. Then they went back to studying their Bibles again. They do it, yet (See Hebrews 10: 29).

September   twenty-second

"..... to Annas first" (John 18: 13).

H ere was a snake in the grass if ever there was one. It is not hard to see why Annas arranged that Jesus should be brought to him, first. When sacrifices were brought to the temple they had to be examined and passed as without blemish. The inspectors under Annas' authority found plenty of flaws, even when there weren't any. The worshipper was then shown where he could buy victims already passed by Annas' inspectors at the temple booths. It all looked very pious but the plain fact was that a pair of doves could cost three times as much inside the temple as outside! Annas had emassed a fortune. The one who had driven Annas' men out of the temple with a whip of cords and overturned the tables of the moneychangers now stood bound and arrested before Annas. He was the power behind the High Priest's throne. Christ, he thought, was now safe within his grasp and power.

Are you in the clutches of an Annas? Has some scheming, ruthless individual got you in a corner and your opposition to his sins looks as if it is going to overwhelm you, rather than him? Just remember that good always wins in the end, always. Even though you crucify good, as Annas did, it will rise to eternally make an open show of evil and overwhelm it.

September   twenty-third

"But Peter stood at the door outside" (John 18:16).

S o near and yet so far. Peter was outside when he should have been inside standing by the One who loved him beyond all others. Outside, indeed. Impetuosity is a cruel master and impulsiveness is a dangerous thing. Emotional thinking that is not Biblical thinking can oust you from the place where you should be. Rash, illogial moves can sideline you from the path of God's will.

Who could not find it in their heart to be sorry for Peter? Look at him, sick at heart that he had fled God's will and yet not so far away as to realise it was the best thing, hence the lingering outside the place where the Saviour was. I would rather be a doorkeeper in the house of my God than dwell in the tents of wickedness, wouldn't you? To be outside the will of God is a very lonely, unhappy miserable place. Whatever you do in your life at this time do not shut yourself out of the will of God to follow your own hot-headed plan. The will of God is not easy but it is, in the end, says Scripture, "good and acceptable". Don't stand, like Peter, outside of it.

September   twenty-fourth

"Now that disciple was known to the High Priest, and went with Jesus into the courtyard of the High Priest" (John 18: 15).

T here is an underlying implication in the detail of today's text, don't you think? We cannot prove that the un-named disciple who went out and brought Peter into the courtyard of Annas was John but one thing is certain, he had an entry into Jerusalem's top society. He was "known" to the High Priest. The word in Greek means "an acquaintance", that is used with the word "kinsfolk" in Luke 2; 44.

Here then is someone known in Sanhedrin circles who was a follower of the Lord Jesus. In John 9 we read that the Jews had agreed "that if anyone confessed that He was the Christ he would be put out of the synagogue". Obviously this rule had not been applied to this disciple who had easy access into the house of Annas. The implication would seem to be that they thought that if Jesus were put out of the way then His disciples would no longer adhere either to Him or His teachings.

Once, though, you have tasted of Christ something happens to you that no regime can remove. The book of Acts shows us that this regime turned back to an unremitting persecution of Christ's disciples when they saw that their faith in Christ was undiminished. My mother used to say to me as a lad, "Once you have tasted of Christ you are spoiled for the world". I have proved her to be gloriously right. Haven't you?

September   twenty-fifth

"Then the servant girl who kept the door said to Peter, 'You are not also one of this Man's disciples, are you?'. He said, 'I am not'" (John 18: 17).

 saucy servant maid taunted him", wrote G.Campbell Morgan. I don't know if that is the kind of girl she was but I am quite sure that there was malice in her voice. Peter felt intimidated by it. The words "not also" caught him off his guard. Did the girl expect a negative answer? It is hard to tell but she certainly implied that a "yes" to Christ's discipleship didn't count much with her.

How could one of the greatest men in history be tripped up so easily? How could he who would later die for Christ go down in history as the one who denied him "for want of face" before one who didn't like Christ? Peter never expected that the supreme trial of his life would come in the form of a servantgirl's question.

Watch it, Christian, watch it. We too would die for Christ but in some room full of friends, at some dinner party, at some hamburger joint, in some corner of our school or university, market place or boardroom, we could let slip a word which we would regret for the rest of our lives. The supreme trial of your life may come today in the form of a question. Watch how you answer it.

September   twenty-sixth

"And the servants and officers who had made a fire of coals stood there, for it was cold, and they warmed themselves. And Peter stood with them and warmed himself" (John 18: 18).

 ires were not normally lit at night when most folk were asleep unless there was an extraordinary reason for staying up. Never was a fire lit in history for a more extraordinary reason. It was a fire lit by the enemies of God Incarnate and Peter stopped to warm himself by it. He never stopped by a more dangerous place. It was a fire that was lit because Christ's enemies were desperately trying to clear up their dastardly business because they wanted to bring the Saviour before Pilate who would, like any other Roman official, begin his duties at dawn and have them over by around 11 a.m.

Let those who are without sin first cast a stone at Peter. Are you too weary from having denied your Lord when you should have spoken up for Him? So, feeling cold in heart, you seek to warm yourself with a film that suddenly starts to have people saying, "For Christ's sake this" or "For Christ's sake that" and they do not in any way mean it in worshipful homage to the Lord. Suddenly there are scenes which debase all that is lovely. "Ah, but, it's only a film", says your heart. Sure, but it was only a fire for Peter. Just a place to warm himself. Isn't it fascinating how that that fire had burned into somebody's memory and that all four Gospels mention it. Are you cold? Be very careful where you warm yourself.

September twenty-seventh

"The High Priest then asked Jesus about His disciples and His doctrine"
(John 18: 19-21).

*T*he examination before Annas was a mockery of justice. It was an essential regulation of the Jewish law that a prisoner must be asked no question which, by answering, he would admit any kind of guilt. Annas violated the principles of Jewish justice when he questioned Jesus.

The Saviour answered Annas by asking him to question those who heard Him. The proper and legal way was, of course, to examine witnesses, not him. Notice how, though, in His answers, the Saviour affirmed that He had nothing to say which He had not already said publicly. Christianity has no secret doctrines for the initiated. It carries no secret symbols or special handshakes or pointing of feet or initiation ceremony held in secret. Even its New Testament baptism's were, if anything, the most public spectacle possible. Nero later killed Christians because he thought them a secret society. He got it all wrong. Christ's teaching and doctrine could not have been more open. It can bear the light of any research or any possible investigation; even the scrutiny of the inscrutable Passover Night.

September twenty-eighth

"And when He had said these things, one of the officers who stood by struck Jesus with the palm of his hand, saying, 'Do you answer the High Priest like that?'. Jesus answered him, 'If I have spoken evil, bear witness of the evil; but if well, why do you strike me?'" (John 18: 22-23).

A profound pathos hangs over this interview of Christ. One of the temple police reached out and slapped the Saviour across the face with an accusation that basically said: "Are you trying to teach the High Priest how to conduct a trial?"

The Saviour did not back down. He pointed out that if He had done anything illegal their witnesses should have been called but if He had but stated the law then why was He being hit for it? The Saviour is asking for a fair trial and He, of course, was facing the most unfair trial in history. These men could not ruin their case by fair means so they were perfectly happy to use means most foul. The case against the Saviour was supported by blows and eventually false witnesses and a case that had to rest on violence and lies was no case at all.

Was the Saviour refusing to "turn the other cheek" by not backing down? Certainly not. As D.A. Carson has written, "Turning the other cheek without bearing witness to the truth is not the fruit of moral resolution but the terrorised cowardice of the wimp". No-one turned the other cheek like the Saviour did. Calvary was turning the cheek like it has never been turned. Yet it bore witness to the truth at every turn. Truth and love with the Saviour always went together. They should do the same with us.

September   twenty-ninth

"Now Simon Peter stood and warmed himself. Therefore they said to him, 'You are not also one of His disciples, are you?' He denied it and said, 'I am not!' One of the servants of the High Priest, a relative of him whose ear Peter cut off, said, 'Did I not see you in the garden with Him'"
(John 18: 25-26).

J ohn now brings his narrative back to the man standing by the charcoal fire. To escape his first denial, Matthew, Mark and Luke, tell us Peter had tried to get out of the building. He got as far as the outer porch when another servant girl pointed him out as one of Christ's acquaintances. He denied his Lord again, this time with an oath, i.e. "By God's Name I don't know Him".

Now, some time later Peter was again at the fire while the lovely Saviour of the world, whom he had left his very fishing boat to follow, the One who had lifted him out of the raging sea as he sank beneath the waves, now goes down to a place where there will be no standing for love of Peter and for love of you and me. And what does Peter do?

He is suddenly challenged by many at once. They say, "Are you not also one of His disciples?" and another says, "Did I not see you in the garden with him?" Badgered, Peter had begun, as Matthew tells us, to curse and to swear in his Galilean accent as he denied his Lord for a third time. "Surely", they said, "You are also one of them, because your speech betrays you".

"Would that someone would say of me,
Surely thy speech betrayeth thee,
Thou hast been with Jesus of Galilee,
With Jesus of Galilee".

September   thirtieth

"Peter then denied again; and immediately a rooster crowed"
(John 18: 27).

ell me, do you think the rooster crowing was a crowing of warning? Was it a crowing like a trumpet blast to Peter's soul threatening damnation? No. What did this rooster know abour morality or theology? Nothing. As the light was breaking over the hills of Moab and touching the pillars of Annas' palace, all the rooster knew was that it was dawn. It was saying to all who slept in the city and surrounding valleys, "It's a new day".

The Saviour loved Peter, dearly. Despite his wicked act and dire failure, Jesus knew the real man and He loved him in spite of what he did. "I have prayed for you", Christ had said earlier, "That your faith fail not". And those prayers carried Peter through and his faith did not fail. Matthew tells us that when the cock crowed "He went out and wept bitterly". He repented and starting from his failure the Lord helped him to achieve true greatness.

The cockerel crows a new day for you, too. The Lord is praying for you. He will wipe away your tears and out of the ashes of your failures He will bring beauty and use you again. It's a new day!

All of us have been given privileges. Jesus plainly taught that to whom much is given is much expected. All across the pathway of history are strewn the wasted lives of people to whom God gave great privileges, great gifts and great opportunities, but, they squandered them. They knew better but lived for themselves and discovered that no human being is big enough to be the goal of their own existence. If you are in a privileged position yours will be the greater sin if you throw it away. Instead; recognise it, thank God for it, and develop it to the glory of God.

OCTOBER

October first

"Then they led Jesus from Caiaphas to the Praetorium, and it was early morning. But they themselves did not go into the Praetorium, lest they should be defiled, but that they might eat the Passover. Pilate then went out to them and said, 'What accusation do you bring against this man?'" (John 18: 28-29).

*H*ypocrisy is a deadly thing. These men took the Saviour to Pilate, the Roman Governor, determined to have Him crucified. Notice, though, that they would not even enter the Praetorium. Why? Because in a pagan Praetorium there were many possibilities for defilement for a Jew: entering the house of a heathen, too close contact with an idolator, contact with leaven, contact with a dead body, etc. These would have made the worshipper ceremonially unclean so that he would not have been able to "eat the Passover". This would seem to prove that these members of the Sanhedrin were so occupied with the arrest and trial of the Lord Jesus that they had not had the time to eat their Passover meal! Everybody else had, but, they were prepared to bring a curse on themselves that night by engaging in all kinds of activity which had nothing to do with the Passover Supper.

Obviously ceremonial defilement was a much more serious matter to them than moral defilement. They were so busy setting up the crucifixion of an innocent man they didn't have time to eat the Passover at the proper hour. Hypocrisy is skin-deep holiness and can have the tongue of an angel and the heart of a devil. Selah.

October second

"Pilate then went out to them and said, 'What accusation do you bring against this man?'. They answered and said to him, 'If He were not an evildoer, we would not have delivered Him up to you'. Then Pilate said to them, 'You take Him and judge Him according to your law'. Therefore the Jews said to him, 'It is not lawful for us to put anyone to death'"
(John 18: 29-31).

*T*he Saviour now moves from being tried by religion to being tried by government. Pilate, the embodiment of the Roman Empire, turns in the early morning to deal with the Jews who have brought a prisoner to him. He has no idea that God Incarnate is standing before him. Right from the start he did everything possible to get rid of this case.

If you study the narrative carefully you will find that the whole scene alternates between the outside and the inside of the Praetorium. There are, in fact, seven movements outside and inside of the Praetorium as Pilate wrestles with the Jews he hated, the Christ who un-nerves him, his conscience that troubles him and the bigger picture of pleasing Caesar in Rome. It brings to the fore the undeniable fact that we all must decide what we are going to do with Jesus. He is the Light who lightens every person who comes into the world and we either respond to that light or turn away from it. Seven times Pilate provocated. Are you provocating or responding?

October third

"Then Pilate said to them, 'You take Him and judge Him according to your law'. Therefore the Jews said to him, 'It is not lawful for us to put anyone to death', that the saying of Jesus might be fulfilled which He spoke, signifying by what death He would die" (John 18: 31-32).

Pilate had not realised that these Jews were out to do Christ to death. He thought they had some scruple with Him which they could deal with themselves. Why should they bother him? But they wanted Christ executed and execution in the Roman Empire could only be carried out by the Romans themselves. The Jews would pronounce a sentence but could not carry it out, that's why they had come to Pilate. They had gone as far as they could.

Of course if the Jews had themselves been able to carry out the death penalty it would have been by stoning. The law laid down that anyone guilty of blaspheming was to be stoned and they certainly accused the Saviour of blasphemy (See Leviticus 24: 16). The Saviour, though, had said that if He was lifted up, that is, if He was crucified He would draw all men to him (John 12: 32). By referring Christ's case to Pilate it made it possible for the sentence of death by crucifixion to be passed on Him. Only by this method was it possible for Christ to be literally "lifted up from the earth". What Christ wanted, the Jews wanted for totally different reasons.

What can we draw from this? We can draw the conclusion that life is complicated, shaped by times and circumstances over which we have no control, while the wicked prosper and the good often don't. Through it all, though, God's ordering of events is inscrutible. It would be well to heed the words of Richard Baxter:

"Ye saints, who toil below,
Adore your Heavenly King,
And onward as ye go,
Some joyful anthem sing.
Take what He gives,
And praise Him still,
Through good and ill,
Who ever lives"

October fourth

"Then Pilate entered the Praetorium again, called Jesus, and said to Him, 'Are you the King of the Jews?'" (John 18: 33).

Was there ever in history a scene like that which now faced Pilate on that infamous spring morning? There Pilate stood sporting on his tunic the "Angusticlavicia", a narrow bordering strip of purple running the length of the garment indicating a class second only to the Senatorial. Before him stood the poor, worn, dishevelled, spitten-upon, outcast, forsaken by every friend in His hour of need. "Are you the King of the Jews?" asked Pilate.

The Governor probably expected that the Saviour would immediately disclaim His title. Instead of doing that He probed Pilate's conscience by asking, 'Are you speaking for yourself on this, or did others tell you this about Me?'

The question still probes our consciences today. Pilate had never met anyone quite like this before and one day the roles would be reversed for Christ is one day going to be the Judge of all the world. (See Matthew 7: 13-27; 25: 31-34; John 5: 22-23, 26-29). For the moment Christ was giving Pilate the opportunity to find out who He was and what He claimed. It was His golden moment if he had but known it.

It is still worth asking ourselves the powerful question: "Is what I say about Christ just what I have heard others say or is it truly the result of my own thinking and experience of Him?" Ultimately the question for us is as it was for Pilate, "Is Christ my King?"

October fifth

"Pilate answered, 'Am I Jew? Your nation and Chief Priests have delivered You to me. What have you done?' Jesus answered, 'My kingdom is not of this world. If my kingdom were of this world, My servants would fight, so that I should be delivered to the Jews but now My kingdom is not from here'" (John 18: 35-36).

Pilate was angry and his strong Roman pride shows up. His indignent question, "Am I a Jew?" was saying that the Royal pretentiousness of any Jew didn't mean a thing to him, personally. His second question, though, is deeper. "What have you done?" suggests that Pilate is less than satisfied with the Sanhedrin's charges against Jesus. Pilate was no fool. He felt the Sanhedrin wouldn't take such pains with someone unless their own interests were at stake.

The Saviour's answer was so restrained yet it was so wonderful. What could He have answered? He could have told him he created the stars, that He created Pilate, that by Him everything consisted. He could have displayed His power, but no, He kept focused on what He had come to do, namely to die for us and to bring many to glory. He must lay aside His glory and define the essence of His kingdom in spiritual terms. Here is no offence against the Roman Empire. Rather it is Christ raising the horizon from the Kingship of a minor Roman in AD30 to the question of eternal Kingship.

As His followers, let us never be ashamed to lift the immediate to the eternal. We belong to an eternal kingdom of which there will be no end. It does not mean that it has nothing to do with everyday life, that it has only to do with "our spirits, not our hands or pockets" but it does mean it is not transitory. Empires crumble, Royal titles are given and taken away but this King remains King forever. Live for Him and His kingdom and your work will also remain forever.

October sixth

"If My kindgom were of this world, My servants would fight, so that I should not be delivered to the Jews; but now My kingdom is not from here" (John 18: 36).

The beauty and majesty of the Saviour never shone more radiantly than when He stood on trial. The Kingship He claimed was not like other Kingships current in the world. The one very conspicuous proof of the foreign origin of His kingdom is its founder's absolute refusal to employ force. Josephus, the Jewish historian, writing of the anarchy in Judea which followed Herod's death in 4 BC said, "Anyone might make himself king by putting himself at the head of a band of rebels whom he fell in with".

This, of course, was the kind of Kingship that Rome wished to root out when it raised its head anywhere in the Empire. The Lord Jesus spelt out His opposition to the use of force, either for Himself or His followers. His behaviour in the Garden of Gethsamane had already proved that because He was so easily taken.

History, of course, has thrown up many examples of Christians blatantly disobeying the Master in this manner. Those who would guard Christianity with force expel its divine spirit. The Master insisted that His kingdom will not be defended by the world's means, its origins and power are elsewhere. And how!

October seventh

"Pilate therefore said to Him, 'Are you a King then?' Jesus answered, 'You say rightly that I am a King. For this cause I was born, and for this cause I have come into the world, that I should bear witness to the truth. Everyone who is of the truth hears My voice'" (John 18: 37).

Who was in control of this amazing conversation? Was it the Roman Governor, whose name "Pilatus" meant "armed with a javelin", a balanced missile six feet long, half wooden handle and half pointed iorn shaft which Roman legionnaries hurled at their enemies with devastating effect? Was it the lonely, penniless, despised prisoner from Nazareth? One cannot help feeling that in this situation Jesus was the judge and Pilate was the one who was in the dock.

Are you being hounded and persecuted and despised for your Christian faith? Are you in a situation where you cannot see the wood for the trees? Do you feel hemmed in a corner and you just cannot see the big picture? Then look at your Saviour hemmed in and captured by the Jewish authorities and being hassled and interrogated by Pilate. Look at how again and again in this conversation He lifts the whole scenario to a higher, wider, universal plain. He asserts that His kingdom is a kingdom of truth and that no-one, in any nation or age who loves truth can fail to instantly recognise that here is something they must either accept or refuse. There is no half-way situation. Everyone who is on the side of truth, Christ says, listens to Him.

October eighth

"Pilate said to Him, 'What is truth?' And when he had said this, he went out again to the Jews, and said to them, 'I find no fault in Him at all'"
(John 18: 38).

Was Pilate jesting? He probably never felt less like jesting in all his life. He had never before heard a prisoner claim that if anyone was on the side of truth they should listen to Him. Here was something startling.

Was Pilate not being cynical rather than jesting? Was he not, in effect, saying, "If Your kingdom is by nature and essence, truth, then You have not got much of a chance of realisation in a world like this?" The nature of eternal truth was not a top priority in the range of activities of any Roman administration. Pilate's attitude had now swung from scornful surprise to that of respectful, puzzled regard.

It is true, though, that Pilate didn't wait for an answer to his question. If only he had! He had asked, "What is truth?" and what he didn't realise was he was looking straight into the eyes of the Way, the Truth and the Life. Here before him stood the self disclosure of God in the person of His Son. But Pilate was busy, he had a Province to run, he had no deeply rooted faith. People were waiting, he shrugged it off, though his very soul actually hung in the balance. Don't be too busy today to listen to the Way, the Truth and the Life.

> Take time to be holy, the world rushes on;
> Spend much time in secret with Jesus alone,
> By looking to Jesus, like Him you shall be,
> Your friends in your conduct, His likeness shall see.

October ninth

"Pilate said to Him, 'What is truth?' And when he had said this, he went out again to the Jews and said to them, 'I find no fault in Him at all'"
(John 18: 38).

When the relentless searchlight of history falls upon Pontius Pilate it finds many faults in him. He once dispatched the Augustan Cohort of Sebastenians to set up their winter quarters in Jerusalem carrying in its identifying colours a special medallion with the Emperor's image. This was sacrilegious to the Jews. When Pilate threatened to kill those Jews who petitioned him and they showed that they were willing to die for their faith, Pilate yielded. He was, at times, a tactless leader even once using money from the Temple treasury to build an aquaduct.

Pilate was also cruel (see Luke 13; 1) and proud (see Luke 19; 10). He was a self-seeking politician who put his position before morality. He was also two-faced for here, according to today's text, he completely acquitted Christ and then sent Him to death. It was the cruelest two-faced action in the history of mankind.

The relentless searchlight of history, though, can pick up no fault in the Saviour. How many lives of great men and women, even from recent history, are now having investigative historians rummaging in their cupboards, unearthing their dark side. In almost two thousand years of history, though, not one single fault has been found in Christ. Should every investigating agency in the history of mankind be turned loose to investigate the Saviour it would never find a fault in Him.

"I find it hard to live up to what is expected of me", said a young member of Parliament to Lord McKay of Clashfern, currently the Lord Chancellor of the United Kingdom. "I have found, though," continued the M.P. "that though I cannot live up to it all, I can point them to the One who is the perfect role model, the Lord Jesus". I happened to be sitting close by when Lord McKay told this story and after he had finished it he began to exalt the perfect Saviour before hundreds of people for about fifteen minutes.

October tenth

"But you have a custom that I should release someone to you at the Passover. Do you therefore want me to release to you the King of the Jews?" (John 18: 39).

Did Pilate wish to do right? I have no doubt that he did. He didn't want to take a positive stand for it, though, did he? The righteous way would have been hard at the time but it would have been easier afterwards. One word would have put him on the moral high ground but fear gripped him, the fear of man. He did not act on what he knew was right and he gave way to fear and arrogance. He simply would not throw his all on the truth and tried to get out of it all by making the people decide between Christ, Barabbas and a man who had participated in insurrection, whose hands were stained with blood (See Mark 15: 7).

Imagine Pilate's consternation when the crowd called for a man who had committed murder in his struggle against Rome while condemning a man falsely accused of being a danger to Rome. The irony was not lost on Pilate but he did nothing about it . He stands forever as a beacon of warning against the fatal error of choosing something that achieves a particular purpose in a particular circumstance but denies an overriding righteous principle. Let's heed the warning.

"Will you evade Him as Pilate tried?
Or will you choose Him whate'er betide?
Vainly you struggle from Him to hide:
What will you do with Jesus?"

October   eleventh

"So Pilate took Jesus and scourged Him" (John 19: 1).

*I*t was an appallingly wicked thing to do. After pronouncing Christ innocent, Pilate now had Christ taken back into the Praetorium and flogged. It was illegal to scourge an acquitted prisoner but Pilate ordered it. Mark records that Pilate had Jesus flogged after the capital sentence was passed, John records a flogging before. Is there a difficulty, here? The answer is that there were two different floggings.

The one John records was a "fustigatio", the least severe form, the one Luke records was the wretched "verberatio", the most terrible flogging of all. The latter was commonly meted out to a person about to be crucified in order to weaken and de-humanise him. It involved being flogged by several torturers and the victim sometimes died. This explains why Christ was too weak to carry His cross. The favoured instrument was a whip whose leather thongs were filled with pieces of bone or lead or other metal. When the Saviour faced this situation He could have told them all to go to hell and it would not have been a blasphemy, it would have been a condemnation. The wonder was not that He survived the whipping post. It was that He stayed there. Selah.

October twelfth

"And the soldiers twisted a crown of thorns and put it on His head, and they put on Him a purple robe. Then they said, 'Hail, King of the Jews!' and they struck Him with their hands" (John 19: 2-3).

Was there ever a scene like it? The soldiers made a crown of thorns, probably taken from the long spikes of the date palm which had thorns up to twelve inches long, and put it on His head; the purple robe, the mocking, the pummelling Him with their fists, it was dreadful. The soldiers could opt to pay Christ mock homage, each one giving Him a blow on the face as he did so. Could they have but known it they were mocking the King of all Kings and Lord of all Lords. They were hailing One who with a word could have called 75,000 angels to His aid.

Yet, as one surveys this awful scene of the mocked King who was in fact a real King, I find my heart bowing in worship. Don't you? In a real world of pain how could you worship a God who is immune to it? Christ laid aside His immunity to pain and mockery. Our sufferings become more manageable in the light of His.

October thirteenth

"Then Jesus came out, wearing the crown of thorns and the purple robe. And Pilate said to them, 'Behold the Man!'. Therefore when the Chief Priests and Officers saw Him, they cried out, saying, 'Crucify Him, crucify Him!'. Pilate said to them, 'You take Him and crucify Him, for I find no fault in Him'" (John 19: 5-6).

Why did Pilate have the Saviour flogged? He was playing on pity. He hoped that the sight of a flogged Jesus dressed up in mockery, thorn-crowned, bruised and bleeding would appeal to their pity. He felt that the flogging of Christ would appease His accusers and the sight of Him touch their hearts. First Pilate, with a dramatic flourish, steps out of the Praetorium and knowing that the people must choose, prepares them for the appearance of Christ, hoping they would set Him free.

There is irony in the famous statement, "Ecce Homo!" (Latin for "Behold the Man"). He is saying, "This poor fellow is surely harmless. He can do no danger. He is no threat". Yet John surely means us to discern a deeper significance to these amazing words. Here is the Word become flesh and we behold His glory, even in His hour of deepest suffering, as of the only begotten of the Father, full of grace and truth. There was a majesty about Him even all these indignities could not suppress or disturb. The Jews wouldn't have Him, though. They cry for His crucifixion for there is no hatred so awful as religious hatred. "You take Him and crucify Him, for I find no fault in Him", said Pilate. Was he transferring power to a Jewish court? No. He was teasing them. And there Christ stood, silent, suffering. My Saviour and yours. Let's take a moment and worship Him.

October fourteenth

"The Jews answered him, 'We have a law, and according to our law He ought to die, because He made Himself the Son of God'. Therefore when Pilate heard that saying, he was the more afraid, and went again into the Praetorium, and said to Jesus, 'Where are you from?'. But Jesus gave him no answer" (John 19: 7-9).

*T*he Jewish leaders now tried another route. If Pilate wouldn't crucify Jesus for rebellion against Rome, he might agree to crucify Him for blasphemy. They then referred Pilate to their law which demanded death for blasphemy, as given in Leviticus 24; 16. "He made Himself the Son of God", they cried.

To Pilate's Graeco-Roman ear, though, this claim meant something different than to a Jewish ear. To a Greek or Roman, a person claiming to be a son of God, was no blasphemy, it meant a person with some quality of the divine in him, someone who enjoyed certain divine powers. It was this that gave Pilate more fear. Had he just whipped such a person?

He took Him back into the Praetorium and asked Him where He came from and Jesus gave him no answer. Why? No answer would have been sufficient for a man who was merely a political manoeuverer and uninterested in facing truth. Yet, is not this silence a quiet fulfilling of the ancient words of the prophet Isaiah whose ministry ranged from about 740-680 B.C. He wrote: "He was oppressed and He was afflicted, yet He opened not His mouth; he was led as a lamb to the slaughter and as a sheep before its shearers is silent, so He opened not His mouth". While Pilate strutted, Christ fulfilled every detail of His Father's will. Selah.

October fifteenth

"Then Pilate said to Him, 'Are you not speaking to me? Do you not know that I have power to crucify You, and power to release You?' Jesus answered, 'You could have no power at all against Me unless it had been given you from above. Therefore the one who delivered Me to you has the greater sin'" (John 19: 10-11).

Here you have a perfect example of God's sovereignty and man's responsibility. The Lord Jesus came to die for our sins so we obviously are responsible for them, yet those very sins are operated under divine sovereignty. Pilate was morally responsible for what he did to and with the Saviour, yet the very power under which he paraded was given to him by God.

"It is a dificult task", wrote C.H. Spurgeon, "to show the meeting place of the purpose of God and the free agency of man. One thing is quite clear, we ought not to deny either of them, for they are both facts. It is a fact that God has purposed all things both great and little; neither will happen but according to His eternal purpose and decree. It is also a sure and certain fact that often- times events hang upon the choice of men and women. How these two things can both be true I cannot tell you; neither probably after long debate could the wisest person in Heaven tell you, not even with the consistence of cherubim and seraphim .... they are true facts that run side by side, like parallel lines .... can you not believe them both? And is not the space between them a very convenient place to kneel in, adoring and worshipping Him whom you cannot understand?"

October sixteenth

"Jesus answered, 'You could have no power at all against Me unless it had been given you from above. Therefore the one who delivered me to you has the greater sin'" (John 19: 11).

In this statement the Saviour shows that there are degrees in sin. He points out that Caiaphas was guilty of greater sin in what he did to Him than he would have been if he had not received from God the huge privileges and responsibilities as High Priest. He should have represented all the blessings of God to Israel over centuries of time. He held the most strategic spiritual office in the world and could have been of immense inspiration to millions but he disintegrated into an impudent, jealous, sly, rude, selfish, calculating, manipulating, devious hypocrite.

It is a warning message to all of us. All of us have been given privileges. Jesus plainly taught that to whom much is given is much expected. All across the pathway of history are strewn the wasted lives of people to whom God gave great privileges, great gifts and great opportunities, but, they squandered them. They knew better but lived for themselves and discovered that no human being is big enough to be the goal of their own existence. If you are in a privileged position yours will be the greater sin if you throw it away. Instead; recognise it, thank God for it, and develop it to the glory of God.

*O*ctober   *seventeenth*

"From then on Pilate sought to release Him, but the Jews cried out, saying, 'If you let this man go you are not Caesar's friend. Whoever makes himself a king speaks against Caesar'" (John 19: 12).

*T*hey had him cornered. The mob were implying that they would report Pilate to Caesar for condoning high treason against Roman authority. The irony of it all was, of course, that they detested Roman authority. The Emperor Tiberias would not take kindly to news of a Galilean preacher delivered up to his Governor in Jerusalem for rebellion, being freed. Tiberias would not know the many intricacies of the case, he would simply read the case as producing a weak, soft, unfaithful Governor. History tells us that Tiberias was a naturally distrustful and morbidly suspicious man. Pilate got the message: he would lose his job.

Before such a threat of terrifying proportions Pilate capitulated. The text tells us that he had been trying to free the Saviour but this all changed before the possibility of no longer being Governor of Jerusalem. Pilate then crossed his Rubicon, he would keep his job, thank you. Innocent or not, Jesus, he felt, was not worth losing a high office over.

The truth of the matter was that Pilate was going to lose his job anyway. A few years later he was recalled to Jerusalem when reported by the Samaritans over another incident in his administration. While Pilate was travelling to Rome, Tiberias died and Pilate goes right off the screen of history. The lesson is obvious. "I'd rather have Jesus", we sing, "than anything this world affords today". May we remember it when the crowd taunt us.

October eighteenth

"When Pilate therefore heard that saying, he brought Jesus out and sat down in the Judgment Seat in a place that is called The Pavement, but in Hebrew, Gabbatha. Now it was the Preparation Day of the Passover, and about the sixth hour" (John 19: 13-14).

John's detail of the crucifixion process, or as Christians would phrase it, "the time of the Atonement", is very moving. The tribunal on which Pilate now sat was a raised platform on which a Roman magistrate sat when discharging his judicial function. This was placed on a magnificent Roman pavement known in Aramaic as "The Ridge", originally measuring almost 3,000 square yards which has been identified as the courtyard of the Antonia Fortress.

John points out that it was towards noon on Passover Eve. What does that imply? It implies that the moment for which the entire history of redemption had been waiting had now arrived. Sentence is about to be passed and Jesus will go to the slaughter of Calvary. There is no doubt that John sees the Lord Jesus as the anti-typical Paschal Lamb of God and that His death coincided with the sacrificing of the lambs in the Temple precincts on Passover's Eve. For centuries the hour of His death had been predicted, enacted in symbol, but now it had come. God's clock never runs slow. God's ultimate will is fulfilled to the month, the day, the hour. The Lamb of God goes to the slaughter for you and me, fulfilling God's will to the minute. What a Saviour!

October nineteenth

"And he said to the Jews, 'Behold your King!'" (John 19:14)

How Pilate hated those people! He means to mock the vassal status of the Jewish people by calling the dishevelled, helpless prisoner standing before them, their King. He acclaims the Lord Jesus as if He were at His coronation seeking all the while to bait the crowd. He stings and infuriates them into crying out that they had no king but Caesar, while they knew very well that the Scriptures insisted that the only true King of Israel is God Himself. Even kings like David and Solomon were but vassal monarchs in covenant with the Lord.

Over and over we see that John's Gospel is an exposition of his prologue contained in the first eighteen verses of the gospel. Here, to the
letter, is the fulfilment of the phrase, "He came to His own, but His own
received Him not". Here was a betrayal of a nation by its own leadership. No king but Caesar? What a choice! What a dead-end decision!
What a denial of the eternal and a trust in the transient!

They were, of course, calling Pilate's loyalty into question in answering his jibes. If he called Christ King, he wasn't Caesar's friend. I wonder, reader, if you call Christ King, whose friendship you will lose? If
people were to investigate our loyalty, on whose side would it fall? You
simply cannot be neutral about the Lord Jesus. Pilate's "neutrality" failed.
So will yours and mine if we try it.

October twentieth

*"So he delivered Him to them to be crucified. So they took Jesus and led
Him away" (John 19: 16).*

For our sakes, He was delivered to them. For our sakes He let
Himself be received by them. Who of us alive does not value
our independence? Who of us does not like to make our own
decisions about where we go today, how we get there, what we do when
we get there? Who likes to be handed over to anyone?

Imagine then, God Incarnate, allowing Himself to be delivered into
the hands of those conniving, two-faced, self-serving hypocrites. The
shame and the humiliation is indescribable. He who thought it not rob-
bery to be equal with God made Himself of no reputation and humbled
Himself and became obedient to the point of death, even the death of
the cross. He must have loved us beyond all telling to allow Himself to
be "delivered to them" for our sakes. What must the countless angels in
Heaven have thought at that moment? "Delivered to them", He who
delivered the worlds by the Word of His power! The whole scene is just
staggering.

If, then, you are humiliated by someone today for the Lord's sake,
just remember this moment. It would make you proud to suffer for His
sake, would it not?

October twenty-first

"And He, bearing His cross, went out to a place called the Place of a Skull, which is called in Hebrew, Golgotha" (John 19: 17).

This is no reluctant victim. He is not compelled to go where He does not want to go. He goes of His own choice. Just as He deliberately left that cosy lamplit Upper Room with the statment, "Rise up, let us go. See, My betrayer is at hand", so now He went out, bearing His cross, not a victim but a victor.

Had you been standing in the crowd on the Via Dolorosa as the Saviour passed by you would never have dreamt that the twice-flogged, frighteningly weakened, blood-stained prisoner was, in fact, leading many sons to glory. That is exactly what He was doing for the way of the cross leads home! No wonder the preaching of the Cross is to millions of unconverted, foolishness. What kind of movement of untold, incalculable blessing begins with a God that is worshipped being punished by His own wrath that should have fallen on the worshipper's guilty head? Mystery of mysteries, indeed. He looked no victor but He was on a divinely marked pathway that led to the greatest victory ever accomplished.

And what is our response? "Whoever desires to come after Me", said the Saviour, "let him deny himself, and take up his cross, and follow Me". The Christian life is a paradox. It looks weak but it is mighty. It seems an irrelevance but it couldn't be more relevant. Its momentum is based on a simple truth: the way up is the way down. Humble yourself and you will be exalted, lose your life for His sake and the Gospels and you will save it.

October twenty-second

"And He bearing His cross, went out to a place called the Place of a Skull, which is called in Hebrew Golgotha" (John 19: 17).

What kind of Man is this? Emperors and kings of earth rule from their palaces; this Man stumbles to His throne. Dynasties of earth surround themselves with armies and panoply, with vast acres of land, with banquets and great occasions of state: this Man goes out, to die at a place called the Place of a Skull.

We don't know why it was called the Place of a Skull. Some reasons given include its topographical shape or the fact that the skulls of the victims lay about it. One thing is certain, it was the place of death. A skull in no way speaks of life. What kind of man is it who identifies with a place of death to found His kingdom? The answer is that the Lord Jesus went to the place of death to destroy death. Who of us but have not looked upon death with deep foreboding? It is an enemy. It comes, if the Lord be not come, to every one sooner or later bearing no relation to whether or not it is deserved. It comes to good people and bad, to wise people or fools, young and old. It comes haphazardly.

Yet, since Christ has conquered death, it has taken on totally different dimensions to the Christian. It may be the king of terror. Jesus is the King of Kings. As William Romaine once said, "Death stung himself to death when he stung Christ". Death is not extinguishing the light, rather it is putting out the light because the dawn has come. Bless the Lord for Calvary!

October twenty-third

"Where they crucified Him ...." (John 19: 17).

Crucifixion! It was a filthy swear word to the Romans and regarded with horror. Cicero called it "The cruelest and foulest of punishments". The commonest form of crucifixion was to fasten the victim's arms or hands to the cross-beam and then to hoist it to the upright post, to which the victim's feet were then fastened. There was also a "sedecula", a kind of seat designed to prolong the victim's life. To breath it was necessary to push with the legs and pull with the arms to keep the chest cavity open and functioning. The "sedecula" prolonged life and agony by supporting the body's weight and therefore encouraged the victim to fight on.

"Let us now pause a while", wrote Matthew Henry, "and with an eye of faith look upon Jesus". Was ever sorrow like unto His sorrow? See Him bleeding, see Him struggling, see Him and love Him .... and study what we shall render".

"We may not know, we cannot tell
What pains He had to bear;
But we believe it was for us
He hung and suffered there."

October   twenty-fourth

"And to others with Him, one on either side, and Jesus in the middle"
(John 19: 18).

John, step by step, shows that every move made during these momentous hours is fulfilling prophesy. What drove Pilate to crucify two others with the Saviour? The other Gospels tell us they were thieves and one of them repented before death. What was the reason for such company for the King of Kings and Lord of Lords? "We receive the due reward of our deeds", said one of them, "but this Man has done nothing amiss". Why, then, must He be placed between two thieves in death? It was, of course, to fulfil prophesy, "He was numbered with the transgressors", wrote Isaiah, "and He bore the sins of many". He was rightly placed for He had taken upon Him the sin of the world. He who was guiltless now had pre-eminence in the guilty place where we should have been.

The great British Prime Minister, William Gladstone, whilst a great church-going, Bible-reading, praying Christian, in mid-life had very real problems with his thought-life through reading marginally salicious literature. He became disgusted with himself and documentary evidence in Gladstone's diaries exists to show that as a mixture of retribution and possible cure, Gladstone had at a period of his life adopted the policy of scourging or self-flagellation. It was a pathetic thing that such a man resorted to self-flagellation for his sins.

Are you plagued, like Gladstone, with guilt of sin? Your Saviour was numbered with the transgressors, in fact put right in the midst of them. He was punished in your place and if you trusted Him as Saviour you can know His forgiveness. Remember, God got even at the cross.

> God will not judgment twice demand,
> First at my bleeding surety's hand,
> And then again at mine.

October   twenty-fifth

"Now Pilate wrote a title and put it on the cross. And the writing was:
'Jesus of Nazareth the King of the Jews'. Then many of the Jews read

this title, for the place where Jesus was crucified was near the city; and it was written in Hebrew, Greek and Latin" (John 19: 19-20).

he title Pilate insisted on putting on Jesus' cross was written in Hebrew, in Latin and in Greek. These were the three great languages of the ancient world. Hebrew was the language of the Palestinian Jews, Latin was the official language of the Roman government and army. Greek was the language of the Eastern Provinces of the Roman Empire.

There is evidence that multi-lingual crucifixion notices were used in Roman times but when the Roman Governor of Jerusalem took his stylus and wrote of Jesus, his hand was being guided of God. Though they may not realise it, unconverted men and women are being guided by God even when they are not seeking His guidance. "Tell it out among the heathen that the Lord is King", says Psalm 96:10. Pilate was unwittingly doing just that.

Think of the antithesis here; think of what Pilate meant by the King of the Jews and what God meant. The King of the Jews will lead them to their eventual salvation and they shall look on Him whom they pierced and trust Him. Pilate wrote the inscription in great anger seeking to humiliate those who had humiliated him but God proved again that He can make even the wrath of man to praise Him. It's helpful to remember this when you are faced with an angry man.

October twenty-sixth

"Then many of the Jews read this title, for the place where Jesus was crucified was near the city; and it was written in Hebrew, Greek and Latin. Then the Chief Priests of the Jews said to Pilate, "Do not write, 'The King of the Jews', but, He said,"I am the King of the Jews""
(John 19: 20-22).

here is a paradox in what Pilate did. He was weak before the coercion and blackmailing of the Jews and faced with a decision of huge and eternal importance and now he is strong, inflexible, adamant and stubborn about an inscription that has the Jewish leaders raging and complaining.

We can all be strong when we want to be but are we strong when we need to be? God did over-rule with what Pilate did and used it but on the human level he represents a foible in all of us: we are strong and refuse to budge on trifles and vacillate and give way on matters that affect our homes, churches, businesses and communities. How many a person has made shipwreck of their lives over some trifle when they could have been holding the line in times of great need? Keep your eye on the essentials today and the unessentials will get sorted out in good time.

October twenty-seventh

"Then the soldiers, when they had crucified Jesus, took His garments and made four parts, to each soldier a part, and also the tunic. Now the tunic was without seam, woven from the top in one piece. They said therefore among themselves, 'Let us not tear it, but cast lots for it, whose it shall be', that the Scripture might be fulfilled which says: 'They divided my garments among them, and for my clothing they cast lots'. Therefore the soldiers did these things" (John 19: 23-24).

The gambling for the clothes of the Lord Jesus certainly shows the indifference of executors towards the executed. The clothes of an executed man were, in fact, the legal perquisite of his executioners. Every Jew wore five articles of clothing, his shoes, his turban, his belt, his tunic, or undergarment, and his outer robe. Four soldiers to five articles of apparel left the inner garment which was woven, seamless. For this one piece they gambled, thus fulfilling Scriptural prophesy (See Psalm 22: 18).

It is those words of re-emphasis of John that bring the horror of it all to us, "Therefore the soldiers did these things": he is saying, "So this is what the soldiers did". Hendriksen makes the point that "Jesus bore for us the curse of nakedness in order to deliver us from it. (cf. Genesis 3: 9-11, 21; 2 Corinthians 5: 4; Revelation 7: 13, 14)". Here is degredation to the last degree. Christ's very last earthly possessions are taken away from Him. He who laid aside His glory is stripped of His very clothes. He who gave us the covering of an eternal robe of righteousness has His very last piece of clothing stripped away. When gazing at that naked, humiliated form,

"Two wonders I confess,
The wonder of His glorious love,
And my own worthlessness".

*O*ctober *twenty-eighth*

"....And Mary Magdalene" (John 19: 25).

*I*t is a very touching thing to see Mary at the cross: Mary from Magdala in the land of Zabulon. She lived among a people who "sat in darkness", says Scripture, in the "region in shadow of death". She could not have been further from the truth. Seven devils had been driven out of her by the resistless power of the Lord Jesus. She had been a stranger from the covenant of promise, having no hope and without God in the world, she walked according to the course of this world, according to the prince of the power of the air.

Mary's life had been transformed by the Saviour and from the day of deliverance out of Satan's power to the day He ascended to His Father, Mary's chief characteristic was an intense desire to never lose sight of Jesus. She had even been watching everything from a distance (See Luke 23: 49). Now, though, she stands by His cross. She was soon to begin the greatest search in history: the search for what was the resurrected body of Jesus. Mark well Mary's chief characteristic and wherever you go today, Christian, never lose sight of Jesus. Day and night, He will keep you right.

*O*ctober *twenty-ninth*

"When Jesus therefore saw His mother, and the disciple whom He loved standing by, He said to His mother, 'Woman, behold your Son!'"
(John 19: 26).

*I*t is not easy to stand by the death and burial of our most cherished hopes, is it? The Lord's dealings with us are not easy to understand. "The Lord gave and the Lord has taken away, blessed be the Name of the Lord", said Job when a house and a storm fell in upon his children. It is so easy to charge God with wrong when our expectations become bitter and sometimes frightening disappointments.

Mary the mother of Jesus could have easily rebelled against the Lord's directions to John to treat her as his mother and she to treat John as her son. She could have said, "John is not my son, You are. You who healed the sick and cleansed the lepers and calmed the raging sea, who fed the multitudes and raised the dead, come down from that cross and save Yourself and me". No word, though, of rebellion crossed Mary's lips. She submitted to the will of God and was quiet and it brought her incredible blessing. It was a blessing greater, purer, higher and better than she could ever have imagined.

What, then, about us? "We", wrote Paul, "had the sentence of death in ourselves, that we should not trust in ourselves but in God who raises the dead, who delivered us from so great a death and does deliver us; in whom we trust that He will still deliver us".

October thirtieth

"After this, Jesus, knowing that all things were now accomplished, that the Scripture might be fulfilled, said, 'I thirst!' Now a vessel full of sour wine was sitting there; and they filled a sponge with sour wine, put it on hyssop, and put it to His mouth" (John 19: 28-29).

The Lord Jesus had fulfilled everything His Father had asked Him to do. He had drunk the cup offered to Him, drained it of all the wrath and suffering it had contained, and now says, as His great spiritual sufferings take their toll of Him physically, "I thirst". It was said spontaneously and naturally but the more spontaneous and natural, the more it fulfilled to the letter the prophesy that had preceded it. (See Psalm 22; 15).

The moral lesson from this plaintive cry, though, was that He had left His own need to the last. When the basis had been laid for our thirst to be eternally quenched by living water so that we need never spiritually thirst again, He speaks of His own burning thirst. It was so deep that, as the prophesy had stated, His very tongue cleaved to His jaws. Climb the hill of Calvary again and see there the utter selflessness of the Saviour. John Stott has succinctly pointed out that to be an enemy of the cross is to lean on your own self- righteousness, instead of looking to Christ's finished cross-work for justification. It is to be self-indulgent, instead of taking up the cross to follow the Saviour. It is to be into self-advertising instead of preaching Christ crucified and it is to be into self-glorification instead of glorying in the cross.

October   thirty-first

"So when Jesus had received the sour wine, He said, 'It is finished.' and bowing His head, He gave up His Spirit" (John 19: 30).

Looking across to the temple precincts the Saviour could see the sacrificial smoke rise from the Passover Lamb, now slain. He knew that He had fulfilled every iota the law demanded against our sin and had obeyed every last request of His Father. Mark and Matthew tell us that He called out, in a loud voice, 'It is finished'. In the Gospel text this loud cry of victory is but a single word, "Tetelestai" which means "It has been and will for ever remain finished". It was no cry of weary defeat.

Immediately the temple curtain, which symbolically barred sinners from the presence of God, was ripped from the top to the bottom. The sin-barrier had been thrown down, the new and living way had now been opened into God's presence. A census was once taken of sacrificial lambs killed in the temple at Passover and the number came to 256,000. This Lamb made one sacrifice for sins forever. He did not die in vain. Horatius Bonner caught it beautifully:

> "Done is the work that saves,
> Once and for ever done,
> Finished the righteousness,
> That clothes the unrighteousness one.
> The love that blesses us below,
> Is flowing freely to us now.
> The gate is opened wide;
> The new and living way,
> Is clear, and free and bright,
> With love, and peace, and day.
> Into the holiest now we come,
> Our present and our endless home".

Not all the blood of beasts,
On Jewish altars slain,
Could give the guilty conscience peace
Or wash away the stain.

But Christ, the heavenly Lamb,
Takes all our sins away;
A sacrifice of nobler name
And richer blood than they.

My faith would lay her hand
On that dear head of Thine,
While like a penitent I stand,
And there confess my sin.

My soul looks back to see
The burden Thou didst bear
When hanging on the cursed tree,
And knows her guilt was there.

Believing, we rejoice
To see the curse remove:
We bless the Lamb with cheerful voice,
And sing His bleeding love!

Isaac Watts

*V*ague and general prayers often spring from vague and general faith. It does not matter how great the request or how trivial, the Lord is still interested in our prayers. He may say, "Yes" or "No" or "Wait" or "Go" and maybe He may send you to answer your own prayer. One thing is for sure, though, He will answer. But there is a nuance in Christ's question that is absolutely revealing. He did not say to Mary, "What do you want?", He said, "Whom do you want?", He is turning our thoughts towards Himself as a living Person, not to a dead corpse. Hallelujah!

NOVEMBER

November first

"And bowing His head, He gave up His spirit" (John 19: 30).

his was not just a fact, it was an act. It is inaccurate to say that the Lord Jesus was dying. They did not kill Him, they crucified Him. There is a difference. Note carefully that John says He "gave up His spirit". Matthew says He "yielded up His spirit". Mark says, "He gave up His spirit". Luke says, "He gave up His spirit". "No man takes my life away from Me", said Christ, "but I lay it down of Myself. I have authority to lay it down, and I have authority to take it again". When people die they drop their head forward. When Jesus died He bowed His head and then voluntarily yielded up His life. Bless His name that He did not give me a fabulous amount of money, or land, or property, or jewels or a social position. None of these could have dealt with my sin and given me peace with God and eternal life. No, He gave Himself for me. Nothing, simply nothing, could compare with that. Sacrifice, then, is the exercise of giving the best we have to the One we love the most.

November second

"Therefore, because it was the Preparation Day, that the bodies should not remain on the cross on the Sabbath, (for that Sabbath was a high day), the Jews asked Pilate that their legs might be broken, and that they might be taken away. Then the soldiers came and broke the legs of the first and of the other who was crucified with Him" (John 19: 31-32).

sn't mere religion an empty thing? Here were Jewish leaders pleading with Pilate for the breaking of the legs of the Lord Jesus in order to keep the Jewish law. This law stated that an executed person must be buried before sundown (Deuteronomy 21: 22), so they wanted Him dead before sundown. After all, for them, the next day was the Sabbath and a very special Sabbath at that. It was the Sabbath of the Passover Feast, a Feast of seven days. The Romans crucified their victims and left them on the cross long after their death to be devoured by vultures. The Jewish leaders, though, insisted that their law be observed punctiliously. How empty, then, is mere religion. These men observed religious law religiously but they violated and abused its every principle and its very essence. They crucified the Light of Life and did pure love to death by every trick they could imagine. Yet, they insisted all the while that God's law be kept to the letter!

Was it any wonder that the prophet Isaiah once cried, "Hear the word of the Lord ..... 'To what purpose is the multitude of your sacrifices to Me?' said the Lord, 'I have had enough of burnt offerings .... the New Moons, the Sabbaths and the calling of assemblies .... I cannot endure iniquity and sacred meetings. Your New Moons and your appointed feasts my soul hates; they are a trouble to Me, I am weary of bearing them'". How very different is this sacrificial Lamb; He will not lead you to mere religion, He will lead you to the Father's heart.

November third

> *"But one of the soldiers pierced His side with a spear, and immediately blood and water came out. And he who has seen has testified, and his testimony is true; and he knows that he is telling the truth, so that you may believe" (John 19: 34-35).*

A lot has been written about these very sensitive verses. Some great physicians claim that the flowing of blood and water from the spear wound prove that Jesus died of a ruptured heart. Much has been made of this in that the theory is then presented that Jesus died of a broken heart. It is surely inaccurate. Such a thing would then contradict the truth that the Lord Jesus voluntarily laid down His life for us. Surely John is not concerned here with the cause of Christ's death but rather with the fact of His death. Notice how John insists on the complete accuracy of what he has written. By the time this Gospel was written the Docetists were denying that Christ was a man and claiming that He never really died, He only appeared to. It seems that even Mohammed's knowledge of the Gospel story seems to have been dependent upon Docetic sources. The Qur'an states, "They did not kill Him, neither did they crucify Him; it only seemed to be so" (Sura 4.156). John stands against it all. Christ was a man, it was real blood and water. Christ died, John saw and testified that it was so. These facts are vital to saving faith. We put faith and trust in One who truly became flesh and also in One who truly died in our place.

November fourth

"For these things were done that the Scripture should be fulfilled, 'Not one of His bones shall be broken'" (John 19: 36).

ven in death the Lord Jesus fitted the anti-typical Passover Lamb to the very last point of the law. As the Passover Lambs were sacrificed in the temple precincts at the very same time as the Lamb of God was being crucified, no Priest was allowed to break their bones. "You shall not carry any of the flesh outside the house, nor shall you break one of its bones", said the Lord to Moses when giving him instructions for the first Passover (See Exodus 12: 46). So the soldiers found Jesus dead and did not need to hurry His death by breaking His legs. They were completely ignorant of the haunting, powerful message this fact had sent out to untold millions of believing hearts. For John and for millions of believers this is more than a historical incident, it is a divine fulfilment.

Many years ago a converted Scottish coalminer, who became a highly gifted Bible Teacher and Evangelist, called David Craig, gave me an outline of the seven active verbs in Exodus 12 where the commands regarding the Passover Lamb were given. I have never forgotten them. I commend them to you, for study. "Take it", speaks of selection (Exodus 12: 3-4). "Keep it", speaks of perfection (Exodus 12; 6). "Kill it", speaks of crucifixion (Exodus 12: 6). "Put it", speaks of application (Exodus 12: 7). "Eat it", speaks of participation (Exodus 12: 7). "Roast it", speaks of expiation (Exodus 12: 8). "Burn it", speaks of incorruption (Exodus 12: 10).

November fifth

"And again another Scripture said, 'They shall look on Him whom they pierced'" (John 19: 37).

s Jesus' body is about to leave the hands of His enemies for the hands of His friends, one great final prophesy is fulfilled. In the book of Zechariah we read of the end-time in Jerusalem when "all nations of the earth are gathered against it" (Zechariah 12; 3). After the defeat of those who lay seige to the great city, God says, "I will pour on the House of David and on the inhabitants of Jerusalem the spirit of grace and supplication; then they will mourn for him as one mourns for his only son and grieve for him as one grieves for a first born" (Zechariah 12: 10). In the New Testament Zechariah's great prophecy is linked with the second coming of the Saviour. "Behold He is coming with clouds", says John in Revelation 1; 7 and "every eye will see Him and they also who pierced Him and the tribes of the earth will mourn because of Him" (See also Matthew 24; 30). For millions who have pierced Christ by persecuting His people through the years, it will be a look of despair, but for John, the immediate fulfilment of the prophesy is for those who literally pierced the Saviour and looked on Him. For the soldiers, as they looked, the wounding meant nothing. For the believer who looks by faith the wounding means everything. No god of earth has a scar like this one. To our wounds, Christ's wounds can speak. The spear wound was man's last brutality and indignity to the lovely Saviour but to the believer it drew forth the evidence of the love of God;

"The very spear that pierced His side,
Drew forth the blood to save".

November sixth

"After this, Joseph of Arimathea, being a disciple of Jesus, but secretly for fear of the Jews, asked Pilate that he might take away the body of Jesus; and Pilate gave him permission. So he came and took the body of Jesus" (John 19: 38).

The Scriptures tell us a fair bit about the man form Arimathea which lay in the hills of Ephraim. Joseph was a member of the Sanhedrin, he was looking for the Kingdom of God, and he was a secret disciple of the Lord Jesus. He had not consented to the counsel and action of his colleagues regarding Jesus. When Jesus died those who loved Him must have wondered what they were going to do with the body of the One they loved.

What could they do? They were poor and the Jewish authorities provided a burial site for criminals just outside the city, instead of allowing them to be put in family tombs, lest they desecrate them. Roman law did not hand the bodies of rebels to the next of kin. The solution came with Joseph's courageous action. He went and asked Pilate for the body of Jesus, intending to bury Him in his own tomb in a garden he owned close at hand to the cross. What brought him out so publicly? What turned a secret disciple into a fearless disciple? It was a dangerous thing to be associated with a crucified criminal, but Joseph had lost his fear. Why? Because perfect love, says Scripture, casts out fear and Christ showed him perfect love like no-one else ever had.

"A man broke my heart with the story of the cross when I was a lad of nine", said a friend of mine to me once, "That was fifty years ago and I want to tell you that Calvary still breaks my heart". With that he wept. Such a breaking leads men and women and young people to follow Joseph of Arimathea's fearless action, inspiring deeds in the cause of Christ: Calvary drew Joseph out and it draws them out to public identification with Christ and witness for Him. What about you?

November seventh

"And Nicodemus, who had first came to Jesus by night, also came, bringing a mixture of myrrh and aloes, about a hundred pounds"
(John 19: 39).

Our old friend Nicodemus suddenly emerges at this tender hour, he who had listened to the Saviour teach him of the New Birth and the things of the Spirit. The cross had melted his heart too and fearlessly he and Joseph took the body of the Saviour down. Who could find words to describe the scene? Was there ever a more precious burden carried by anyone? The body of God Incarnate marred more than any man's was with the rich in His death. Obviously Joseph had used his rank to persuade Pilate to let them have Christ's body and he had brought the linen bandages. It was Nicodemus who personally procured the spices, about a hundred weight.

Why so much? The feeling is that to bring such a quantity he must have had the help of a servant. It was a mixture of myrrh, a fragrant resin turned into a powdered form and aloes, which was a powder of aromatic sandalwood. It was fit for a king and in the eyes of these two men it was a King they were burying. There is, though, no hint whatsoever here of any resurrection. The spices were to take away the stench of death. Mary of Bethany, though, days before, had realised that spices would not be needed for her Lord because her Lord would rise again and so she gave Him her costly ointment beforehand. His body was not to see corruption. There was no stench. What Joseph and Nicodemus lost in their secrecy, Mary gained in her open commitment. Come on, then, secret disciple, come out into the open and the Lord will give you light!

November eighth

"Now in the place where He was crucified there was a garden, and in the garden a new tomb in which no-one had yet been laid. So there they laid Jesus, because of the Jew's Preparation Day, for the tomb was nearby"
(John 19: 41-42).

All of my Christian life I have loved those words, "Now in the place where He was crucified there was a garden". Somehow the contrast between the cruelty and wickedness of the cross with its attendant noise and ribaldry and milling crowds passing from the adjoining road out of the city and the quietness and beauty of the nearby garden touches something deep in my heart. In a garden a first Adam fell and death came. In a garden a second Adam from Heaven was laid in death and resurrection life came. In a garden a first Adam hid from God because of his sin and silence reigned. In a garden God Incarnate was sought by a woman who had sinned deeply and a cry of joy and recognition erupted from its depths. In a garden Satan came to damn mankind to Hell. In the very place where there was a garden, Christ was crucified and Heaven was open to all who repent. In the first garden because of sin, loneliness, heartbreak, sorrow, grief and pain came into the world. In this garden, fellowship, peace, joy and healing came to which there will be no end. A wilderness, in Christ, has blossomed indeed as a rose. Aren't you glad you know Him?

November ninth

"On the first day of the week Mary Magdalene came to the tomb early, while it was still dark, and saw that the stone had been taken from the tomb" (John 20:1).

Isn't it strange how what you think is the very worst day of your life turns out to be the very best? You may be saying today that you could bear anything but that which you are facing? Yet, what you are facing, in fact, be the dawning of a new day for you.

What did Mary want? She wanted to find Christ in the sepulchre but if she had got what she wanted it would have been the saddest day for her. The fact that she did not find Him there turned out to be her greatest good. What you and I think is our greatest good often turns out to be our greatest trial, a real albatross around our necks. What we think is our greatest trail and sorrow often brings future life and joy. "Before I was afflicted I went astray," said the Psalmist, "but now I obey your Word ... it was good for me to be afflicted so that I might learn Your statutes" (Psalm 119: 67, 71).

November tenth

"Then she ran and came to Simon Peter, and to the other disciple, whom Jesus loved, and said to them, 'The have taken away the Lord out of the tomb, and we do not know where they have laid Him.' Peter therefore went out, and the other disciple, and were going to the tomb, so they both ran together, and the other disciple outran Peter and came to the tomb first" (John 20: 2-4).

*A*mazing: the enemies of Christ had more fear and jealously of His resurrection than his friends and disciples had hope! The enemies of Christ had made sure that a seal had been put on the tomb and a Roman armed guard placed there only on hearing some words of a resurrection. Yet, the Lord had specifically spoken of the matter over and over again to His disciples, even but a few hours before and their unbelief had brought forgetfulness.

It's so easy when things seem to go wrong in our lives to forget that the Scriptures say, "All things work together for good to them that love God." The enemies of the Gospel had listened more carefully to Christ's words than His friends had! The mobs, the wickedness of the leaders, the mocking and jeering, the running away in the garden had all contributed to a confused and unbelieving state in Christ's friends.

The lesson is that we must not let people upset us and divert us from listening to the Lord. The treacherous memory of unbelief can make us forget the Lord's promises just when we need them most.

November eleventh

"Peter therefore went out, and the other disciple, and were going to the tomb. So they both ran together, and the other disciple outran Peter and came to the tomb first" (John 19: 3-4).

There is a delicate and moving piece of information given to us from our text. It tells us where Peter was during the long and torturous hours between the crucifixion and the resurrection. Have you ever wondered where Peter went after denying his precious Lord with oaths and curses? The last glimpse we have of him is seeing him weeping and broken in spirit after the cock crowed. Where did Peter go knowing fine well that the One he deserted in His hour of need had subsequently been taken to the skull-like hill and crucified? The whole city was astir with the news of it all. But there had been no sign of Peter on the Via Dolorosa. There was no word of Peter at the cross. Then John tells us in this verse that Peter had eventually ended up with him. Mary ran to where she knew Peter was and found him with John.

It's good to have a John to go to when your life caves in. Judas went out and committed suicide but Peter went to John and John had taken him in. Who knows what kind words the beloved disciple spoke to the heartbroken, backslidden Peter? He must have calmed him by some word or deed that got him to a place where news of the empty tomb had him immediately sprinting for the Garden! Lesson? Be a John to some Peter today.

November twelfth

"And he, stooping down and looking in, saw the linen clothes lying there; but he did not go in. Then Peter came, following him, and went in to the tomb; and he saw the linen clothes lying there, and the handkerchief that had been around His head, not lying with the linen clothes, but folded together in a place by itself. Then the other disciple, who came to the tomb first, went in also; and he saw and believed" (John 20: 5-8).

Long have I puzzled over what John saw. Mary "saw" the stone rolled away. John came and "saw" the way the clothes lay but did not go in to the sepulchre. Peter "saw", after looking carefully how things were but then John came in to the tomb and "saw" in a way the others didn't: he "saw and believed". By what he saw he was absolutely convinced Jesus was alive. What, then, was it about the way the grave clothes lay that convinced John? Some say the spices would have stiffened the linen clothes wrapped around the body of the Lord Jesus and that they were lying there in his body shape. John does not say that. The thing that dawned on John's mind, surely, was that the clothes were not unwound. Even the napkin which covered the Saviour's head which would have been laid on a slightly elevated ledge, had been undisturbed. No thief had stolen into that tomb, he wouldn't have got by the guard. No friend had disturbed those clothes, either. They had neither been put off or taken off. It was as if the body of Christ had passed clean through them. The grave clothes were still in their folds.

As Christ later appeared by coming clean through a door, so He rose clean through His grave clothes. The stone had not been rolled away to let Christ out, rather, it had been rolled away to let the disciples in. When John saw it he became the first person in history to believe in the resurrection. Ah! No wonder he wrote a book! And how many millions of people, because of his testimony, have believed? And, how many because of ours? Selah.

$\mathcal{N}$ovember thirteenth

"Then the disciples went away to their own homes but Mary stood outside by the tomb weeping ...." (John 19: 10-11).

I have always been challenged by these words of Moody Stuart and I share them with you. "Mary's love, in fact, sought more and obtained more than John's knowledge and faith. He saw, believed and returned to his own home. He was satisfied without seeing Jesus. Mary believed less and knew less but she loved more. No well-ordered but empty tomb could ever satisfy her soul. John did better than Mary in believing; Mary did better than John in waiting; John got sooner but Mary got more". So Mary waited on. She came in company but she waited alone. She must find the Saviour for herself. She will do nothing until this is accomplished. Let's make sure that in all our busy service for the Lord that we are passing on to others what we have learned for ourselves. Better to speak of things that you know in your experience. A lot of witnessing and preaching is powerless because a lot of what is said is second hand, it doesn't come from first-hand experience and knowledge. Mary sought Christ for herself. Christianity is not knowing about Jesus, it is knowing Jesus. Wait on the Lord and you will find things you have not yet even dreamt of. Wait, I say, on the Lord.

November fourteenth

".... and as she wept she stooped down and looked into the tomb. And she saw two angels in white sitting, one at the head and the other at the feet, where the body of Jesus had lain" (John 20: 11-12).

There is no fear, whatsoever, in Mary. "There is no fear in love", the Bible says and she had a love for Christ which nothing could shake, even though she believed Him to be dead. She wasn't afraid of the dark for she came to the tomb "while it was yet dark". Friends were very hasty in all their movements, for fear of the Jews. They scurried here and there not wanting to be seen. Such things do not move Mary. Friend nor enemy make no difference to her. Note, though, that Mary's love was so great it overcame fear of the supernatural. The soldiers at the tomb were so scared of the angels at the tomb that they shook and became as dead men. Another of Mary's companions, at the sight of the angels, "ran with fear to bring the disciples word". The angels had to say to the other woman, "Be not afraid" but not to Mary. Mary didn't need comfort, she needed the Lord.

Would you not be awed if you saw a couple of angels in white sitting in a tomb? What was it then that swamped the fear in Mary? It was that no angel had driven seven devils out of her life. Can you imagine what it must have been like to have the devil possess you to that strength? One word from the Saviour and they were gone. After that Mary feared no-one. Perfect love had cast out fear. It was a tremendous demonstration of Romans 8: 38-39.

November fifteenth

"Then they said to her, 'Woman, why are you weeping?'. She said to them, 'Because they have taken away my Lord ...." (John 20: 13).

My, what a grief was in this woman's heart! The absence of her Lord had taken away all purpose. "What are you weeping for?", they ask. " .... my Lord", she answered. "They have taken away the Lord", she had said to the disciples. Now she emphasises that "the Lord" is "my Lord". The angels penetrate her sorrow to its deepest point. Just think for one moment, Christian, if you felt that your Lord had died and that you would never see Him again. Where would you turn? What would you live for? The very thought is unthinkable, isn't it? For you to live is Christ, is it not? That very truth proves that Christ is not a Lord, or just the Lord, to us. We can stand before the very angels of Heaven and say, "He is my Lord".

If someone told me that my neighbour's children had been in a tragedy I would be very upset but if someone told me that my children had been in a tragedy, it would be different. Why? Because I am in a different relationship to other children in comparison to my own children. I can't help it. That's the way it is. Bless God, though, Mary was in a few seconds to learn that she could say that Christ was not only "her Lord" but "her Living Lord".

November sixteenth

"...And I do not know where they have laid Him" (John 20: 13).

The other women were told by the angels to "Come, see the place where the Lord lay". Mary, though, is not interested as to where the Lord lay. Rather she is interested as to where He is now! Her devotion to the Saviour is matchless but it brings with it a message to us all. Who of us have not lived with stories of what the Lord did? When Gideon was told that the Lord was with him he replied, "Oh my Lord, if the Lord is with us, why then has all this happened to us? And where are all His miracles which our fathers told us about, saying, 'Did the Lord not bring us up from Egypt?'" Gideon was soon to find out that in a very dramatic way the God of his fathers had not changed.

In the course of human life, people can change radically, but not God. He never becomes less truthful or merciful or just or loving or good or powerful as He used to be. We must not, though, merely live on stories of the past. We must have Mary's attitude, where are we with the Lord, now, today. Her seeking changed to finding, the Lord's absence turned to presence, darkness turned to light. Mary proved that if we draw near to God He will draw near to us, but it was the Jesus Christ who is the same today, that she found. Praise God she did not need to study where the Lord lay any more. I approached the Garden Tomb in Jerusalem with a beating heart, one summer's day, expecting some great feeling when I was brought up sharp by a sign on the door. It read, "He is not here, He is risen". "Sorry, Lord", I prayed, "I forgot!" Selah.

November seventeenth

"Now when she had said this, she turned around and saw Jesus standing there, and did not know that it was Jesus" (John 20: 14).

ascinating, isn't it, that Mary did not recognise Christ when she found Him? There He was, standing quietly behind her and when she saw Him she thought He was the gardener. What was wrong? Perhaps tears were blinding her for she was weeping. Yet, it is a phenomenon that happened to more than Mary. The two on the way to Emmaus, later, did not recognise Him as He walked and talked with them. Later, again, the disciples in the boat did not recognise the Man on the shore. What was going on? Again I find Moody Stuart's suggestion helpful. He says, "She seeks for a Christ of her own conception ... having before heard the image of what Christ to her mind ought to be, she cannot recognise Him in what He actually is". He adds that people are running to the ends of the earth in quest of Christ, turning from Him where He is to where He is not. "We have a vague idea of a Christ we must climb for, or dig for, or traverse sea and land for and no other Christ will satisfy us. We often repeat our enquiry after a distant Saviour and refuse the Saviour who is talking with us". Meditate well on these words, today. "Do not say in your heart, 'Who will ascend into Heaven?' (that is to bring Christ down from above) or, 'Who will descend into the abyss?' (that is to bring Christ up from the dead). But what does it say? "The word is near you, even in your mouth and in your heart" (Romans 10: 6-8).

November eighteenth

"Jesus said to her, 'Woman, why are you weeping? Whom are you seeking?' She, supposing Him to be the gardener, said to Him, 'Sir, if you have carried Him away, tell me where you have laid Him, and I will take Him away'" (John 20: 15).

hese questions to the Saviour of Mary are indicative of what He constantly does. He wants Mary to be specific. Is that not, for example, what He did to blind Bartimaeus? "Have mercy on me", said Bartimaeus. "What would you that I do to you?", asked Christ. "Lord, that I might receive my sight", he answered. And he was healed. We are often very vague in our asking of God. We pray general prayers, we are not specific. Vague and general prayers often spring from vague and general faith. It does not matter how great the request or how trivial, the Lord is still interested in our prayers. He may say, "Yes" or "No" or "Wait" or "Go" and maybe He may send you to answer your own prayer. One thing is for sure, though, He will answer. But there is a nuance in Christ's question that is absolutely revealing. He did not say to Mary, "What do you want?", He said, "Whom do you want?". He is turning our thoughts towards Himself as a living Person, not to a dead corpse. Hallelujah!

November nineteenth

"Jesus said to her, 'Woman, why are you weeping? Whom are you seeking?'. She, supposing Him to be the gardener, said to Him, 'Sir, if you have carried Him away, tell me where you have laid Him, and I will take Him away'" (John 20: 15).

Let's not rush over today's very precious text. It tells us a lot. It tells us that the resurrected Jesus had a common, human form, else Mary would not have recognised Him as the gardener. It tells us that Mary had found the supposed gardener courteous and kind as she called him, "Sir" and asked a favour of Him. She may have wondered if the owner of the garden had ordered his gardener to remove the body of the supposed executed criminal from the new tomb in which He had been placed in a hurry. What does Mary's desire to fetch Christ's body and give it a burial, suggest? It suggests that she was a woman of some wealth and standing. Over the past year she had ministered to Him by travelling with Him amongst other women and giving from her substance (See Matthew 27: 55 and Luke 8: 2-3).

Mary had substance and because of her standing had time and she gladly gave it to the Lord. Even in death she would give Him what she had for a decent burial. What have you got? Give it to the Master. Solomon had a temple, David had a sling, Dorcas had a needle, Moses had a stammer, Paul had a quill, Aquila and Priscilla had a home, Joseph of Arimathea had a tomb and Peter had a boat. Think of the myriads of people recorded in Scripture who gave what they had to the Lord and look at the consequences! Remember the words of Henry Ward Beecher, famous brother of Harriet Beecher Stowe; "In this world it is not what we take up but what we give up makes us rich".

November twentieth

"Jesus said to her, 'Mary!'" (John 20:16).

*I*t was just one word. He didn't say, "I am the Lord Jesus Christ". He didn't say, "I am the Living Bread", or "I am the True Vine", or "I am the King of Kings or the Lord of Lords". He simply said, "Mary!" How did she know it was Him? Sheep always know the shepherd's voice. How often have you heard some speakers speak thousands of words about the Lord and it leaves you cold? Suddenly, though, someone speaks one word or two by the Spirit and your heart is touched or someone is converted or there follows great spiritual blessing. It is the Lord speaking. "Mary", He said. Mary, possessed by the Devil. Mary, delivered from the Devil. Mary, following and ministering to the Lord of her substance. Mary, bereaved, weeping, forgetful. Mary, who knew sin and grace, evil and good, light and darkness, wandering and faithfulness. Who could ever interpret the tone of voice so as to reveal the full impact and signifance of that one word, "Mary"? Of all the novels ever written, of all the films ever scripted, of all the plays ever acted, of all the articles ever penned, of all the events that have ever happened, there never has been or ever will be again anything to quite equal what that one word conveyed. "Mary!" It meant death had been defeated and our lovely Saviour now lives in the power of an endless life. What a word!

November twenty-first

"She turned and said to Him, 'Rabboni!' (which is to say Teacher)"
(John 20: 16).

*T*he word "Rabboni" literally means, "My Great One". It was a common term of honour addressed by a student to his master or his teacher. It was applied by respectful people to those recognised as public teachers of divine subject matter. Notice, though, that Mary turned to Him and said, "Rabboni!" It was as if she was despairing of an answer from the gardener and that she had turned herself back towards the tomb. She must have turned and walked away. What a revelation to her soul in the sound of that voice that made her turn back to Him and say, "Rabboni".

And what a teacher! From Him she learned salvation. His word was a lamp to her feet and a light to her path. He was her joy, her peace, "the treasure of her soul", restored to her. And He is our teacher too. He has revealed to us the very heart of God. Without Him we would know nothing. We all have many teachers in our lives, some good, some great, some inspiring, some challenging and very helpful, but this is the teacher we return to from them all. He is the teacher by whom the Christian judges the words, content and principles of all other teachers. Smoking flaxes He does not quench, bruised reeds He does not break. Pray, then, today Christian this simple prayer; "Teach me Your way, Lord". And He will.

November   twenty-second

"Jesus said to her, 'Do not cling to Me, for I have not yet ascended to My Father .... " (John 20: 17).

Our text is not an easy one to interpret. The other women held Jesus by the feet and had no restraint imposed on them (See Matthew 28: 8). Thomas was even asked by Jesus to touch Jesus' wounds to remove his doubts (See John 2O: 27). Mary had neither fear nor doubt. Why then was she told by Jesus not to touch Him? Many interpretations have been written and expounded on this question and we are by no means certain as to its exact meaning. The clue may lie in the meaning of the word, "touch". The more accurate rendering is "Hold" or "Cling". He is saying, 'Don't hold on to Me"!. He is not saying, "Don't lay a finger on Me", rather He is implying, "Don't detain Me, Mary".

What is the lesson for us in this incident? Surely it has to do with the fact that we have a more wonderful relationship with the Lord Jesus now that He has ascended to His Father. Mary wanted longer communion with the Saviour in the Garden. Now that she had found Him she did not want to let Him go. Who could blame her? But He must go in order to assure her of a far deeper fellowship and a completely new relationship through the Holy Spirit that she could never have known when He was here in the days of His flesh. The old mode of fellowship was over and a richer fellowship would be put in its place. He also must go for our sake, too, that He might fill us with His Holy Spirit wherever we are today. Aren't you glad that He told Mary not to hold on to Him? It means He can now fill you through and through with Himself.

November   twenty-third

" .... but go to My brethren and say to them, 'I am ascending to My Father and your Father, and to My God and your God'" (John 20: 17).

Who would ever have thought it? A woman in whom seven devils had lived now becomes God's chosen messenger. Of all the people in the world God chose Mary Magdalene to declare the news of the resurrection and ascension of His Son. How God loves to take the weak things of this world to coufound the mighty and the foolish to confound the wise! Do not think that because your past is bad your future is not good. The burden of this text is that Mary was not to wait for more but to go out and declare what she had got. Going was better than staying. She was commanded not to touch but to tell! It was the moment for which she was ordained, it was the greatest work of her life. Again and again from Joseph in Egypt to Mary in Jerusalem, from Gideon threshing wheat to Ananias reaching out to the newly converted Paul, from the lonely Ruth to the busy couple, Aquila and Priscilla, from your life to mine, we go through a labyrinth of ways to a moment where, if we are faithful, we speak "what we do know and testify of what we have seen" and incalculable blessing ensues.

That moment may come in your life today. Mary didn't know when she got up early that morning that before the day was out she would pass on the most incredible news the world had ever heard. You and I are called to pass on the same message to our generation. Let's not spend our Christian lives worshipping the risen Lord and forgetting to tell others about Him.

November   twenty-fourth

" .... but go to My brethren and say to them, 'I am ascending to My Father and your Father and to My God and your God'" (John 20: 17).

My brethren! What, the men who had forsaken Him and fled? The men, who on receiving Mary's message, did not believe it (See Mark 16: 11)? Here is a new name for them, a name even more intimate than "friends". Mary obviously understood what was meant by "brethren" for she did not go with the news to His natural brothers but to the disciples. He does not, though, say, "I am ascending (or returning) to our Father" but to "My Father". There is a difference of relationship. He is a natural Son, believers are adopted sons. Yet, we are called His "brethren". What a brotherhood! Heirs of God and joint-heirs with Jesus. Rebels against His truth, sinners against His law, fugitives from His grace and love, Godless and without hope and now "both He who sanctifies and those of us who are sanctified are all one for which reason He is not ashamed to call them brethren, saying: 'I will declare your name to My brethren; in the midst of the congregation I will sing praise to You' ... and again: 'Here am I and the children whom God has given Me' (Hebrews 2: 11-12). It was a great message then and it is a heart throbbing message still. I am so glad I am a part of the family of God, aren't you?

$\mathcal{N}$ovember twenty-fifth

"Mary Magdalene came and told the disciples that she had seen the Lord, and that He had spoken these things to her" (John 20: 18).

I have seen the Lord", she said, not, "I've read about the Lord" or "heard about the Lord", or "had a vision of the Lord", but "I've seen Him!" For the rest of her life she must have talked of it. Did she marry and tell her children? Did she later join some local church and its people hold her in awe as the woman who first saw the resurrected Christ? Imagine Mary at your supper table. Where did she go after telling the disciples? Where did she live and where did she die? We don't know. We never meet her in Scripture again, but the last glimpse of her is going to find those doubting, erring, men and bursting in with "I've seen the Lord!".

The whole episode has, wrote C.H. Dodd, "Something indefinably first-hand about it. It stands in any case alone. There is nothing quite like it in the Gospels. Is there anything quite like it in all ancient literature?" Certainly not. But Mary told the disciples, and the disciples told the Roman world, and the Roman world is now Mediterranean rubble and its people gone into eternity. Yet, still, across the centuries, every day, somewhere in the world someone experiences that resurrected Lord Jesus for the first time and tells his or her friends, or father or mother, or neighbour, or family, "I have, by faith, seen the Lord!"

Mary Magdalene, we do not know what happened to you on earth after your wonderful testimony but we will meet you in Heaven when side by side with incalculable millions we shall say, "There He is Mary, the One you first told us of, and He is the fairest among ten thousand

and He is the altogether lovely One". Wherever you are Christian, our cry must still be, "We would see Jesus". Perhaps we shall literally see Him, today. Even so come Lord Jesus!

November twenty-sixth

"Then, the same day at evening, being the first day of the week, when the doors were shut where the disciples were assembled, for fear of the Jews, Jesus came and stood in the midst, and said to them, 'Peace be with you'" (John 20: 19).

What brought them back? News of His resurrection. The disciples had scattered but now they gather, particularly it would seem, on the word of the two who had seen Him at Emmaus and the word of the women who had seen Him. Frightened for their very lives they meet behind closed doors, and supernaturally, the Saviour appears before them. And what was His first word? "Peace". They didn't deserve such a greeting, did they? No disciple had appeared to take the Saviour's body down from the cross. The two who had the most to fear, both rulers of the Jews, had fearlessly identified with Him in His death. Here were his closest circle who had deserted Him in His hour of need and they are now locked in a room "for fear of the Jews". And their Lord says, "Peace". They deserved a severe dressing down but, no, He said, "Peace".

When you have failed. When your heart is filled with terror and the fear of man. When agony and darkness swamp you. When it all seems beyond solving, that same Saviour still says, "Peace" to your soul. Is it any wonder that it appears alongside the word "Grace" in greeting after greeting at the beginning of Paul's great letters? May it breathe comfort to you wherever you are today.

November twenty-seventh

"Now when He had said this, He showed them His hands and His side. Then the disciples were glad when they saw the Lord" (John 20: 20).

The Lord Jesus always turns grief to joy but the disciples' joy on this occasion was special. Luke gives us further detail of how and why the disciples were glad when they saw the Lord. At first, says Luke, "they were terrified and frightened and supposed they had seen a spirit". To feel you are in the presence of a disembodied spirit is a terrifying experience. "Behold", said Christ, "My hands and My feet, that it is I myself!"

What He was doing, of course, was establishing that in resurrection He still possessed a body of flesh and bones. They still "did not believe for joy", said Luke. What a fascinating phrase! It means that they still thought it was too good to be true. The Saviour was determined to prove to the disciples that He was the same Jesus as He was when He was with them. He had eaten with them before He suffered and now He eats with them again to demonstrate the physical reality of His resurrection. As He eats the broiled fish and some honeycomb they saw Him in a new light. The word for "saw" is the same word used of John when he saw and believed. It means more than seeing with the eye, it refers to seeing which produces understanding. At last, then, the disciples believed. These are infallible proofs we are dealing with. This resurrection actually happened. Don't be one who thinks it's too good to be true, be one who thinks it's too true to be bad!

November twenty-eighth

"Then Jesus said to them again, 'Peace to you! As the Father has sent Me, I also send you'" (John 20: 21).

This was the second time, in this incident, that the Saviour used the common greeting, "Peace to you". The first time it was used to allay the disciples' fears but now it is used for another purpose. It was to create within them a courage for the work which lay ahead of them. Their joy overflowed when they realised that the Lord was truly resurrected, yet, on that first resurrection day He quickly reminded them of their responsibility. Their own peace, joy and safety was not the final thing, they had a responsibility to bring this good news to others that they too might have their own peace, joy and safety.

As the Savioiur showed them those sorely wounded hands, He was not sending them on an easy pathway. They too must go the way of the cross. What does that imply? It implies that they would not be able to fight with arms to spread their Gospel. They would not be calling on governments to defend the Gospel. They would be depending on spiritual power from Heaven to do their work. The Saviour would not physically fight for His Kingdom and that is why He was so easily crucified. We will need courage to have such an attitude today. That courage is as available now as then.

November twenty-ninth

"And when He had said this, He breathed on them, and said to them,
'Receive the Holy Spirit'" (John 20: 22).

Here is the secret of power. Obviously the disciples did not receive the Holy Spirit on this occasion. Christ was soon to tell them to wait at Jerusalem until they were endued with "power from on high". This breathing on them is prophetic, powerfully symbolic and deeply suggestive. They had just been told of their responsibilities to spread the good news and of the peace and courage available to spread it. But here we have the power available. It is the power of the Holy Spirit.

Years ago I sat one evening in the debating chamber of the Cambridge Union listening to Martyn Lloyd-Jones speaking. He told the story of a woman who came one evening to listen to him speaking at Westminster Chapel in London and who had been converted to Christ during the service. She had been a Spiritualist and Dr. Lloyd-Jones asked her what she felt was the difference between the Spiritualist meeting she had been used to and the Christian meeting in which she had been converted. She replied, "There was a power in both meetings. One was an unclean power and the other was a clean power". Is that what people feel when they enter your local church services? Is that what they feel when they hear your witness? It should be. The world does not have this power but the Christian does. Take of the Holy Spirit's power today. He will give you power for service. You are equal for this task only in the power of the Holy Spirit. It is a clean power!

November thirtieth

"If you forgive the sins of any, they are forgiven them; if you retain the
sins of any, they are retained" (John 20: 23).

When we take the Gospel to people we will soon find we have to deal with the problem of sin. If I may speak from my experience I have found when people are exposed to the teaching and preaching of God's Word it draws their sins out like needles to a magnet. All over the world I have found it to be the same. Expound the Scriptures and the Gospel they contain and you will find yourself spending hours listening to people pouring out their sins.

Does any Christian, then, being sent by Christ have the right to say to any individual, "Your sins are forgiven you?" or "Your sins are not forgiven?". Let me quote Dr. Cambell Morgan on the subject. He writes, "The answer is unquestionably, "Yes". To whom have I the right to say, "Your sins are forgiven?" To any man, to any woman, to any youth or maiden, who, conscious of sin, repents toward God, and believes on the Lord Jesus Christ. I have done it hundreds of times, and after a man or woman has said, 'I do repent, I will trust Him'; I have replied, 'Therefore your sins which are many, are all forgiven in the Name of the Redeemer.' And when, for some reason or supposed intellectual pride, more often of moral delinquency, the soul has persisted in sin, saying, 'No, I cannot give this up'; then I have had to say to that soul, 'Your sins are not forgiven; they are retained, they remain with you'". So the messenger's role is declaratory but it is God who effectively remits or retains. No servant of Christ has authority independent of His.

*L*ove always involves sacrifice, always. The Saviour's love for us involved His coming from unimaginable glory to a lowly stable, making Himself of no reputation. He lived for thirty-three and a half years with the reality of the cross over His head. Peter in turn lived for Christ for thirty years knowing it would cost him his life. We too know that it will be costly for us in the coming days to live for the Lord Jesus. Yet, as we stand by Bethlehem's manger and by Calvary's cross and hear that incredible call of our Saviour saying, "Follow Me", we gladly say, by God's grace, "Anywhere with Jesus we will follow on".

DECEMBER

December first

"But Thomas, called Didymus, one of the twelve, was not with them when Jesus came. The other disciples therefore said to Him, 'We have seen the Lord'. When he said to them, 'Unless I see in His hands the print of the nails, and put my finger into the print of the nails, and put my hand into His side, I will not believe'" (John 20: 24-25)

Let no-one ever say that the Scriptures are removed from reality. There is nothing more real than God's Word. If some romantic writer were handling this story I doubt if he or she would ever insist that the whole thing was called into question by one of Christ's nearest and dearest followers. Let's never forget that Thomas had been perfectly prepared to die for Christ. He had said so (See John 11: 16). But he like the rest had run away and now, no doubt, filled with grief and remorse, on hearing the disciples speak of the Saviour's resurrection, he reacts with great caution and doubt.

I don't think Thomas was a natural sceptic. He didn't doubt everything as a matter of principle. Rather Thomas was a man who had a faith in two minds. His questions were from the standpoint of faith. Faith and doubt aren't mutually exclusive but faith and unbelief are. Thomas did not say he did not love the Saviour or deny belief in His teaching. What he did do, though, was doubt that Christ could have survived the awful treatment and wounding He had received at the cross. He must see and touch those wounds or he would not believe. After all he had not been present at Christ's appearing and he was no more unbelieving than the disciples had been before it. It proves one thing, though, the resurrection of Christ was subjected to the severest tests at the time of the resurrection.

You doubt the resurrection? Then remember this statement of Francis Bacon: "If a man will begin with certainties, he will end in doubts; if he is content to begin with doubts, he will end in certainties"

December second

"After eight days His disciples were again inside, and Thomas with them. Jesus came, the doors being shut, and stood in the midst, and said, 'Peace to you!'" (John 20: 26).

*L*ong have I seen and known it: Christ does not, as Isaiah teaches, break bruised reeds and throw them away, nor does He quench smoking flaxes despite their fitful burning. If He turned away from every doubter He would have to turn away from the entire Christian church. Life is, as any medical practitioner will tell you, a permanent battle against all sorts of diseases and good health is an ability to keep disease at bay. The life of faith is a permanent battle against doubts. All Christians doubt at some stage in their life of faith. To doubt is not a sin, it does not invalidate your conversion experience. Just study how Christ handled the doubts of John the Baptist, if you don't believe me.

Christ did not come to damn Thomas. He didn't even come to scold him. For eight whole days Thomas had heard the disciples speak of the risen Lord and how he must have tossed and turned in his soul that week. And now Christ appears again and who would doubt that He appeared just for Thomas' sake? He had come to restore him. Would He do such a thing? He certainly would. If there had been no-one on this earth but you, He would have come all the way and died just for you. Christian, walk in the common knowledge that you are beloved of the Lord, doubts and all.

December third

"The disciples therefore said to him, 'We have seen the Lord'. But he said to them, 'Unless I see in His hands the print of the nails, and put my finger into the print of the nails, and put my hand into His side, I will not believe'" (John 20: 25).

*T*he pathos and emotion of this incident is a lot deeper than words. Yet, apart from the feelings it stirs in all of us, a principle of the spiritual life lies at the very heart of it. The principle is that Christ hears all our conversations, even though we don't see Him. The Lord knew exactly what Thomas said when expressing his doubts about the resurrection even though he was not physically present in the room at the time. Indeed, not only does the Lord know our private conversations, He knows our every thought.

I doubt if Thomas availed himself of Christ's invitation by coldly scrutinising the wounds of the Saviour. Such an act would be incompatible with the immediate spontaneous words he spoke, "My Lord and my God". Thomas may have appeared a hopeless case to those who might have heard him express his doubts during that momentous week but of all the disciples he made the greatest confession of any. He reached a higher level than all the rest. Don't judge a doubter too hard for "when the Queen of Sheba heard of the fame of Solomon concerning the name of the Lord, she came to test him with hard questions". Before she was finished she was saying, "Blessed be the Lord your God, who delighted in you, setting you on the Throne of Israel". Sometimes the toughest of doubters become the greatest of believers.

December fourth

"Jesus said to them, 'Thomas, because you have seen Me, you have believed. Blessed are those who have not seen and yet have believed"'
(John 20: 29).

Here is the Saviour's last beatitude. He is not talking to His disciples, now. They had experienced the privilege of seeing Him and believing on Him. Just like Thomas they had not believed until they saw; if they had believed a week earlier than Thomas, it was simply because they saw the resurrected Lord a week earlier than he did. The Lord is now looking down the coming centuries seeing all those people from every corner of the earth who would believe on Him without seeing Him. They are pronounced "Blessed", i.e., not simply "happy" but "accepted by God".

Peter put it beautifully, later. "Whom not having seen you love. Though now you do not see Him, yet believing, you rejoice with joy inexpressible and full of glory, receiving the end of your faith - the salvation of your souls". And how do we believe, even though we don't see? Through the reading and teaching of the Scriptures, for, "Faith comes by hearing and hearing by the Word of God". Keep on reading and teaching the Word of God, Christian, and just as you claim to love the One you have never seen, others will come to love Him too.

December fifth

"And truly Jesus did many other signs in the presence of His disciples, which are not written in this book; but these are written that you may

believe that Jesus is the Christ, the Son of God, and that believing you
may have life in His Name" (John 20: 30-31).

I once knew a man in my youth who said that he was only interested in the Bible from a historical point of view. He read it for its
history, he said. Poor man! Notice how John's purpose is not academic or merely historical, it is evangelistic. He carefully selects his
material from all the material available in order that people might personally believe the truth at the heart of it all. He deliberately set out to
show that the Messiah is the Jesus he has just written a beautifully drawn
portrait of in his Gospel. The end result of such belief was "life in His
Name", not just a lot of facts in his readers' heads.

To say that John was successful in his noble purpose is an under-
statement. In the intervening centuries millions have taken up his invitation to believe the message. John's goal in evangelism is the goal of
all evangelism. In this area, as Christians, we dare not be tepid. God
forgive us if we have no emotion, no enthusiasm, no urgency and no
compassion regarding the lost. How can we ever possibly say we are
evangelical without being evangelistic? Leon Morris once said, "When
Christians evangelise, they are not engaging in some harmless and pleasant past-time. They are engaging in a fearful struggle, the issues of which
are eternal". We would also be well reminded of the words of Vance
Havner when he stated that, "The Gospel is for lifeboats, not show-
boats, and a man must make up his mind which he is going to operate".

December sixth

"After these things Jesus showed Himself again to the disciples at the Sea
of Tiberias, and in this way He showed Himself" (John 21: 1).

*A*s the first eighteen verses of John's Gospel are known as the
prologue, so this twenty-first chapter of the Gospel is known
as the epilogue. Notice the word, "We" in verse 24 of this chapter: "This is the disciple who testifies of these things, and wrote these
things; and we know that his testimony is true". This would seem to
indicate that John's associates added this epilogue which they heard
from John in the form in which he had told it. Why is it added?

Is not the resurrection the climax of John's story? Yes, it certainly is.
Yet, here we are given a demonstration of the reality of the resurrection.
There were at least twelve post-resurrection appearances of the Lord

Jesus and this is number seven. It is an interesting study. He appeared to Mary Magdalene (Matthew 16: 9), to the women (Matthew 28: 9), to Cleopas and his companion (Luke 24: 13-35), to Simon (Luke 24: 34), to the disciples with and without Thomas (John 20: 24-29), to the seven at the sea of Tiberias (John 21: 1-14), to the disciples on a mountain (Matthew 28: 16-20), to the five hundred (1 Corinthians 15: 6), to James the Lord's brother (1 Corinthians 15: 7), to the eleven on Olivet (Acts 1: 4-11) and to Paul (Acts 9: 3-7). They all show that the resurrected Christ was not a spirit, not an hallucination, not a vision but a real, live, flesh and blood person. The pre-resurrected Jesus has come back as the very same Jesus. He has forced open a door that had been locked since the death of Adam. He has beaten him who had the power of death, that is the Devil, and now everything is different.

December   seventh

"Simon Peter, Thomas called Didymus, Nathanael of Cana in Galilee, the sons of Zebedee, and two others of His disciples were together"
John 21: 2).

I like to meditate on the fact that Nathanael was there at the end of Christ's public ministry because he had been there at the beginning. The man whom Christ said was guileless, who had first wondered if any good thing could ever have come out of Nazareth, who had then declared to the Saviour, "You are the Son of God, you are the King of Israel!" had remained faithful, right to the end.

How many there are who begin well. They flourish in the things of God, they enthuse about the joy of sins forgiven and peace with God, they witness for their Master, they give to His work, they live for Him. Then they go missing from their usual place of worship, they no longer raise a song to Christ at the unusual hour, never to speak of the usual. They have grown cold. They are "splendidly null". They have left their "first love" for Christ. There is some disease at the root of their faith and the lovely blossom is gone. I tell you it is impossible to witness for Christ in the darkness of the world except in the power of first love. Nathanael never forgot his beginnings, that's why he was there at the end. Don't you think consistency is one of the best jewels you could possess?

December eighth

"Simon Peter said to them 'I am going fishing'. They said to him, 'We are going with you also'" (John 21: 3).

People have always disagreed as to whether or not to blame Peter and his friends for going fishing on this occasion. Surely he had to eat, so the action in itself was not wrong. It would not be unreasonable to assume that they had gone to Galilee in obedience to their Lord's command and there is no indication that they had gone there to assume their old career as fishermen.

There is, though, an underlying restlessness in this story. Peter was a man of action, a leader, and he must do something. When you are restless you can find relief in action. They knew too much to go back, and not enough to go on, it was the waiting that was a killer. Jesus had told them to wait. I can't see anything wrong in filling in waiting time with something useful. But we must beware of restlessness. Just last evening I was involved in a very public way in evangelistic preaching and when I got to my bed I tossed and turned in the wee small hours over what I had just done and said. I was very restless when suddenly a verse from the Bible entered my mind like lightening. It simply said, "My Word shall not return to Me void". I was suddenly filled with this incredible calm at the thought that God's Word always fulfils that purpose for which God sent it. God was saying, "Trust Me on this". I rolled over and slept like a baby. You can wait for the fulfilment of a promise like that, can't you? But you don't need to be restless in the interim.

December ninth

"They went out and immediately got into the boat, and that night they caught nothing" (John 21: 3).

What good can failure do? A lot. All things that happen to us as believers are not necessarily good but they all work together for good. There is not a loss, not a disappointment, not a failure, not a heartache, not a difficulty, not a turn on the road of your life but a loving Saviour can, through it all, teach you a lesson. Was it by chance that Peter and his friends caught nothing? No, it had been carefully arranged by the Lord. Lessons were about to be taught which would not only help these men but which would enrich the whole Church of Christ forever.

So, you caught nothing? So, you have outwardly failed in some enterprise for the Master? Read then, these words by F. B. Meyer: "But what good can failure do? It may shut up a path which you were pursuing too eagerly. It may put you out of heart with things seen and temporal, and give you an appetite for things unseen and eternal. It may teach you your own helplessness, and turn you to trust more implicity in the provision of Christ. It is clear that Christians have often toiled all night in vain, that Christ may have a background black and sombre enough to set forth all the glories of His inter- position".

December   tenth

"But when the morning had now come, Jesus stood on the shore; yet the disciples did not know that it was Jesus" (John 21: 4).

It was most probably the early morning mist that obscured the Saviour. I don't think it was unbelief that had closed their eyes, do you? Yet, how often the Lord is near us and we don't know Him? There He is in your place of work, today. There He is by the bedside of that sick patient as you do your best to help them. There He is, standing, despite your marital row, or family disagreement, or heartbreaking exam failures. There He is when you were passed over for promotion. There He is, standing on the shore, when your nets are empty.

Learn to discern the presence of the Lord. You will reach no shore in life where He isn't present. As David put it long ago: "Where can I flee from Your presence? If I ascend into Heaven, You are there: .... if I take the wings of the morning, and dwell in the uttermost parts of the sea, even there Your hand shall lead me, and Your right hand shall hold me. If I say, 'Surely the darkness shall fall on me', even the night shall be light about me: indeed, the darkness shall not hide from You, but the night shines as the day, the darkness and the night are both alike to You". See your Lord everywhere, Christian. If you truly love Him, as Peter soon showed, you will detect His presence.

December   eleventh

"Then Jesus said to them, 'Children, have you any food?'. They
answered Him, 'No'. And He said to them, 'Cast the net on the right side
of the boat, and you will find some'. So they cast, and now they were not
able to draw it in because of the multitude of fish" (John 21: 5-6).

*D*A. Carson makes a very interesting point regarding this command, which was obviously given by a Man whom the disciples did not recognise! Why should they listen to the voice
of someone calling in the early dawn mist from the shore of the lake?
Carson points out that since the disciples did not recognise the Lord, "It
is hard to see how Jesus' exhortation to throw the net on the starboard
side greatly differs from advice that temporary sports fishermen have
to endure: "Try casting over there, you often catch them over there'".
He says if there are those who haven't experienced this delight he rec-
ommends they take his children with them on their next fishing trip!

The point was, of course, that there was a shoal of fish on that side of
the boat and Jesus knew all about them. Just like He knew there was a
coin in the fish's mouth so that Peter could pay his tribute money, just
like He had earlier in His ministry asked Peter, in whose boat He had
preached, to "launch out into the deep and let down your nets for a
catch". It is obvious that the Lord Jesus knows the flip of every tail of
every fish in every ocean on earth. If He knows that much detail about
fish, how much more does He know about you? Talk about fish: His
thoughts about you are more, says Scripture, than the sand on the seashore! As for those lonely, bewildered disciples, He is able to do for you,
too, exceedingly, abundantly, above all that you could ever ask or think.

December   twelfth

"Therefore that disciple whom Jesus loved said to Peter, 'It is the Lord!'"
(John 21: 7).

*T*he relationship between Peter and John is full of lessons. They
were obviously great friends. They are recorded in Scripture as
often being together (John 1: 35-41; 13: 23-24; 18: 15-16; 20: 1-10;
21: 2, 7, 20-22; Acts 3: 1-4; 8: 14-17; Galatians 2: 9). They were as great
friends often are, very different. Peter was the man of action, John the

man of insight. Quick action and quick insight in the hand of God, in the Kingdom of God, are a great complement to one another.

Why, so often, do so many people want to stereotype Christians? Who do people think that when a person finds Christ he or she loses their personality, their "colour and flair"? Look at these two: Peter the impulsive, articulate, fervent, spontaneous leader: John the literate, pondering, sensitive, retiring visionary. Between them they and their friends were about to turn the Roman world upside down for Christ. You are in your personality the person God made you, don't try to be anyone else. You are, in all the world, the person best qualified to be you. Let God use you to His glory just like Peter and John.

December   thirteenth

"Now when Simon Peter heard that it was the Lord, he put on his outer garment (for he had removed it) and plunged into the sea" (John 21: 7).

et no-one ever say that deep in his heart Peter did not love the Lord. Cowardly, wayward and weak he had been. Sinful, certainly. A disastrous denial of his Lord had no doubt led to the dark night of his soul. Who of us is there who have not known it? Pressurised by this, that or the other, instigated by Satan, we have let the Lord down. We have, like Peter, gone out and wept. As Dr. Alan Redpath said one evening as he and I were preaching together in Greystones in Co. Wicklow, "There is no sin that I am not capable of committing two minutes after this service is over". I have long thought on that statement by that great servant of God.

The meaning of our text seems to be that Peter put on his outer garment when he knew it was the Lord. He had obviously stripped to his loincloth for fishing purposes. He did this out of respect tucking up the lower part of his outer garment into his belt, so as not to impede his legs, and swam for the shore. "It is the Lord!" was all he needed to hear. Gone was fear, gone was hopelessness and restlessness, the Lord was there and that was enough. He couldn't wait to see Him. He didn't even wait to help with the immediate haul of fish, he must see the Lord. He must welcome Him.

We know that Peter had said on one occasion previously, when he had failed, "Depart from me for I am a sinful man, oh Lord". He had asked the Lord to give him up because of his personal failure. But the Lord will never leave us nor forsake us. So then, discouraged, broken, down-hearted Christian, be up with you and away to your new risen Lord. He loves you still with the very same love as He showed you at Calvary. He is Jesus Christ, the same yesterday and today and forever.

December   fourteenth

"Then, as soon as they had come to land, they saw a fire of coals there, and fish laid on it, and bread. Jesus said to them, 'Bring some of the fish which you have just caught'" (John 21: 9-10).

You may have had a bad night but the Lord Jesus can give you a good morning. How very typical of the Master to show His servant nature as much in post-resurrection days as pre-resurrection days. And when we pass through the chill waters of death, or we are called by the Lord's shout at the Second Coming, we shall dine with Him as these men did.

We shall, we are told, gather from every clime and nation. Not, then, by a fire with its curling smoke on a stretch of deserted beach in Galilee, but on a celestial shore on Heaven's morning. We shall hear stories which will thrill our hearts as to how multitudes were found by the Saviour, and who will serve at the table? The Lord will. We serve a Servant-King who came not to be ministered to, but to minister. Have we the same nature? Ask not what your local church or community can do for you but rather what you can do for your local church or community, for the Lord's sake.

December   fifteenth

"Simon Peter went up and dragged the net to land, full of large fish, one hundred and fifty-three" (John 21: 11).

He has not been nicknamed "The big fisherman" for nothing, has he? Peter, single-handedly, hauled the net with one hundred and fifty-three fish up the beach. Interesting interpretations, especially from some of the early church fathers, have been given as to the significance of the number of fish: obviously somebody thought to count them and remembered how many there were.

It is very hard not to catch a subliminal message through this haul of fish. Surely it was a parable to the disciples of the kind of work in which they would be involved in the future. Not only would the Lord provide for their needs but they were going to become fishermen for the Lord and catch people. They will have to learn to cast their nets by His direction, they will have to learn great patience, as they go through the contrasts of storm and calm, wind and sunshine, summer and winter, for His sake. One thing is certain, though, the Gospel net will never break no matter how many fish you land. The net may have broken in the haul recorded in Luke 5: 1-11 but not here. So, Christian, keep casting! Remember though these four little rules as you fish:

"Keep your face towards the sun,
Study the fishes' curious ways,
Keep yourself well out of sight,
Study patience all your days".

December sixteenth

"Jesus said to them, 'Come and eat breakfast,' yet one of His disciples dared ask Him, 'Who are you?' - knowing that it was the Lord"
(John 21:12).

When the Lord calls you to do something for Him, He means it. He decided you should do it, He provided the circumstances in which to call you, He organises the sphere in which you should serve Him. Sometimes the events of life are so overwhelming that we forget our calling. The pressures of the immediate crowd out the big picture, we lose our sense of direction.

Look at these men sitting by a fire of crackling charcoal which is chasing away the morning chill. Every word of their Saviour is hung upon eagerly, every movement watched. Notice that John does not merely say that they did not ask Him who He was, He tells us that they dared not ask Him.

There is no doubt that Christ's presence by that fire that morning reminded them of something vitally important - their calling. He had called them to serve Him three years before and that calling still stood. So does yours. Don't let anything obscure that which the Lord has called you to do.

December seventeenth

"Jesus then came and took the bread and gave it to them, and likewise the fish. This is now the third time Jesus showed Himself to the disciples after He was raised from the dead" (John 21:13-14).

Two things are important to note in this part of this beautiful epilogue of John's Gospel. The first is that the Lord personally does the feeding here. Back in Jerusalem they gave Him a piece of "broiled fish" and He strengthened their faith by eating it. Here the Lord Jesus feeds them symbolically, showing as He did by the lake with the multitudes, that this is what He loves to do.

How many times, weary with life's burdens and heartaches has He said to you, as He did to those men that morning, "Come and eat"? He has fed you on food this world knows nothing of for it suffers from a wasting disease called, by the French philosopher, Albert Camus, "absurdism". Life, such people believe, is a bad joke. Millions more suffer from a complaint called "Marie Antionette's fever". She who could have virtually anything she wanted complained that "Nothing tastes". So many are like the Duchess of York who recently told Alexandra Shulman of "Vogue" Magazine: "You know what, when you're down and you've got nowhere to go, you're going to try everything." She talked of her search for "inner peace" and the "mammoth journey" she had embarked upon. To all such, the Saviour of the world says, "Come and eat." When He feeds you there is a satisfaction which results which cannot be beaten. Taste and see, said the Psalmist, that the Lord is good. You need journey no more. He has what you need.

December eighteenth

"So when they had eaten breakfast, Jesus said to Simon Peter, 'Simon, son of Jonas, do you love Me more than these?'. He said to Him, 'Yes, Lord; you know that I love You'. He said to him, 'Feed My Lambs'"
(John 21: 15).

And how did it fare with Peter? How did he feel in his heart and mind as he gazed into the face of the One who died for him and whom he had so cruelly and selfishly denied? What right had he to serve the One he had caused the enemy to blaspheme? Was Peter finished?

The Lord singled him out from the rest and, notice, He addressed him by his old name. He was taking him right back to his natural roots, right back to where he had been, where He had found him and He re-issues the call to serve Him. He is the God of second chance.

Notice, though, the basis on which all Christian service rests. He didn't say, "Do you believe in Me?", or "Will you obey Me?" or even "What on earth were you doing denying Me?" There was no scolding, no checking out his present doctrinal position, He simply said, "Do you love Me?"

The story is told of a young woman in Edinburgh who applied for fellowship in a church but the minister was not happy with her inability to answer certain basic questions. On his third refusal she answered, "Weel, sir, I mayna and I dinna ken sae muckle as mony: but when ye preach a sermon aboot my Lord and Saviour, I fin my heart going out to Him, like linseed out of a bag". If you have ever seen the process you'll understand why the minister admitted her to the fellowship of that local church immediately.

December   nineteenth

"He said to him a second time, 'Simon, Son of Jonas, do you love Me?' He said to Him, 'Yes, Lord; you know that I love You'. He said to him, 'Tend my sheep'" (John 21: 16).

Being a shepherd is not the easy pastoral idyll it always appears. In Romania I was up a mountain at 10,000 feet with some friends when we met a shepherd. He told us with great animation that a bear had come upon his flock in the night and I could very clearly see that being a shepherd was not all quiet meadows and sheep grazing safely. Shepherding is not always done beside still waters. It may mean having the wolf burying his fangs in you to save the lambs.

The Lord had spoken earlier of the sheep He would bring into His fold and now Peter is specifically given the job of shepherding them. No-one did a better job than Peter was to do in this very special area of ministry. He was to write two letters in the New Testament addressed to Christians who were facing hostility and suspicion in the Roman Empire and who were being reviled and abused for their lifestyles. His letters are filled with encouragement and inspiration for the suffering lambs and sheep of Christ's fold. His letters minister to millions of Christians today. Standing on the shore of Galilee that misty morning Peter had no idea of the ministry that lay ahead of him. Neither do you. Never say that you know the will of God for the rest of your life. You don't. Your greatest work for the Lord may lie just ahead of you.

$\mathcal{D}$ecember   twentieth

"He said to him the third time,'Simon, son of Jonas, do you love Me?'.
Peter was grieved because He said to him the third time, 'Do you love
Me' (John 21:17).

A lot of textual discussion has taken place around the different levels of meaning of the word "love" in the Lord's questions to Peter. I am not scholastically qualified to adjudicate on it all but surely the point of the three questions is that as Peter had denied his Lord three times, he is now required to profoundly confess Him three times. Peter is grieved that the Lord asked him the third time about his love for Him but it must be done. Peter, on his third confession, is now fully restored for service.

Have you, like Peter, let your Lord down? The Lord would draw you back to the point where you went wrong and there He would restore you. At Bethel Abraham went astray and went off into Egypt to lie his way out of a crisis. He had to be brought back to Bethel and restored to his calling. He built an altar there and became the epitomy of faith in all generations.

"No chastening", says the Bible, "seems to be joyful for the present, but grievous; nevertheless afterward it yields the peaceable fruit of right-eousness to those who have been trained by it". The Lord's chastening grieved Peter but what incredible fruit it produced. So, be patient, Christian, if you are experiencing the chastening of the Lord, it will yield a great harvest in your life.

$\mathcal{D}$ecember   twenty-first

"Jesus said to Him, 'Feed My sheep'" (John 21: 17).

F or the third time Peter is told of the work the Lord has for him. Aware of his great weakness and failure it must have been one of the greatest revelations of his life to discover that the Lord still loved him and wanted him to continue in Christian service.

Time changes us all. Affections between people cool, opinions alter, but the Lord Jesus does not change. He loved Peter just as He loves you, as much as He ever did. Time has no effect on Him whatsoever. Our moods change, we are "like oranges one day and lemons the next". But not with the Saviour - He is never put out, He is never variable. He is, says Scripture, "without shadow cast by turning".

Have you not found that circumstances change people? Someone gets promoted and suddenly forgets their roots and doesn't want to know their old friends. New surroundings, new friends, new opportunities alter people. But the Lord Jesus, though, now exalted to the highest place in the Universe is just the same Lord Jesus as He was here on earth.

Even sin and provocation from Peter did not change the Saviour's attitude to him. Peter must have been staggered at the Lord's constancy. He certainly found out in no uncertain terms that his Lord was the same yesterday, today and forever.

Peter's Lord is yours, "He who has begun a good work in you will complete it until the day of Jesus Christ", wrote Paul. Nothing will stop the Lord's determination to make you holy. Nothing.

$\mathcal{D}$ecember twenty-second

"Most assuredly, I say to you, when you were younger, you girded yourself and walked where you wished; but when you are old you will stretch out your hands, and another will gird you and carry you where you do not wish" (John 21: 18).

By the time John wrote this Gospel Peter had been martyred and he now well understood the meaning of the Saviour's words to Peter. The Lord contrasts Peter's youth with what lay ahead. As with any young person Peter was free to move as he wished; literally, the words mean "you used to put on your belt, you used to get dressed to travel". Peter could have walked wherever he wished to walk. The hour was coming, though, when Peter would have to raise his arms so that a rope could be tied around him as he was prepared for crucifixion. Then Peter would later have to stretch out his hands on the crossbeam of a cross.

Serving God, would, for Peter, not be to go where he wished. He would have to be prepared to go to a place where he did not wish to go. So often that is how it is in God's work. Ask people who have obeyed the Lord in service if their sphere of activity is where they would have naturally chosen to serve and you will find almost, invariably, that it isn't. They are given grace to do it, though. The question, "Would you be prepared to die as a martyr?" is sometime used. The answer is that if you have to die for Christ you will get the grace from God to do so. Meanwhile you will get the grace from God to live for Him and that is often just as difficult.

December twenty-third

"This he spoke, signifying by what death he would glorify God"
(John 21: 19).

*D*ying a good death for the Lord is just as possible as living a good life for Him. I know we have arrived at the Christmas season and you are probably surrounded with every sign of life but, then, we do not know the moment our earthly life will be taken from us. Even Bethlehem's manger had the shadow of death upon it and as the Lord Jesus brought glory to the Father in His death (see John 13: 31-32; 17: 1) so Peter was to do the same.

There is a message of tremendous hope here. Do we despise Peter forever for his dreadful denial of the Lord Jesus? Certainly not. In fact we love his tender, sensitive and sympathetic writing in the New Testament letters. He became a pillar in the church. Peter's dreadful and shameful denial was overcome by thirty years of dedicated service that followed the faithfulness to his Lord, even to the point of martyrdom. If you have failed your Lord, repent, be restored and live the rest of your days to His glory and, if the Lord be not come, die a death to His glory. I tell you it is harder to live for the Lord Jesus when you are older than it is when you are younger, but remember the young are looking to see if it works. By God's grace, show them.

December twenty-fourth

"And when He had spoken this, He said to them, 'Follow Me'"
(John 21: 19).

*T*his verse could immediately mean that the Lord invited Peter for a walk and a private conversation along the seashore but surely there is more to it than that. Just as Peter had been recommended to service, so now the Lord re-issues that original simple, clear, unequivocal call. Peter had first heard it when he and Andrew had been casting a net into the Sea of Galilee three and a half years before (See Matthew 4; 18). The words, I'm told, more literally mean "travel with Me".

Those words come to you and me on this Christmas Eve. Love always involves sacrifice, always. The Saviour's love for us involved His coming from unimaginable glory to a lowly stable, making Himself of no reputation. He lived for thirty-three and a half years with the reality of the cross over His head. Peter in turn lived for Christ for thirty years knowing it would cost him his life. We too know that it will be costly for us in the coming days to live for the Lord Jesus. Yet, as we stand by Bethlehem's manger and by Calvary's cross and hear that incredible call of our Saviour saying, "Follow Me", we gladly say, by God's grace, "Anywhere with Jesus we will follow on".

December   twenty-fifth

"Peter, turning around, saw the disciple whom Jesus loved following, who also had leaned on His breast at the supper, and said, 'Lord, who is the one who betrays you?'" (John 21: 20).

J ohn, from the very beginning of his Gospel, constantly veiled himself but what better description to be veiled by than this one? It does not imply in the slightest that Jesus did not love the other disciples. Our reading of John's Gospel shows that without any doubt. It was, though, the phrase that John wanted to be known by.

On this Christmas Day the T.V. listings will be full of programmes featuring famous people, highlighting actors famous for their part in the films shown, interviews given with interesting people who have accomplished great things, etc. Who, in any of the films will be highlighted as having one great feature above all others, the feature that they are loved by the Lord? On this day millions are reminded of Christ's birth but how many have personally responded to the incredible love that led Him to Bethlehem and Calvary? How may count it the greatest distinction of all to be loved by the Lord? On every continent there are such and if you and I are amongst them then there is one call we should heed above all others today. In the light of such love that call says, "Come, let us adore Him".

December   twenty-sixth

"'But Lord, what about this man?' Jesus said to him, 'If I will that he remain till I come, what is that to you? You follow Me'" (John 21: 22).

Peter had just been told what following Christ would cost him. It would cost him his life. Peter's question about what would happen to John was understandable. These two were very close and if Peter was going to die he was concerned about John. The Lord saw deeper into Peter's heart than anyone else. He saw that Peter had not fully understood what He had meant by the words "Follow Me". He meant that Peter had a task to accomplish and it would be well for him to concentrate on it rather than on what another should be doing and what might happen to him.

The answer was very straight. He had obviously told Peter to mind his own business. It was a call not to interfere in the life of another. And isn't it a message to all of us? We can be so busy asking questions about others that we fail to fulfil the mission to which we are called ourselves. We are to be faithful to our own commission and that will take all our time and energy. It is not necesssary for me to know the Lord's plans for others. His plan for me is enough to be getting on with. I am called to play out the part He has written for me, not to be spoiling my own soul's condition by fussing about another's part.

December   twenty-seventh

"Jesus said to him, 'If I will that he remain till I come, what is that to you?'" (John 21: 22).

This amazing statement shows very clearly that our lives are not the victims of chance nor the creatures of circumstance. Our steps are ordered by the Lord. He has adapted our lives in such a way that our past is suited to our limitations, temperaments and capabilities. The words, "If I will" shows the sovereignty the Lord has over our lives and deaths. We can now look back upon the amazing paths the Lord laid out for these two men. They had no idea, that misty morning by the sea, just how significant they were to be. Peter was to see huge success as a preacher of the Gospel but even more as a writer to sufferers. His pastoral ministry through his letters will be a help to people "going through the mill" to the end of time. Yet, how could he have ever been such a pastor if he had not proved God to be his comforter as he lived out his ministry with the anticipation of his martyrdom hanging over his head?

John, though, was to write the book of Revelation. He became a lonely exile on the island of Patmos and lived through the time of the fall of Jerusalem, the destruction of the Temple and the scattering of the Jews worldwide. It was because of his lonely exile that he was able to write of those sublime visions given to him by God and his great emphasis on the unchanging Saviour. It was his personal circumstances that gave his writing such potency, even to this day. The words, "If I will" should not make us afraid, rather they should comfort us in that they remind us that the Lord knows what He is doing with our lives. All our circumstances are used to bring about His purposes.

December   twenty-eighth

"Then this saying went out among the brethren that this disciple would not die. Yet Jesus did not say to him that he would not die, but, 'If I will that he remain till I come, what is that to you?'" (John 21: 23).

eople do not always listen to what is being said, do they? The disciples did not pay close enough attention to the Lord's words and for many a day it was believed by them and through them by the wider Christian circle that John would not die until the Second Coming. Therefore the longer John lived the closer they felt the coming of the Lord to be. You can imagine the sense of anticipation must have reached fever pitch as John grew older! On his death Christians were bound to be disappointed and non-Christians caused to mock. That's why this verse is carefully included in John's Gospel to warn us to pay close attention to the detail of Scripture.

How many another person have you heard saying that they believe they will not die until the return of Christ? How many have through the generations predicted a date and a time for His coming? When those Christians died and when those many predictions did not happen it all led to mockery from the uncoverted. Jesus told us that only the Father knows the day and the hour of His return. Nobody else does. So let's stick by His words. If He wills that we remain until His coming, or if He wishes us to pass through death, His will is paramount. Believing this would bring confidence to us and stop un-necessary mocking from the unconverted.

December   twenty-ninth

"This is the disciple who testifies of these things, and wrote these things ..... " (John 21: 24).

oday's text establishes beyond all doubt that "the beloved disciple" whom we have met through this Gospel is none other than John. It also indicates that he was still orally testifying for Christ even after he had written his Gospel. Right through his long life he still spoke far and wide of the years of communion he had had with the Saviour and also of that turning point in his life when, because of the way the clothes lay, he had first believed that Christ had risen from the dead.

Don't you love the way John's tongue and pen are linked in our text? His Gospel writing is unsurpassed, indeed as a friend of mine said to me just yesterday, "If we had nothing but John's Gospel it would be enough". John's writing has left its mark. Indeed checking on the Internet for references to John's Gospel recently I found there were tens of thousands of references. I have tried to imagine what it must have been to hear John speak. As he wrote in one of his letters, "What we have seen and heard we declare to you also", but as he declared it what must have been the look in his eye? What must have been the tone in his voice? He who had seen Him, bore Him an incredibly faithful witness.

And you and I? Christ declared that we who have not seen yet who have believed are more blessed. How, then, runs our pen and our tongue? John's witness to his Saviour to the very last How about ours? Is ours Wesley's cry?

"Happy, if with my latest breath,
I may but gasp His Name:
Preach Him to all and cry in death,
'Behold, behold the Lamb!'".

December   thirtieth

"... and we know that his testimony is true" (John 21: 24).

ho are the "we" in our text? Some say the church to which John belonged, some say the church at Ephesus, some say a group of John's disciples who preserved his record and gave it to the world. Others suggest it is an editorial "we", a form by which the writer is underlining the truthfulness of his own witness. In the end, though, whoever the "we" refers to, they could not have known John's witness was true because they were not present at the events he writes about. They weren't there! It surely must refer to what F.F. Bruce calls, "the inward witness of the Holy Spirit ... that witness had begun to validate itself in their personal experience and thus they knew it to be true".

We too, in our day and generation, also know the very same experience. There is a ring of authenticity in this Gospel that touches our lives as we face a new century as it has touched millions in the last two. The Spirit of God witnesses with our spirit that this Gospel is true. What we once guessed about we now know, through John, as fixed guiding pole star in our journey to eternity. As the great preacher W.E. Sangster was dying of a wasting disease, he wrote to the evangelist Dr. Billy Graham and said, "Tell them it's true, Billy, tell them it's true".

December   thirty-first

"And there are also many other things that Jesus did, which if they were written one by one, I suppose that even the world itself could not contain the books that would be written. Amen" (John 21: 25).

At the very beginning of this Gospel John wrote of the Saviour who "was in the world, and the world was made through Him, and the world did not know Him". Through his wonderful Gospel John testified of the Saviour, of His words, His deeds, His acts. He then tells us that his Gospel was one great invitation to believe that Christ is the Son of God. Now, at the very end of the greatest story ever told, John re-asserts himself and for the one and only time in his Gospel refers to himself as "I". (See 1 John for John's use of "we" and "I"). He says that the world that did not know Christ when He came, would be a very small library to contain all the books that could be written if all of the Saviour's deeds were put into writing.

Let us be reminded again that God never ends with an end but always ends with a beginning. As C.S. Lewis put it, "This is a story which goes on for ever, in which every chapter is better than the one before." John's invitation comes down the centuries to us again. Are we going to be part of this unending story too or are we going to live merely for ourselves? John's one aim in life had been to glorify Christ. In that he gloriously succeeded. May we do the same.

Bibliography

F. F. Bruce, *The Gospel of John,* Pickering and Inglis 1983

William Barclay, *The Gospel of John Vol 1 and 2,* The St. Andrew Press, Edinburgh, 1955

D. A. Carson, *The Gospel According to John,* Inter Varsity Press/William B. Eerdeman's Publishing Company, 1991

David W. Gooding, *In the School of Christ,* Gospel Folio Press, Grand Rapids, Michigan, 1995. Also taped seminars on the Gospel of John, Myrtlefield Trust

F. B. Meyer, *The Gospel of John,* Marshall, Morgan and Scott 1950

Bruce Milne, *The Message of John,* Inter Varsity Press, 1993

*If you would like information
on other books by Derick Bingham
please write to the publishers*